Praise for *Laboring Positions:
Black Women, Mothering and the Academy*

An array of theoretical frameworks and naturalistic research approaches inform the volume and the contributors' critical analyses of academe, scholarship production, and the politics and artfulness involved in simultaneously crafting lives as academics and mothers. Contributors offer keen and diverse insight into the ways one can navigate the paradoxes of creative privilege and structural oppression found within the academy. The narratives also thoughtfully reveal how one can negotiate commitments to self-actualization, communal nurturing, scholarly excellence, institutional leadership, and student, family, and self-care. Together, contributors to this volume offer valuable lessons about both the border crossing and boundary setting work that academic careers warrant given complex racial, gendered, economic, and maternal contexts.
—CAMILLE M. WILSON, Educational Leadership and Policy Studies, Wayne State University, Detroit, Michigan

This collection offers significant insight into the material conditions, struggles and triumphs of Black mothers working in largely North American academic institutions. This rich subjective dimension—the combination of research and data on conditions of work for Black women in the academy, carried by detailed personal accounts and interview excerpts—makes a needed contribution to current literature on motherhood, and diversity in academic institutions. Broad structural issues are highlighted through the standpoint of a diverse group of Black mothers, an approach that is importantly informative in a time when the discourse of diversity, and myriad equity mandates can mask the stark reality of most university cultures.
—MAKI MOTAPANYANE, Women's Studies/Dept. of Humanities, Mount Royal University, Calgary, Alberta

Laboring Positions brings to the forefront the social locations of black mothering in the academy. The articles reveal "the transgressive, testimonial and transcendent power of the 'other' mothers of the academy" in vivid fashion. This is a critical read and a challenging text.
—DEIDRE HILL BUTLER, Director of Africana Studies, Union College, Schenectady, New York

Laboring Positions: Black Women, Mothering and the Academy makes a very important and timely contribution to scholarship in the field of motherhood studies. The personal narratives and voices of multiple generations of Black mothers both in the academy, as well as in the community, are stories that have been mostly individualized and rendered invisible in the academy. The diverse contributions highlight the complexities of Black women who are mothering in the academy and put a real face on the multiple realities of mothering, othermothering and community mothering as experienced by Black mothers. The treatment of the three interrelated themes transgression, testimony and transcendence will help students of Women's Studies, Gender Studies and Motherhood Studies build knowledge of the experiences of Black women mothering and their work in the academy. Finally, it pushes institutions to take institutional ownership of some of struggles and to co-create solutions.
—WANDA THOMAS BERNARD, **School of Social Work, Dalhousie University, Halifax, Nova Scotia**

Laboring Positions
Black Women, Mothering and the Academy

Edited by

Sekile Nzinga-Johnson

DEMETER PRESS

Copyright © 2013 Demeter Press

Individual copyright to their work is retained by the authors. All rights reserved. No part of this book may be reproduced or transmitted in any form by any means without permission in writing from the publisher.

Published by:
Demeter Press
c/o Motherhood Initiative for Research and
 Community Involvement (MIRCI)
140 Holland St. West, P.O. 13022
Bradford, ON, L3Z 2Y5
Telephone: 905.775.9089
Email: info@demeterpress.org
Website: www.demeterpress.org

Demeter Press logo based on the sculpture, "Demeter" by Maria-Luise Bodirsky <www.keramik-atelier.bodirsky.de>

Cover photograph: Ramatu Bangura

Printed and Bound in Canada

Library and Archives Canada Cataloguing in Publication

 Laboring positions : Black women, mothering and the academy / edited by Sekile Nzinga-Johnson

Includes bibliographical references.
ISBN 978-1-927335-02-4

Cataloguing data available from Library and Archives Canada.

*for my children,
Kimathi, Cabral, and Zora*

Table of Contents

Acknowledgements
xi

Introduction:
Extending the Boundaries
Sekile Nzinga-Johnson
1

PART I. TRANSGRESSION

1.
Community Property:
Black Mothers' Communal Ownership of their
Daughters' Degrees
Giovanni N. Dortch and Candice Bledsoe
35

2.
Teaching for Change:
Notes from a Broke Queer Hustling Mama
Vanessa L. Marr
58

3.
"I Am My Child's First Teacher":
Black Motherhood and Homeschooling as Activism
Within and Beyond the Academy
Marcelle M. Haddix and LaToya L. Sawyer
75

4.
Resisting with Child:
Black Women's Embodied Negotiations of Motherhood
in the Academy
Sekile Nzinga-Johnson
91

5.
"I'm Not Your Mama; Do Your Work":
The Black Female Academic as Surrogate Mother
Tokeya C. Graham
111

PART II. TESTIMONY

6.
Black Academic and Single Mother: Colliding Statuses
Rosalyn Terborg-Penn
127

7.
And There Went My Adventurer's Spirit:
Motherhood and Fieldwork Post-9/11
Patricia Williams Lessane
147

8.
Walking Tightropes Without Nets:
The Adjunct as Single Mother
Stacia L. Brown
164

9.
Mothering Black: A Cross-Cultural Perspective
on Mothering in the Nigerian Academy
Rose A. Sackeyfio
175

10.
Clashing Clocks: Black American Women Professors'
Perceptions of Parenting on the Tenure Clock
Markesha McWilliams Henderson and Natalie T. J. Tindall
192

PART III. TRANSCENDENCE

11.
Daughter Dreams and the Teaching Life of Audre Lorde
Alexis Pauline Gumbs
211

12.
Fighting Phantoms:
Mammy, Matriarch and Other Ghosts Haunting
Black Mothers in the Academy
Yolanda Covington-Ward
236

13.
Mothering and Mentoring:
Relational Dynamics Among Black Women in the Academy
Karen T. Craddock
257

14.
Black Women Occupying the Academy: Merging Critical
Mothering and Mentoring to Survive and Thrive
Julia S. Jordan-Zachery
273

Contributor Notes
292

Index
298

Acknowledgements

There are many people who I would like to acknowledge who have provided me with insurmountable instrumental and emotional support through the production of this volume. I would like to first thank the many scholars who responded to the call for papers but ultimately were unable to contribute to the final volume. Your ideas and overwhelming interest were inspiring and demonstrated the depth of scholarly possibilities on the topic of Black women, mothering and the academy. I also would like to thank my fellow contributors as well as my publishing editor, Andrea O'Reilly. I am grateful for your perennial patience with me in my present and past multiplicities as a professor/ Women's Studies program director/mother/volume editor/partner/human. I especially would like to acknowledge Karen Craddock and Michelle Dunlap for their developmental support and Lisa Carley Hotaling for her editorial and conceptual support for the book. Your feedback, input, and insights were invaluable to moving this project forward. This volume would not have been completed without the welcomed and critical feedback and mentorship of Julia Jordan-Zachery. Words cannot express the deep gratitude I feel for you joining me on this journey and dragging me kicking and screaming across the finish line. Your encouraging texts and sisterhood have sustained me. I would also like to offer special thanks to my friend Ramatu Bangura for granting me permission to use her photo of her beautiful daughter for the book's cover.

My effort toward the completion of this volume was sustained by the unwavering support of my wonderful circle of sister friends, Chiara Santos Browning, Tiffani Walker Bullock, Gay Byron, Hilda Chacon, Natasha Chen, Tonia Cook, LaShunda Echols-Smith, Akilah Folami, Nikol Alexander-Floyd, Tokeya Graham, Carlnita Greene, Kimberly Jenkins, Richelle Patterson, Danielle Ponder, Doreen Rice, Connie Rodriguez, Valeria Sinclair Chapman, Tanya Shuford, Serina Tetenov, Roxana Walker Canton, Renee Williams, Ronette Williams, Nikkee Williams-McGainey and Gillian Young-Miller. I appreciate your reassurance when I wavered and doubted whether I was indeed on the right path. I also want to thank RocCity Roller Derby of Rochester, New York, and Black Girls Run of Chicago. Your lessons of perseverance and endurance, whether skating the last lap or running the last mile, stay with me as a writer and editor.

I would be remiss if I did not end my note of gratitude without thanking my dear family. To my sister, brother, mother, nieces, nephews, aunts, uncles, cousins, grandmother, great grandmother and in-laws, your collective love, support and sacrifice have always propelled me forward on this journey. I especially want to thank my aunt Latrice Robinson and my cousins, Chedrena Brown-Pyburn, Marquita Byrd, Belinda Wilkerson and Annisha Lewis. Your prayer filled family-love was especially edifying on this voyage.

I would like to thank my partner, Cedric Johnson, for all of his critical feedback wrapped in love and encouragement. I am so thankful for all the sacrifices you have made on behalf of my life dreams and passions. As I have said in the past, I am blessed to have you as a partner on this journey. Finally, I would like to thank Kimathi, Cabral, and Zora, my beautifully intelligent children, for blessing me with mutual gifts of connectedness and sovereignty. Your love, kindness, unwavering patience and fun-loving spirits eased my internal conflict of perceived maternal neglect and provided me with the wherewithal to produce this volume. I am eternally grateful.

Introduction

Extending the Boundaries

SEKILE NZINGA-JOHNSON

Black daughters must learn how to survive in interlocking structures of race, class and gender oppression while rejecting and transcending those very same structures.
—Patricia Hill Collins ("The Meaning of Motherhood" 54)

LABORING POSITIONS aims to disrupt the dominant discourse on women's mothering experiences within the academy, which largely focuses on contemporary work-life concerns and career disruption of White middle class biological mothers. This volume acknowledges the salience of the institutional challenges facing contemporary caregiving academics; yet it is also concerned with expanding the academic mothering conversation. This collection speaks against mind/body dualism and private/public spheres by privileging the interactions between Black women's mothering experiences and their working lives within and beyond the academy. In doing so, the perspectives captured herein offer us cogent starting points from which to interrogate the interlocking cultural, political, and economic hierarchies of the academy.

Consider the following case: Everest University, a large, for-profit, technical college conglomerate, frequently airs a commercial that features a woman student/actor of color who self-identifies as a teen mother. During the commercial, the student tours a sampling of the college's experiential classes and eventually "bumps into" one of her professors who happens to be a Black woman. Upon seeing her professor, the student's face lights up and she unabashedly wraps her arms around the faculty member as they warmly embrace. The student/actor exclaims, "She is like a second mom to me! She taught me everything!" The commercial later shows the same student/actor greeting two job placement staff members who are White women. She warmly greets them but in this instance she offers no verbalized testimony of her level of shared intimacy with either of them. Every time I view the commercial from my couch with remote control in hand and my finger triggered on the turn channel button, I am evermore indignant by Everest's commodification of nurturance that is performed by both student and faculty member. It is unclear to me whether what I am witnessing is scripted or if the connections are authentic in their expression.

Nonetheless, I am intrigued by the Everest marketing department's manipulation and production of both the faculty member's/actor's assumed maternal role and Black women's survivalist legacy of *other-mothering*.[1] I wonder, does the faculty member freely embrace the identity of the student's "second mom"? Is she compensated and rewarded for her maternal labor on behalf of Everest? My panicked heart races as I consider the depiction of a Black woman working in a setting such as Everest as becoming more and more indicative of Black women's stagnated plight as intellectual workers. I also consider the plausibility of a more insidious plot undergirding Everest's marketing department's intentions. Specifically, I am curious to know if Everest has calculatedly marketed their commercial to showcase a racially maternalized faculty member to their most likely first generation, working class, and/or working adult student population pool. Does their not so subliminal confounding of the packaged promise of education and nurturance serve as a telling statement regarding the expected and subordinated servant role of women faculty of color within the academy?

More central to this current volume, I often question how this performance of maternity fits within the current discourse on mothering in the academia. What would the student's "second mom" reveal if she were allowed to speak from her own standpoint and of her own understanding of "mothering?" Would her story include other realms of mothering/caregiving? In short, I wonder if the current academic mothering discourse fully captures the complexities and extensiveness of mothering practices and performances of all women in the academy.

I have been preoccupied with this line of curiosities for over a decade. My interest in motherhood studies dovetails with my grounding in Black feminist and intersectional feminist understandings of motherhood/mothering. In Patricia Hill Collins' now classic essay, "Shifting the Center: Race, Class and Feminist Theorizing About Motherhood," she reminds us that we can turn to women of color's narratives and their creative endeavors to gain insight into their self-defined articulations of their "standpoints on mothering and motherhood" (641). It is those underrepresented narratives and understandings that drive this volume. The contributors herein collectively offer counter narratives, which complicate current interpretations of maternal subjectivities within the academy. Like their Black womanist/feminist foremothers, the forthcoming essays continue to defiantly offer intersectional analyses, critiques of contemporary academia and transcendent possibilities of the academy and society. In doing so, the volume locks arms with the documented and undocumented narratives of many academic "others" who continue to confront erasure as they create embodied intellectual resistances and counter locations from within.

My editorial goal for *Laboring Positions* is to offer a poly-vocal collection of essays whose themes privilege and arouse Black mothering as central in the narratives, research, and models of existence and resistance for the Black women's survival within academy. The contributors do so using a wide variety of methods and perspectives including Womanist research ethics, hip-hop feminism, literary analysis, autoethnography, memoir, qualitative research, theory and practice driven frameworks and practical guidance and everyday testimony that are all collectively bound by Black women's intellectual lives and mothering experiences.

Some might raise eyebrows at the significance of unsheathing an intersectional distinction on the issue of mothering and academic work when there are so many "others" languishing from within and in search of a unified front for mobilization. Fellow maternal scholar, D. Lynn O'Brien Hallstein, cautions that decentering of gender as the primary unit of analysis may be a counterproductive exercise and serve a divisive function against feminist struggles concerned with the goal of building strategic alliances to address the motherhood penalty faced by academic women. O'Brien Hallstein argues that "contemporary intersectionality itself is apolitical and shifts the focus away from the feminism and thus the direct focus of social justice that mothers need now" (373). An interpretation of intersectionality that is void of politics is unproductive. Each essay featured in *Laboring Positions* exposes structural inequities, which produce the material conditions that influence Black women's professional and personal trajectories. Thus, contributors to *Laboring Positions* engage intersectionality as a necessary tool for understanding the complexities of the compounding oppressions facing Black women and their political work both inside and outside of the academy.

Feminist scholars, Karen Ramsay and Gayle Letherby, rightfully warn against scapegoating academic non-mothers by creating a false binary of mothers and others. Specifically, their work underscores the dangers of privileging biological and legal motherhood over other forms of care work expected or performed by non-mothers in the gendered university. Ramsay and Letherby argue that favoring the burden of "motherhood" is not a fruitful exercise for the collective who equally deserve claim to their lives within and outside of the academy (26). In response, I borrow the words of fellow mother-academic-radical, Sara Motta, by stressing that this collection does not seek to preclude or minimize others' actualities or feminist projects but instead extends "the possibilities of solidarities across difference by affirming that we exist and demand the right for our truth to be heard" (1).

In sum, *Laboring Positions* provides an intellectual and sociopolitical location for the broadening discourses of mothering in the academy. This collection, not unlike childbirth and labor, embodies threads of joy, dissonance, resistance, and struggle in its attempt to stretch the scope and impact of current academic mothering discourse. In sum, the works herein are foregrounded by the maternal practices and experiences of those academic laborers whose silence has been loud, yet has been excluded from the conversation.

BLACK WOMEN IN THE ACADEMY IN THE TWENTY-FIRST CENTURY

Both women's and Black people's intelligence have always been deemed inferior under patriarchy and racism. Both civil rights and feminist movements buttress Black women's struggle for access to formal education. In theory, advance degreed Black women represent a subpopulation that has achieved the pinnacle of educational success. "Get a good education and then a good job" is a common aspirational message bequeathed to many Black children by parents, teachers, community leaders and policy makers. Black women have complied and are earning more doctorates than ever before. However, these data on Black women's increased rate of educational attainment does not parallel their reality within the academy. Thus the sacred grove remains a site of struggle for many.

Currently, Black women comprise approximately three percent of full time instructional faculty in the United States (21,689 of 728, 977) and just two and a half percent of all full time faculty ranked at assistant, associate, or full professor level (Table 260, Digest of Education Statistics 2010). In 2010, data from the U.S. Department of Education also reports that Black academic women were employed (21,609) at a rate higher than Black men (18,026). However, the data also suggest that there were more tenured Black men faculty (7,935) than Black women faculty (6,314) during the same year. These numbers should be interpreted with caution otherwise they distract us from the real issues of inequity in the professoriate. A more central question remains, why do both groups' tenure rates pale in comparison to the overall number of tenured faculty (326,562) reported for that year (Table 264, Digest of Education Statistics 2010)? In a related vein, why do these slight within-group gender variances often cloud our discussion of the unwavering overrepresentation of White men faculty (215,896) and White women faculty (110,996), who continue to comprise the vast majority of senior academic positions? I argue that these equally dismal circumstances are of concern for both Black women and men and are not simply concerns of representation. Instead, the aforementioned data are indicative of the complex and perpetual interplay of racism and sexism, which continue to sustain a racial and gender hierarchy in academia.

How might we explain the meager representation of Black women in academia? Samuel Myers and Caroline Turner contend that the disparity in the numbers between assistant and full professors can been partially attributed to the disproportionate number of Black women professors who are denied tenure (296). Additionally, the tenure and promotion process has been criticized as a subjective gate-keeping practice that rewards narrow dimensions and modes of academic labor and unjustly penalizes a great number of women and people of color (Villalpando and Delgado Bernarl 244). In 2010, the U.S. Department of Education reports only 2,331 of 6,411 Black women were promoted to full professor during this same timeframe. Conversely, 49,650 White women were promoted to full professor (Table 264, Digest of Education Statistics 2010). Lack of scholarly productivity has often been used to justify the discrepancy in these numbers. Yet Black women and other women of color are often at risk of being penalized professionally for not choosing paths of disembodied individualism when they participate in collaborative projects, relational work, engaged pedagogies, applied research, or social justice work. Targeted attacks on their intellectual worth and contributions not only diminish their existence within the academy, but the tenure denial case of former University of Michigan faculty member and renowned Native American scholar-activist, Andrea Smith, reminds us that the careers of women of color are indeed subject to professional backlash and erasure. These systemic injustices speak to the academy's steadfastness against restructuring itself maintains the exclusion of academic outsiders.

Many women of color academics minimize their circumstance by rationalizing their privileged status in comparison to the struggles of other women in their communities. Others pull strength from prior generations who may have sacrificed for them to occupy these coveted positions. Black women, particularly Black womanists/feminists, have a long history of transformation and resistance that is documented by their prolific knowledge production and their social justice work within and beyond the academy. Yet these accomplishments are tempered as Black women continue to endure structural injustices and daily microaggressions as they navigate the contemporary academy.

Examining the nature of Black women's academic appointments within this context is of increasing significance in the neoliberal environment of the twenty-first century. The contemporary academy continues to embrace corporate and capitalist modes of operation in its hiring and management of its intellectual labor force with less tenure track positions available and more vulnerable contingent posts being created. Marc Bousquet's cautionary essay, "Lady Academe and Labor-Market Segmentation," reminds us that the gender segmentation of the labor market is not limited to manufacturing but is rapidly occurring within the neoliberal academy. He argues that the contemporary academy has both normalized and feminized contingency faculty. In doing so, academia has enacted extreme economic penalties for women, especially those women who are members of underrepresented groups, those women who belong to underpaid fields and who are employed at second tier institutions or community colleges (1-4). Women of color most often occupy all of these spaces and are extremely vulnerable to work based exploitation within this context. Feminist scholar, Ann duCille reminds us that for Black women "the principal sites of exploitation are not simply the cabaret, the speakeasy, the music video, the glamour magazine; they are also the academy, the publishing industry, the intellectual community" (592). Not surprisingly, a 2010 report from U.S. Department of Education revealed that 8,964 of 21,609 Black women faculty work as adjuncts, instructors and other low wage workers. Additionally, studies have reported higher rates of isolation and job dissatisfaction amongst Black academic women (Moses 23-48). In the end, it seems that education is only a relative buffer which provides some material gain for Black women but not at the same rates for White women and Black men.

Black women faculty, like other underrepresented groups, also are economically and professionally vulnerable given that their status within the contemporary academy often mirrors and is intimately connected to Black women's economic and labor status within the United States. The United States' rapidly advancing neoliberal economic and political environment has severely assaulted all workers; however, Black women are facing the highest unemployment and underemployment rates despite President Barack Obama's 2009 economic recovery and job creation campaign (National Women's Law Center). The privatization of care work, health care and education has placed significant strain on informal care systems, which has increased Black women's caregiver burden and compromised their wealth attainment (Washington Post-Kaiser Family Foundation). These current economic conditions exacerbated outside the academy also impact Black women and their work within the academy, particularly those faculty members who are caring for others within their families and demand justice for those in vulnerable communities. In addition, the academy's hetero-patriarchal culture of disembodied individualism, unbound work demands, assumed infinite availability, and institutional profit over collective gain intensifies the career vulnerability of women of color academics and risks straining faculty members' connections in their familial and community lives as well as their personal well-being.

BLACK WOMANIST/FEMINIST THEORIZING ON MOTHERHOOD

Black womanist/feminist theorists have contributed extensively to historicizing Black women's reproduction and motherhood within the United States. As early as the seventeenth century Black feminists have advanced theories of "both motherhood and motherhood disposed" (Spillers 78). A key thrust of Black womanists/feminists has been to problematize feminist theorizing by locating black women "outside of the view of the traditional symbolics of female gender" (Spillers 78), which has created alternate border zones for locating Black motherhood and reproduction. In her definitive essay, "Mama's Baby, Papa Maybe," Hortense Spillers confronts White western middle-class feminists' monolithic reading of women's gender roles and motherhood by asserting that Black feminists maintain "a specialized reading of female gender as an outcome of certain political, socio-cultural empowerment within the context of the United States" (77) thus they "regard dispossession as the loss of gender, or one of the chief elements in an altered reading of gender"(77). Spillers complicates essentialist motherhood through her assertion that "even though the female slave reproduces other enslaved persons we do not read birth in this instance as a reproduction of mothering precisely because the female like the male, has been robbed of the parental right, the parental function" (78). Spillers' work foregrounds the joint forces of capitalism, racism, patriarchy, and heterosexism, which undergird hegemonic constructions of Black motherhood and womanhood. Thus, Spillers' work serves as a critical forerunner in extending the feminist subfield of maternal or motherhood studies.

The early sentiment of Anna Julia Cooper prophetically eclipses Spillers' motherhood dispossessed thesis as she envisions a day when Black women would have the rights of their daughters' bodies in her address to the World Conference of Representative Women in 1893 (711). Though contemporary Black women are free from enslavement, they continue to struggle to protect the lives of Black children as we bear witness to the failing health, educational and legal systems that seek to control and limit their lives. In response to these assaulting conditions, bell hooks theorized that *homeplace* serves as a both safe haven for Black families after encountering the daily hostilities of broader society, and as a location for political teaching and activism against those very structures and institutions that oppress both Black adults and children.

Both Angela Davis' essay "Racism, Birth Control and Reproductive Rights" and Dorothy Roberts' groundbreaking book, *Killing the Black Body* illustrate Black women's reproductive struggles under slavery as being intimately linked to their continued struggles for reproductive freedom in the U.S. Collectively these Black feminist scholars confront liberalism's construction of a private/public sphere, which views the private sphere as the dominant location for reproduction and motherhood. Thus, Black feminists' interrogation of the political and economic history of the United States has disentangled reproduction from mothering practices. Mothering/motherhood or being mothered, unbound by biology or legality yet bound by oppression and economic circumstance, entails a wide range of subjectivities. The fluidity of Black women's roles within their communities included providing care for a variety of children and assuming valued roles as *"othermothers"* (James 45) or *"surrogate mothers"* (Cole xv).

Building upon Cooper's and Roberts' contextualization of Black women's histories of physical, reproductive and psychic bondage, Alice Walker privileges the existence of Black women's daily acts of resistance against the suppression of their bodies and lives. In Walker's essay *In Search of Our Mothers' Gardens*, she writes of Black women's miraculous and necessary ability to maintain desire to save fragments of themselves solely for their own joys in the midst of their full and constrained lives. Walker's work counterbalances criticisms that all Black women most readily occupy essentialist positions of self-sacrificing maternity. Most importantly, Walker's work speaks to Black women's and mothers' tradition of cherishing their own desires, whether as gardeners, artists, or scholars. Walker's piece offers validation and inspiration to Black women who embrace their own self-defined passions. More directly, Walker offers a critical compass for Black women academics who must withstand the controlling rhetoric of selfishness as they carve out their intellectual endeavors, make peace with saying "No," or participate in wellness affirming activities.

Black women also have histories of resisting racist and sexist critiques waged against the legitimacy of their motherhood due to their working lives and their economic independence from men. In response, Patricia Hill Collins offers yet another conceptual dimension of mothering in her essay, "The Meaning of Motherhood in Black Culture and Black Mother/Daughter Relationships," by suggesting that economic provision is a central aspect of *motherwork* and has historically been consistent with good mothering for Black women. Hill Collins reframes Black women's economic contributions to their families, which has often been demonized as unfeminine and paradoxically defined as bad mothering. Contemporary Black mothers, including those who are academics, continue to resist retrograde domesticating pressures that feminists have identified as *intensive mothering* (Hays) and the *new momism* (Douglas and Michaels), which are discussed more fully in a later section.

Finally, Audre Lorde's radical intellectual legacy as a self-identified Black lesbian mother scholar poet activist continues to create new crevices for feminist praxis. Many academics are forced to splinter ourselves, our lives, work, and our politics to better "fit" within the academy. This state of splitting off and disembodiment has lead many to exist and persist disjointedly as intellectual workers. Lordes' intellectual contributions, as illuminated by Alexis Pauline Gumbs (this volume), offer us an epistemological road map for living our own reality. Lorde's legacy is rich with theory, praxis, testimony, poetry, dreams, resistance, and life narrative. She utilizes the location of mother as a component in her knowledge production as she bonds her maternal role to her sociopolitical struggles within and outside of the academy. Her radical decision to not privilege one aspect of her identity or politics over the other remains a necessary project for all who desire to remain integrated and whole.

In sum, this sampling of Black feminist theory denotes a prolific history of womanist/feminist thinking that pushes back against master narratives of motherhood and mothering and work. This rich yet under-utilized intellectual tradition has confronted state and economic based control of Black women's bodies, reproduction, relationships, and family systems; expanded the conceptualization of maternal labor; reframed the boundaries of motherhood that exist outside of biology and legality; drawn parallels between Black mothers' and daughters' experiences; privileged non-heteronormative family structures including queer families, single parent families, intergenerational families, and non-kin family networks; acknowledged mothering as intertwined with Black women's working lives; utilized motherhood as a location for womanist/feminist theory building and praxis; and advanced mothering as a mode of resistance against social, economic, and political oppression. Collectively these interpretations complicate our understanding of the fluidity and scope of the mothering practices and ideologies and remain relevant for contemporary womanists/feminists. The works included in *Laboring Positions* represent a personified embrace of this intellectual tradition articulated by our Black womanist/feminist foremothers.

BLACK WOMEN, MOTHERING AND THE ACADEMY

Laboring Positions enacts the academy as a situated location in which to examine both the intersectional contours of Black women's maternal labor as well as Black women's mothering experiences as marginalized academics within a historically patriarchal, antifamily, individualist, and increasingly marketized professional context. Yet, the dominant academic mothering discourse primarily centers on the ways in which women's behaviors and bodies are read within the academy or focus on how women negotiate their private lives within this context. The research and policy contributions of scholars featured in Susan Bracken, Jeanie Allen and Diane Dean's volume *The Balancing Act: Gendered Perspectives on Faculty Roles and Work Lives* has advanced an important line of critical research focusing on the particular structural barriers that academic-mothers experience within the work place. Work-life research approppriately names many of the gendered practices of the academy and has advocated for widespread policy and cultural change. For example, Carol Hollingshead, Beth Sullivan, Gilia Smith, Louise August and Susan Hamilton examined policy recommendations which range from tenure clock extension to institutional policies that grant caregivers leave from the moment they claim a new dependent on their taxes. These trends in policy development are greatly needed and some institutions have made significant strides; however, the authors note many institutions continue to lag behind when it comes to the development of work-life balance and family friendly policies (63). In addition, their analyses reveal that despite policy development, many academics remain hesitant in utilizing these provisions due to fear of penalty (62). These data add particular cautionary weight for those faculty members who are most vulnerable.

There has been a tendency to marvel at the alleged droves of women who leave or "opt out" of the academy under such pressures. However, *Laboring Positions'* contributors reminds us that these paths are for the privileged few. We know little of those who stay. It is important to acknowledge that there has been a plethora of anthologies that focus on the dual challenges of being both parents and academics, which emerged in the past decade. However, volumes such as *Mama PhD*, edited by Elrena Evans and Caroline Grant often expose common themes of racial privilege in the narratives of academic women who tend to contribute to these volumes. For instance, in *Mama PhD* several contributors reported that it was not until they became pregnant or became mothers, that they began to experience overt work place discrimination. That is, despite their subordinated status as women, they perceived their colleagues as generally accepting of them and their competence as intellectual workers.

Conversely, women of color academics' narratives regularly encompass themes of alienation and exclusion due to racism, sexism and elitism. We can sample from the testimonies penned by disenfranchised Black academic women in Joy James' and Ruth Farmer's *Spirit, Space and Survival: African American Women in (White) Academe*, as well as refer to the disturbing data from the 62 Black academic women who participated in Lena Wright Meyers' published study, *A Broken Silence: Voices of African American Women in the Academy* to gain a sense of Black women's alienation within the constraining politics, culture and economy of the academy. We can also point to more recent and timely volumes such as *Presumed Incompetent: The Intersections of Race and Class for Women in Academia,* edited by Gabriella Gutierrez y Muhs, Yolanda Flores, Carmen G. Gonzalez and Angela P. Harris, as an indication of the continued racialized, gendered and class-based struggles that women of color confront as academics. Thus, pregnancy and mothering issues are interactive with other intersectional disadvantages that have been well established in the literature. Additionally, many Black women's notions of mothering and working extend beyond these narrow constructions. We require a wider scope if we are to truly gain a sense of Black women's work-life issues in the contemporary academy.

In response, Lynn O'Brien Hallstein and Andrea O'Reilly offer a compelling framework for examining contemporary academic mothers' circumstance as representative of the dual conflict between the unbound work expectations of the contemporary academy and the unbound work expectations of twenty-first century *intensive mothering*.[2] O'Brien Hallstein and O'Reilly argue that the contemporary unbounded expectation of intensive mothering operates as both a function of racial and class privilege and is an oppressive force against which all mothers should actively resist. This twenty-first century Western White middle-class construction of intensive mothering is indeed today's measuring stick; however, it offers little novelty concerning the normalized diminishment of Black women's femininity, womanhood, and motherhood. As stated earlier, Black women have historically confronted and defended themselves against White middle-class women's norms.

Structural injustices continue to create wide-reaching instabilities and vulnerabilities in communities of color and many Black women, regardless of their educational attainment, often respond to these disparities through the performances of other mothering, maternal activism, mentoring, intellectual mothering, educational motherwork, intergenerational mothering, sister mothering, and community mothering. Many of the contributors in *Laboring Positions* do indeed frame their testimonies around their tensions between their academic careers, their children, and their home lives. Yet, most chapters evoke themes that elucidate the many ways in which Black women continue to take responsibility to others' children, other family members and community members. In fact, some argue that these commitments drive their scholarly and activist agendas.

Many essays speak from the position of daughter and bring both their literal and figurative mothers' intellectual labor into focus. Specifically, these contributors focus on the significance of being mothered by others in order to pursue their intellectual careers. Other contributors see value in drawing upon mother-daughter dynamics or maternal experiences to construct survival strategies for navigating the academy. This reciprocal intergenerational politics of motherhood counters feminists' prior characterizations of third wave feminists' matrophobia[3] in that the work herein acknowledges mother figures who have provided ongoing instrumental, spiritual, psychological and intellectual support for the success of Black women academics' careers.

This protective motherwork deliberately crosses the domesticated borders of "motherhood" and complicates the unbound dimensions of both academic work and mothering. Upon entering the academy, Black women academics find their futures and the futures of their students and their junior colleagues more vulnerable than ever. As such, Black academic women, both mothers and non-mothers, are overrepresented in the performance of care work on campus through their intellectual legacies, social justice work, campus service, and mentoring of vulnerable students and junior faculty in their desperate attempt to retain their fellow academic "others." These mothering performances also are messy, boundless, expected and imposed and they deserve more integration into mothering discourse. Thus, *Laboring Positions* purposefully endows an inclusive scholarly location to interrogate the care work of women who *mother* others within academic spaces by choice, imposition or circumstance. *Academic other mothering* or *mothering the mind* within the context of the academy illuminates the undocumented, undervalued, exploitive, and I would argue, *racialized* nature of these forms of feminized labor. The aforementioned Everest recruitment commercial reminds us that these forms of labor are expected for women of color faculty and function as uncompensated retention services with profit potential for self-serving institutions.

The feminized and maternalized labor of "other-mothering" students has been criticized as an expected performance of all women marked by gender within the academy (Ramsay and Letherby 26) yet women's refusal to embrace these imposed identities has been linked to negative outcomes on women's teaching assessments and formal evaluations (Myers 57-58). Debra Harley's notion of "maids of the academy" and Tammy Henderson, Andrea Hunter and Gladys J. Hildreth's closely related "academic domestic," frames the exploitative subservience that Black women face as academics and complicate prior assertions that Black women uniformly choose and desire these "maternalized" forms of labor. Arlene E. Edwards also suggests that the subservient role of the women faculty members of color ignites additional struggle as they attempt to transcend their designated status with little formalized recognition or support from their institution (150).

In turn, Judith Butler reminds us that gender is an incessant activity performed with or for another, even if the other is only imaginary (1). However, some women of color academics embrace these identities and view their function as both vehicles for social justice and the praxis of an ethic of care that resists the individualistic norms of the academy. For many marginalized women, including Black academics, gender interacts with other social forces and active commitments to social justice that complicate Butler's notion of gender performance. bell hooks cautions us not to assume that a "Black woman who works hard to be a responsible caretaker is only doing what she should be doing" as a woman (386). She further argues that our "failure to recognize the realm of CHOICE, and the remarkable re-visioning of both woman's role and the idea of 'home' the Black woman consciously exercised in practice, obscures Black women's political commitment to eradicating racism and other forms of social injustice" (hooks 386). Several contributors' works embody these choices, impositions and dilemmas and provide us with deeper analysis of the extensiveness of Black women's maternal labor with the academy. Their work joins others who argue that academic leaders and institutions pay lip service to diversity, yet do little to address the expectation and devaluation of gendered, maternalized, and invisibilized labor.

As a collection, *Laboring Positions* necessitates a situated extension of the parameters of the unbound and intertwined nature of mothering and labor for twenty-first century women of color academics. Considering the aforementioned breadth of maternal practices performed by Black women, as noted in this volume, within and outside of the academy, it is safe to say that in addition to the expectation of *intensive mothering* as suggested by O'Brien and O'Reilly, Black women simultaneously face the realities of *extensive mothering*.[4] Building on Laurel Ulrich's dichotomy of intensive/extensive mothering, a contemporary interpretation of *extensive mothering* best captures the *scope and impact* of Black women's maternal performance and labor. This expansive net of maternal practices circulates throughout the chapters in *Laboring Positions,* and for many it co-exists with the pressures of intensive mothering. These extensive practices signify, as Black feminists have long argued, that Black women are not merely responsible for mothering their children with few resources and much resistance but are often doing so within hostile work place (and sometimes home) environments. In addition, to mothering their own children in the context of a capitalist, patriarchal and racist society, they are also expected to perform mothering and care work to a wide swath of others due to structural inequities both within and outside of the academy. In sum, contemporary *extensive mothering* encompasses the sociopolitical interventions undergirding much of the Black women's work and mothering practices (hooks 42).

This theoretical extension engages a rift within the present literature on academic mothering. The omission of the complexities and expansive scope of Black academic women's extensive mothering has rendered their experiences further invisible in the current bio-legal mothering discourse. As Lisa William-White recently decried "Where is this research? Where are those voices?" (7). The contributors in this volume respond to these queries and join feminist scholars such as Lisa William-White and Arlene E. Edwards whose works reveal that these joint realities, mothering and intergenerational academic work, when engaged together dictate alternative border zones of meaning making and modes of resistance for many Black women. They also may demand more comprehensive responses from institutions, researchers and policy makers who are currently considering "motherhood penalty," "the maternal wall," the "leaking pipeline" and other structural barriers that have largely centered on gendered inequities as the primary location for intervention.

Policy concerns of work-family conflict are central tensions in several essays; however, structural critiques, and resistances against institutionalized barriers and injustices course throughout the volume. The contributors' wonderfully transgressive essays and critical research serve as evidence that Black women exist beyond the institutional and ideological boundaries that have attempted to define their journeys. The contributors speak to each other and some conversations are louder than others; yet together they offer us a complexly nuanced portrait of the emergent literature on race, gender, mothering, and work.

Finally, Black women scholars continue to serve as a critical location to confront the massive loss and exploitation of intellectual workers in the academy. In them we find the invisibilized body, the sexualized, the gendered body, the racialized body, the underpaid body, the unpaid body, the contingent body, the teaching body, the uninsured body, the radically thinking body, the caregiving body, and we find the servant body of both community and academic institutions. All these locations demand our intervention. The collective works within *Laboring Positions* reveal that Black women's success has largely been because of the tireless labor of other Black women and their communities of origin. It is time for a comprehensive response from the academy. We must take institutional ownership and stabilize the hemorrhaging of Black academic women and place value on their intellectual labor and humanity. In doing so we may be able to address some of the greatest challenges of the contemporary academy.

CONTRIBUTORS

Both singularity and commonality of experience and perspective animate *Laboring Positions*. All of the writers share identities as Black women scholars, yet they offer a variety of intersectional feminist contributions and analyses to motherhood studies. The contributors labor from small liberal arts colleges and large research institutions; historically Black colleges and universities, predominantly White institutions as well as large African universities; graduate programs and undergraduate programs; four year institutions and two year community colleges; they represent the humanities, the professions and the behavioral and social sciences, as well as interdisciplinary fields. They are activists and leaders within and outside of the academy.

The authors are faculty members, graduate students, administrators and independent scholars. Some are journeying toward tenure while others are well respected senior scholars. Still others are part-time or adjunct faculty who cobble together their positions with no employee benefits, no permanent offices, and little professional autonomy. The authors are diverse in socioeconomic status, with some receiving financial assistance from the government to support their families and others are economically privileged. Some of us write from the location of mothering or being mothered by those who are biologically or legally connected to us while others theorize and frame their chapters from the realms of other-mothering, intellectual mothering, educational motherwork, communal mothering, intergenerational mothering or mentoring. Some contributors embrace maternal roles in others' lives while others view the unbound nature of these relationships as potentially threatening to their professional lives and well-being. Collectively, we are staking claim and advancing motherhood studies through the kaleidoscopic lens of Black feminist theory.

OVERVIEW

Laboring Positions is organized by three interconnected themes: Transgression, Testimony and Transcendence. Yet, several themes may flow throughout many of the chapters. Essays located in the first section predominantly embody the theme of *Transgression* and collectively interrogate the multitude of ways in which Black women construct their careers as intellectuals who engage in critical border crossing by disobeying the rules and boundaries of the academy. The authors' essays evoke a keen awareness of the contested ground upon which they tread and traverse. They frame their intellectual journeys from within the sociopolitical struggles that are ever-present within and outside the academy. These authors push back by naming, reframing, and reclaiming Black women's space as embodied intellectuals. For some this entails redefining what being and living as a Black mother scholar means.

In "Community Property: Black Mothers' Communal Ownership of Their Daughters' Degrees," Giovanni Dortch and Candice Bledsoe reframe academia's individualistic model of success and secluded achievement. Their research on Black women's shared educational achievement gives appropriate weight for the invisibilized "educational motherwork" of many African American mothers. The authors' research contributes to radical educational and feminist scholarship by defining daughters' educational successes and reframing intellectual achievement as communally earned. The collaborative and intergenerational owning of education and achievement is at once an act of humility and one of defiance against the academy's tradition of excluding Black women's bodies and work. Their work, grounded in a Womanist research ethic, honors prior generations of Black women's and mothers' intellectual pursuits, which have been historically suppressed in conjunction with the silenced joys and freedoms of their bodies.

Despite the neoliberalization of the academy, which has lead to an increase in economically and professionally vulnerable contingent faculty, Vanessa Marr's chapter, "Teaching for Change: Notes from a Broke Queer Hustling Mama," offers us a location of resistance in her analysis of its economy, politics and culture. Marr puts forth a critical testimony in which she refuses to be invisibilized as an intellectual worker. Her professional, economic and social location as an underpaid and exploited "broke queer hustling professional adjunct" who is also a mother of three, is situated within an environment that privileges White middle class married heterosexual male tenured professors. Her essay deliberately illustrates how her performance as an "academic hustler" at home, in the classroom, and in the community ignites multiple modes of survival and resistance. In doing so, Marr invites readers to consider her full existence despite inherent structural barriers she faces both within the academy and society.

Marcelle M. Haddix and LaToya W. Sawyer's chapter "'I Am My Child's First Teacher': Black Motherhood and Homeschooling as Activism Within and Beyond the Academy," documents the authors' involvement in a homeschooling community, which is fueled by their interrelated roles as Black mothers and as activist scholars. Their work is timely given the continued defunding of public school education in the U.S., which has direct negative consequences for communities of color. Haddix and Sawyer embrace a hip-hop feminist theoretical framework to privilege the counter-stories of contemporary Black mothers in homeschooling communities as they confront master narratives that position Black parents as absent, uninvolved, unengaged, and/or not caring about their children's education. They employ autoethnographic methods to ground their analysis of their intellectual and advocacy work as Black mothers of Black boys. The authors share their personal experiences of making deliberate choices to homeschool their sons as a result of the overwhelming miseducation of African American male students in public school systems. The authors network with other home schooling Black parents through the use of new media forms, which facilitate and create opportunities for contemporary modes of community building. Haddix and Sawyer frame African American homeschooling in the twenty first century as an expression of contemporary Black feminist praxis. They offer, from their self-defined locations as mother-scholar-activists, a multipronged multilevel model for addressing educational inequity by simultaneously educating future public school teachers, partnering with other local parents to advocate for high quality education for their community's children while also providing a nurturing education for their own children outside of failing public schools systems.

My own chapter, "Resisting with Child: Black Women's Embodied Negotiations of Motherhood in the Academy," draws upon the dual interactive discourses on corporeal control concerning Black women's reproduction and academic women's reproduction.

Specifically, my chapter examines the professional, structural and personal issues surrounding Black academic women's constrained choices regarding reproduction and their careers. Using interview data, I consider the ways in which the academy enacts corporal control over women's bodies and thus, rewards and penalizes faculty based on their level of compliance with disembodied patriarchal workplace norms. I argue that Black women, like other women of color, act as transgressive foot soldiers as they simultaneously claim embodied intellectual space by disrupting the mind/body dualism of academia.

Tokeya C. Graham's chapter, "'I'm Not Your Mama': The Plight of the Black Female Academic as Surrogate Mother," reflexively explores the complexities of the professor-student dynamic when it is woven together with shared cultural histories. Her essay deftly interrogates the unique context of the community college setting which she argues encourages a blurring of these boundaries and a fulfillment of racialized and feminized care work. Graham confronts the multiple ways that students seek to position her professional role as one of a surrogate mother. Graham raises key issues for Black women faculty to consider regarding imposed and desired maternal labor. This work is exemplary in its articulation of the internal struggles faculty of color face who are both committed to social justice and who are at high risk of being exploited by the academy. Graham's essay speaks loudly against this second force and reasserts her self-defined path as an academic that sits outside of others' expectations.

The collection's second section focuses on the situated *Testimonies* of Black academic women and offers a collage of the many faces of academic mothering and motherwork informed by race, class and gender. Stories provide food for the soul and many will be edified and inspired by the diverse perspectives offered in this section. The mother-academic narratives include subthemes of struggle and triumph both at home and within academia. They collectively reveal the strengths, vulnerabilities, roadblocks and successes of the contributors as evidence of survival from within. "Black Academic and Single Mother: Colliding Statuses," by Rosalyn Terborg-Penn, offers us a historical backdrop to consider the personal and professional challenges faced by Black women academics who chose to parent prior to the implementation of maternity leave polices. Through Terborg-Penn's memoir, we witness a Black mother academic trailblazer who also simultaneously resists the familiar strong Black woman trope of the "superwoman." Terborg-Penn is best known as a pioneering historian whose scholarship placed Black women's history at its center; however, her essay reveals that she established her career while concurrently parenting as a single mother and care-giving daughter. Her memoir is enriched by her maternal decision to include exchanges with her daughter, which reveals a shared intergenerational retrospective of her journey. Her testimony is a reminder of the many structural barriers Black women, scholars, and mothers navigated just one generation earlier yet remain significant today.

Patricia Williams Lessane's chapter, "And There Went My Adventurer's Spirit: Motherhood and Fieldwork Post-9/11" offers an autoethnographic account of her maternal experiences and professional journey, which redefined her approach to her career as an anthropologist following several traumatic world events and personal loss. Lessanne's testimony takes the reader on her intellectual, psychological and spiritual journey towards personal and professional clarity. Her essay, like several others herein, draws life and career lessons from her relationships with her mother. Lessane's essay offers encouragement to other mother-academics who may have to creatively rework their career trajectories when trauma, familial crises and external events arise. Her testimony assures readers that the journey can and does continue.

Stacia Brown's mother-academic testimony, "Walking Tightropes Without Nets: The Adjunct as Single Mother," reminds us that we still have much ground to cover to meet the complex needs of working mothers. Brown's status as an adjunct discloses her economic and professional vulnerability in the absence of institutional policies and benefits for part-time academic workers. Her essay challenges popularized assumptions that academic and other professional mothers are "opting out" of work and instead reveal that many are often "pushed out" or "kept down" due to structural inequities and the mass reduction of tenure track positions available in the increasingly economically streamlined profession of higher education. Brown's narrative enriches our understanding of many academics' current reality of a shrinking academic job market and the denial and elimination of benefits for part-time workers. Like others in this collection, Brown's sociopolitical understanding of her circumstance fuels her connections to other "others" and drives her mother-activism. Specifically, Brown draws strength and activist vision from her dually belittled locations of adjunct and single mother to create safe spaces in the classroom and via the Internet for other single parents of color. Brown's essay also serves as a telling reminder of the crucial role of extended family members in the caretaking of young children and the stabilization of mothers' working lives.

Rose Sackeyfio's chapter entitled, "Mothering Black: A Cross-Cultural Perspective on Mothering in the Nigerian Academy" is in conversation with Terborg-Penn in that race is not a direct barrier that they must confront within their institutions. The racialized climate in the U.S. did, however, inform Sackeyfio's decision to move her family to West Africa. It was within the historical and sociopolitical moment that Sackeyfio frames the complexity of being a cultural outsider as a Black woman and single mother-academic within the Northern Nigerian academic environment. Sackeyfio's testimony exposes the paradox between the alienation she felt due to her single motherhood status while living within a hetero-patriarchal nation and the support her family experienced while living within a Western African communal context. Sackeyfio's testimony illuminates the compounded interplay between Nigerian cultural and religious milieu, women's subjugated role and status, women's careers, and motherhood. She offers a critical reflexive analysis of the patriarchal and religious constraints that women academics must navigate in Nigerian academic institutions that inhibit their advancement and professional development. Her essay deepens our understanding of Black academic women's subjectivities outside of the Western context.

Markesha McWilliams Henderson and Natalie T. J. Tindall's qualitative research reported in "Clashing Clocks: Black Women Professors' Perceptions of Parenting on Tenure Clock" and is conversant with my chapter. McWilliams Henderson and Tindall's work further highlights the heavily weighed decisions or circumstances surrounding starting and maintaining a family for a sample of Black women professors who were mothers. Using qualitative interview data from ten Black professor mothers who are tenured or who hold tenure track positions, Henderson and Tindall provide readers with a sharpened insight into how their participants navigate the responsibilities of their professional pursuits and family obligations. In doing so, we gain a deeper understanding of how these Black academic-mothers make meaning of their coexisting and sometimes conflicting professional-familial experiences. Henderson and Tindall's research also sheds light on gender role dynamics that academic women confront in their professional and private lives.

The final section, *Transcendence* encompasses chapters that utilize motherhood as the transformative and active resource for reaching beyond the boundaries of the academy. These contributors collectively attempt to redefine the academy's future possibilities by presenting us with intellectual and activist roadmaps for navigating the challenges that await us. Their works cogently conjure Patricia Hill Collins' sage advice highlighted in this Introduction's epigraph. These contributors complete the volume by offering us momentum as they revision the possibilities for Black women in the academy as mothers, daughters, mentors, scholars and activists.

Specifically, in "Daughter Dreams and the Teaching Life of Audre Lorde," Alexis Pauline Gumbs lyrically honors the intellectual motherwork of Audre Lorde. Focusing on mother-daughter subjectivity as a focal point for critical praxis, Gumbs' essay centers on Lorde's dreams about teaching and mothering and her journal documentation of her daughter Elizabeth's dreams. She argues that the dream archive and dream work of Lorde—lesbian, poet, mother, warrior, teacher—serves as a road map for contemporary and future Black mothers survival in the academy. Gumbs' interpretation of Lorde's life and work positions her as a critical figure in the creation of a radical, intergenerational Black feminist praxis of mothering. Most importantly, Gumbs' essay evokes the legacy of prior generations of Black feminist scholars whose intellectual work will continue to reverberate through the thinking and radical feminist praxis of their sister-daughters (and sons) for generations to come.

In her autobiographical essay "Fighting Phantoms: Mammy,

Matriarch and Other Ghosts Haunting Black Mothers in the Academy," Yolanda Covington-Ward locates the gravity of stereotypes on Black women's experiences both within and outside of the academy. Covington-Ward frames and eloquently pronounces the racialized and gendered discourses that often devalue Black women's motherhood. Covington-Ward's expertly applies Marvin Carlson's theatrical construction of "ghosting" to suggest that the academy serves as a repository of cultural and social memory. Covington-Ward builds on this construction by offering her own narrative of resistance and provides suggestions for those who might join her on this journey into the sacred grove. Covington-Ward's work challenges Black women to stay put and to resist being swayed by the backlash that they may face with the academy. She reminds us not to be surprised but to continue to challenge and confront the academy when met with resistance. Her work encourages Black women to transcend boundaries, both imagined and real, that often steer us away from spaces where we rightfully belong.

Karen Craddock's chapter "Mothering and Mentoring: Relational Dynamics Among Black Women in the Academy" considers the role of Black women academics positioned as mother/mentors to other Black women in the academy. Emergent ideas on this "mothering" context are put forth by exploring dynamics of power and relationship between both women while resisting the stressors in the academy. Building on extant qualitative research of psychological resistance to marginalization and mother-daughter relationships among young Black mothers, Craddock uses salient themes and constructs of the Profiles of Resistance and Models of Mother Involvement that were revealed. Parallels are drawn between mother/daughter dyads and the role of Black women graduate students or junior scholars and their senior colleagues or professors. Her exploration offers a mother/mentor comparative framework that can be used to examine patterns of psychological resistance and relational dynamics among Black women and other under-represented women of color who are navigating the often stressful and often marginalizing context of academic institutions.

Finally, the volume closes with a visionary piece by Julia Jordan-Zachery. This essay responds to many of the professional and personal issues raised in the volume and provides us with a useful framework that is organically built from Jordan Zachery's own exemplary experiences. Her chapter, "Black Women Occupying the Academy: Merging Critical Mothering and Mentoring to Survive and Thrive," is reciprocally conversant with Craddock's and responds to concerns raised in Graham's essay by inviting other Black women to critically reflect on the nature and purpose of their service to others. Jordan-Zachery's builds her framework by considering the parallels between her roles as both a Black mother and an academic mentor. She thoughtfully responds to many mentors within the academy by offering a balanced model of mentorship that resists the essentialist trope of the perennially selfless and self-sacrificing Black mother by centering her essay on the needs of the faculty mentor. Jordan-Zachery's model, like Gumbs' is built from Black mother-daughter dynamism and compels us to utilize the organic models and metaphors we have before us in our journeys as academics. Her mentor framework serves social justice minded faculty who yearn to support their students and junior colleagues' survival within the marginalizing environment of the academy while they simultaneously transcend the very same positions.

CONCLUSION

Babies typically exit women's bodies at a designated gestational age of nine months/forty weeks. Sometimes delivery takes place at home, sometimes in a hospital and other times on the side of the road. However, I and only I had to decide when this body of work would be born unto the world. It was I who had to decide that the topic was worth laboring for. It was also I, who decided who I would co-create this product with and what form the volume would take. It was an empowering and painfully personal journey for which I am thankful to have had sista (and brother)-doulas along the way to comfort and support me. In the end, I am pleased with the process and the product.

However, for all the ground that I hoped to cover with this collection, there are notable lacking perspectives and voices that are critical to consider in this area of maternal and feminist theory and research. Topics that are in need of being further examined include issues germane to mothering and women in the academy from the African diaspora and other women of color; issues of queer parenthood, fathering and the care work of academic Black men and other academic men of color; student mother voices, Black mother academics on issues of disabilities; and the oft silenced voices and perspectives of child-free and childless Black academic women. I invite my fellow scholars to explore these unintended omissions that are also opportunities for knowledge production waiting in disguise within this budding subfield of motherhood studies.

I join Andrea O'Reilly in her declaration that Motherhood Studies continues to be a viable area of scholarly inquiry. I notice as I share this volume's focus, that others' eyes clouded over, possibly questioning the legitimacy of a scholarly focus on professional Black women's working lives and mothering experiences. Were they questioning those that dared to speak our truth? This I will never know, but my fellow contributors and I view our collective labor as worthy.

In closing, I offer this collection not as a panacea or a rebuttal of prior work on mothering in the academy. It is not a celebration nor condemnation of motherhood and academia—struggle, joy, resistance agency and ambivalence weave throughout. I do envision the volume as a structure for a fuller conversation on academic mothering and Black women's working lives. I also hope that the essays that follow will inspire and activate other academic "others" to dialog across borders.

NOTES

[1] Stanlie M. James defined the concept of the community *othermother* as the women in Black communities who support birth mothers both formally and informally in the responsibilities in child rearing.
[2] Lynn O'Brien Hallstein suggests third wave and intersectional feminists are matrophobic in their assertions of feminism. However, I have not found this to be the case. Intersectional feminists, like many of the scholars in this book, pay homage to the feminists of color who have come before them and build their works from the foundational texts that have theorized more complexly around constructions and the politics of mothering.

[3] Julia Grant tracked the genealogy of *intensive mothering* and framed it as a retrograde mothering ideology that has placed undo pressures upon contemporary women and mothers. Sharon Hays, Susan Douglas and Meredith Michaels, and Andrea O'Reilly contend that intensive mothering is defined by three core beliefs 1) children need and require constant nurturing by their mothers who are exclusively responsible for meeting the child's needs/desires; 2) "good mothers" are under the direct guidance of experts; and 3) that mothers must channel all of their time, energy and resources into their children at the expense of their own lives as women.

[4] Laurel Ulrich's concept of *extensive mothering* involves the care of many young rather than the deep investment of a few as in "intensive mothering." Julia Grant argues that intensive mothering has become more central in contemporary societies however, many groups, including women of color, poor women and women who work outside of the home continue to engage in extensive mothering practices.

WORKS CITED

Bousquet, Marc. "Lady Academe and Labor Market Segmentation." *The Chronicle of Higher Education*. Web. Retrieved on December 30, 2012.

Butler, Judith. *Undoing Gender*. New York: Routledge, 2004. Print.

Cole, Johnetta B. "Preface." *Double Stitch: Black Women Write About Mothers and Daughters*. Eds. Patricia Bell Scott, Beverly Guy-Sheftall, and the SAGE Women's Educational Press, Inc. New York: Harper Collins Publishers, Inc., 1991. xiii-v. Print.

Collins, Patricia Hill. "The Meaning of Motherhood in Black Culture and Black Mother-Daughter Relationships." *Double Stitch*. Eds. Patricia Bell-Scott, Beverly Guy-Sheftall, Jacqueline Jones Royster, Janet Sims-Wood, Miriam DeCosta-Willis and Lucille P. Fultz. New York: Harper Perennial, 1991. 42-57. Print.

Collins, Patricia Hill. "Shifting the Center: Race, Class, and Feminist Theorizing about Motherhood." *Mothering: Ideology, Experience and Agency*. Ed. Evelyn Nakano Glenn, Grace Chang, and Linda Forcey. New York: Routledge, 1994. 45-65. Print.

Collins, Patricia Hill. "The Meaning of Motherhood in Black Culture and Black Mother/Daughter Relationships." *SAGE Journal* 4.2 (1987): 7. Print.

Cooper, Anna Julia. "Women's Cause is One and Universal." *The World's Congress of Representative Women*. Ed. May Wright Sewell. Chicago: Rand McNally, 1894. 711-15. Print.

Davis, Angela. *Women, Race and Class*. Toronto: Random House, 1981. Print.

Douglas, Susan J., and Meredith W. Michaels. *The Mommy Myth: The Idealization of Motherhood and How It Has Undermined Women*. New York: Free Press, 2004. Print.

duCille, Ann "The Occult of True Black Womanhood: Critical Demeanor and Black Feminist Studies." *Signs* 19.1 (1994): 72-92. Print.

Edwards, Arlene "Mothering the Mind Women of Colour Creating Supportive Communities to Increase the Academic Success Rates of Minority Students." *Journal of the Association of Research on Mothering*. 5.2 (2003): 144-153. Print.

Evans, Elrena and Caroline Grant. *Mama PhD: Women Write About Motherhood and Academic Life*. Piscataway, NJ: Rutgers University Press, 2008. Print.

Grant, Julia. *Raising Baby by the Book: The Education of American Mothers*. New Haven: Yale University Press, 1998. Print.

Gregory, Sheila T. "Black Faculty Women in the Academy: History, Status, and Future." *Journal of Negro Education* 70.3 (2001): 124-138. Print.

Gutierrez y Muhs, Gabriella Yolanda Flores, Carmen G. Gonzalez and Angela P. Harris, eds. *Presumed Incompetent: The Intersections of Race and Class for Women in Academia*. Boulder: University of Colorado Press, 2012. Print.

Harley, Debra A. "Maids of Academe: African-American Women Faculty at Predominately White Institutions." *Journal of African American Studies* 12 (2008): 19-36. Print.

Hays, Sharon. *The Cultural Contradictions of Motherhood*. New Haven: Yale University Press, 1996. Print.

Henderson, Tammy, Andrea Hunter, and Gladys Hildreth. "Outsiders within the Academy: Strategies for Resistance and Mentoring African American Women." *Michigan Family Review* 14.1

(2010): 28-41. Print.

Hollingshead, Carol S., Beth Sullivan, Gilia Smith, Louise August and Susan Hamilton. "Work/Family Policies in Higher Education: Survey Data and Case Studies of Policy Implementation." *The Challenges of Balancing Faculty Careers and Family Work, New Directions in Higher Education*. Ed. John W. Curtis. 130 (Summer 2005): 641-65. Print.

hooks, bell. "Homeplace: A Site of Resistance." *Yearning: Race, Gender, and Cultural Politics*. Boston: South End Press, 1990. 45-53. Print.

James, Joy and Ruth Famer. *Spirit, Space and Survival*. New York: Routledge, 1993. Print.

James, Stanlie M. "Mothering: A Possible Black Feminist Link to Social Transformation." *Theorizing Black Feminisms: The Visionary Pragmatism of Black Women*. Eds. Stanlie M. James and Abena P.A. Busia. London: Routledge, 1993. 44-52. Print.

Mason, Mary Ann, Marc Goulden and Nicholas Wolfinger. "Babies Matter: Pushing the Gender Equity Revolution Forward." *The Balancing Act: Gendered Perspectives in Faculty Roles and Work Lives*. Eds. Susan Bracken, Jeanie Allen and Diane Dean. Sterling: Stylus, 2006. 9-30. Print.

Moses, Yolanda T. "Black Women in Academe: Issues and Strategies." *Black Women in the Academy: Promises and Perils*. Ed. Lois Benjamin. Gainesville: University Press of Florida, 1997. 23-38. Print.

Motta, Sara. "The Messiness of Motherhood in the Marketised University." *Beautiful Transgressions, Ceasefire*. June 2012. Web. June 30, 2012.

Myers, Lena Wright. *A Broken Silence: Voices of African American Women in the Academy*. Westport, CN: Greenwood, 2012. Print.

Myers, Samuel and Caroline Turner. "The Effects of Ph.D. Supply on Minority Faculty Representation." Papers and Proceedings of the One Hundredth Sixteenth Annual Meeting of the American Economic Association. San Diego, CA, January 3-5, 2004. *The American Economic Review* 94.2 (2004): 296-301. Print.

National Women's Law Center. "Employment Crisis Worsens for Black Women during the Recovery." 2011. Web. Retrieved July 25, 2012.

O'Brien Hallstein, D. Lynn. "Being and Thinking Between Second and Third Wave Feminisms: Theorizing a Strategic Alliance Frame to Understand Academic Motherhood." *Academic Motherhood in Post-Second Wave Context: Challenges, Strategies and Possibilities*. Eds. D. Lynn O'Brien Hallstein and Andrea O'Reilly. Bradford, ON: Demeter, 2012. 354-380. Print.

O'Brien Hallstein, D. Lynn and Andrea O'Reilly, Eds. *Academic Motherhood in Post-Second Wave Context: Challenges, Strategies and Possibilities*. Bradford, ON: Demeter, 2012. Print.

O'Reilly, Andrea. *From Motherhood to Mothering: The Legacy of Adrienne Rich's "Of Woman Born."* Albany, NY: SUNY Press. Print.

Ramsay, Karen and Gayle Letherby. "The Experience of Academic Non-Mothers in the Gendered University." *Gender, Work and Organization* 13.1 (January 2006): 25-44. Print.

Roberts, Dorothy. *Killing the Black Body: Race, Reproduction, and the Meaning of Liberty*. New York: Random House, 1998. Print.

Spillers, Hortense. "Mama's Baby, Papa's Maybe: An American Grammar Book." *Feminisms: An Anthology of Literary Theory and Criticism*. 2nd ed. Eds. Robyn Warhol and Diane Price-Herndl. Brunswick, NJ: Rutgers University Press, 1997. 384–405. Print.

Ulrich, Laurel Thatcher. *Good Wives: Image and Reality in the Lives of Women in Northern New England, 1650-1750*. New York: Knopf, 1982. Print.

United States Department of Education (USDoE), National Center for Education Statistics. "Fast Facts: Degrees Conferred by Sex and Race." Web. Retrieved April 7 2012.

Villalpando, Octavio and Dolores Delgado Benarl. "A Critical Race Theory Analysis of the Barriers that Impede the Success of Faculty of Color." *The Racial Crisis in American Higher Education: Continuing Challenges for the Twenty First Century*. Eds. William Smith, Philip G. Altbach and Kofi Lomotey. Albany: State University of New York Press, 2002. 243-270. Print.

Walker, Alice. *In Search of Our Mothers' Gardens: Womanist Prose*. New York: Harcourt, 1983. Print.

Washington Post-Kaiser Family Foundation Poll of Black Women in America. Web. Retrieved March 31, 2012.

William-White, Lisa. "Seeking Emancipation from Gender Regulation: Reflections of Home Space for a Black Woman Academic/Single Mother." *Qualitative Research in Education* 1.1 (2012): 4-35. Print.

I.
TRANSGRESSION

1.
Community Property

Black Mothers' Communal Ownership of their Daughters' Degrees

GIOVANNI N. DORTCH AND CANDICE BLEDSOE

If you educate a man, you educate an individual; if you educate a woman; you educate a family (nation).
—Dr. James Emmanuel Kwegyir-Aggrey (1875-1927)

I (GIOVANNI) *first became interested in examining motherhood and African American women in academia during the first year of my doctoral program when I worked in the front office of my department as a graduate assistant. One of the senior graduate students came in and asked the secretary to attend her graduation. I chuckled to myself, recognizing how tedious and long graduations are, and the audacity of this woman asking the secretary to basically come to work on her day off. It reeked of classism from my perspective. Many of the older students had informal relationships with the secretary. However to impose a parental or familial role upon her was for me, a violation of the staff and student boundaries. I continued to listen as the secretary inquired why the student's family would not be attending her graduation. The student replied, "My dad's mad because I'm not going to be a 'real' doctor." I was stunned; this woman's family would not attend the awarding of her Doctorate of Philosophy because she was not receiving a Doctorate of Medicine? Because this encounter occurred between two white women, I could only attribute the situation to class difference and dominance, and I knew, for me, it was a glimpse into a different world, one in which I would never fully occupy. In my community and from my experience, mothers spearheaded their children's' educations. In the absence of a mother, I wondered where her community was, her support system, the people she was connected to prior to entering the university and grad school. In the end, reflecting on my own mother, my personal practices as a mother, and the experiences of the women I surrounded myself with, I could only wonder, where is this woman's mother? Her father and his ignorance could avoid and boycott all he wanted, but* WHERE *was this woman's mother?*

Many Black female students have completely different histories and unique experiences at the graduate levels of education when it comes to being mothered. Whereas academia is a notoriously isolating singular endeavor, we, as well as a significant portion of our colleagues who are Black women have experienced the process of obtaining advanced degrees as a communal one. Consequently, our degrees and the process of completing them belong not only to us but to our communities of origin, and especially to our primary caregivers, our mothers and grandmothers.

Being mothered as a graduate student has the potential of transforming mother-daughter relationships in powerful ways. The notion of ownership, communal work and physical, emotional, moral and mental support often grow exponentially when a daughter enters academia. As mothers of graduate students, our parents bear witness to our struggles not only as students and teachers, but as mothers, wives, lovers and friends as well. Our entrance into disciplines that are overwhelmingly "white" spaces intellectually and physically trigger a myriad of reactions, from protection to pride at the work we produce and the challenges to which we subject ourselves.

While "making it their business" to nurture and mother us through the process, they also envision our success as their own success, with Doctoral and Master's degrees becoming "our" achievements, as indeed they are the product of communal work in multiple ways. Our research explores, through the lives of African American women, the community property notion of academic achievement among mothers and daughters.

We ground our research in a womanist research ethic, which, as Marsha Houston explains, is community cognizant. Community cognizant research is described by the following characteristics: a research agenda that is set by the concerns of ordinary speakers;

it employs community based theories; it accepts that members are heterogeneous; it problematizes privilege and power; and it is written in an accessible way" (677). We recognize and use the normal protocols of academic research (informed consent, specified releases, etc.) while incorporating the specific methodologies significant to womanist methods. We also recognize that our proximity to our interviewees in social status and strata presents its own set of privileges and consequences (Few, Stephens and Rouse-Arnett).

Our research extends from our own experiences and those of women in our particular scholarly community. They consist of multi-generational, extended family and communal ownership of and investment in our advanced degrees, starting at the most basic levels of the graduate school process, extending to graduation. While well educated and erudite, we strive for accessibility in our language, terminology and explanations, as indeed, mothering is an experience for multitudes of women. We specifically identify the differences and highlight those differences in our community member participants' experiences while acknowledging the shared experiences of being mothered, obtaining higher education, and returning that education or the benefits thereof to the community. We also recognize that the experiences we discuss are not the experiences of all Black women who enter into graduate study, and are not exclusive to Black women. They are the experiences that we have discussed widely in our various geographic, academic, familial, social, religious, and created communities and locations.

PARTICIPANTS

We examined the experiences of five women who are at different phases of their graduate school education, different places in their careers, in different disciplines and from various geographic locations and institutions to discover the ways in which their advanced degrees become the community property of mothers and women elders in the community as well as their daughters. The stories of five women, Giovanni N. Dortch, a sociology doctoral student, Candice Lucas Bledsoe, a Human Rights graduate certificate and education doctoral student, Erma Johnson Hadley, the Chancellor of Tarrant County College, Chandra Harkins, a playwright, business owner and soon to be graduate certificate student and English doctoral student, and Whitney Peoples, a Women's Studies doctoral student, explain that regardless of location, time, academic program, age, and level of achievement, Black mothers make significant investments in their daughters degrees, and feel a sense of communal ownership. Whether or not they had previously attended college, understood their daughters' scholarly work, or understood the full purpose of higher education, the mothers we discuss took their roles seriously and aggressively invested in their daughters' degrees, which they also subsequently use and claim communally.

Case #1

For Giovanni, the initial investment of mothering occurred when she decided to move out of state to study for her doctorate. As a single parent, her community, including master's degree advisers and administrators, former classmates, neighbors and parents were invested in her success. They encouraged her to further her studies while simultaneously expressing concern over how she would balance her coursework, employment and parenting duties. After negotiating, seeking advice and conversing with various members of the community, it was collectively decided that Giovanni should leave her children with her own parents, and go off to school for a year, and then send for her children. The practice of women seeking education while mothering has existed for generations among women of color. From antebellum periods until the modern day, obtaining an education while mothering has been seen as a way to increase the quality of life for both single and married mothers and their children. (Guy-Sheftall; Hunter; Battle-Waters; Watkins). Giovanni's decision parallels that of poet, novelist and professor, Margaret Walker Alexander, who chronicles her efforts to complete her doctorate while mothering four children; Walker ultimately decides to leave her younger children with her mother while she completes her doctorate, and her older children attend college (Guy-Sheftall 459).

This decision proved crucial to Giovanni's success as a first year doctoral student. She was able to attend school full time, work on campus as an instructor and departmental assistant, maintain a 4.0

GPA, and fulfill her residency requirement for the degree program. She made monthly visits back to her hometown to visit and care for her children, and enjoy the fellowship of her family.

Despite Giovanni's family serving as an extended community for her children, Giovanni's mother, Mrs. Dortch, also undertook the majority of childcare, including, meal preparation, clothing, transportation, academic support and emotional concern. Hence in this situation she not only mothered Giovanni from afar, but mothered her own grandchildren who resided with her and Giovanni's family of origin.

Another investment that Mrs. Dortch made into her daughter's graduate school education was being interested in and seeking to understand the process. Prior to Giovanni's departure, her mother was uncertain as to why one would seek graduate level education; she encouraged her to pursue work avenues instead, and argued that Giovanni was not utilizing her network to find employment. Once Giovanni began her program, her mother took the time to sit with Giovanni, understand the graduate school process, negotiate the logistics of childcare and even accompany her to academic conferences.

Mrs. Dortch also took it upon her self to invest financially in Giovanni's success by funding Giovanni's attendance to academic conferences, contributing to childcare costs, and funding Giovanni's trips home for very necessary and nourishing family time. These trips provided Giovanni a reprieve from the often isolating and stressful environs of the academy.

This investment in Giovanni's academic endeavor became a source of pride and the degree expanded to a sort of communal ownership as Mrs. Dortch regularly inquired into Giovanni's progress, requested drafts of research presentations, and even monitored Giovanni's leisure time with phone calls, Facebook check-ins and e-mail correspondence. In this way, Giovanni has been able to maintain her academic progress and parental duties over the course of graduate school with the multifaceted wrap around support of her mother. She is currently writing her dissertation proposal in preparation for her dissertation research, and plans to pursue a career in academia as a professor of Women's Studies and Sociology.

Case #2

Like Giovanni Dortch, Candice Bledsoe knew that after graduating from Baylor University with her BA, she was going to take a different path from most of her friends. Many of them began relocating and working for companies. They would often share their starting salaries with one another to see who would win. Candice knew that she did not want a traditional corporate job. As a result, her first post-graduate experience teaching as an Instructor of English at Yonok College, in Lampang, Thailand reassured her that she wanted a career in academia.

Her mother, Geraldine Perry continuously supported Candice's travels and education. She would often say, "You are not the first to go to college, but you have obtained many 'firsts' in our family. Don't stop with travel. Please, continue your education, too." Candice's travels allowed her to experience educational opportunities and public speaking opportunities in uplift and motivate citizens of Burma, Cambodia, Malaysia, Thailand, Germany, France, England, Italy, Belgium, the Netherlands, Scotland, and Luxembourg. After completing her stay at Yonok College, Candice returned to the United States.

Candice decided to obtain her Masters in Liberal Studies at Southern Methodist University. Her classes focused primarily on Human Rights and African American Literature. She worked and attended graduate school, while being married and having a child. Her mother would provide emotional and spiritual support on a daily basis by calling Candice to reassure her that her sacrifices were worth the cause. This proved helpful as Candice maintained her friendships from her prestigious alma mater, Baylor University, and witnessed the economic success of her peers, while she focused on putting her passion and talent for writing to use in a way that would not only benefit her, but allow her to eventually serve a larger community.

Candice's mother-in-law, Renette Bledsoe would also assist Candice with childcare, so that Candice could focus on her studies. Renette would often prep dinners for the week to make the task of cooking easier for Candice. "I see everything that you are doing Candice: working, going to school, being married, and taking care of your children. I'm proud of you. That takes work, and I will help anyway that I can." Even her grandmother, Madea (during this time she was in her late eighties), and Aunt Joyce Hackworth would help Candice with her family, too. The community beamed with pride when she graduated with her master's degree.

Although, several women in her family had obtained a master's degree, Candice received her degree from a Predominately White Institution as opposed to the Historically Black College and Universities (HBCUs) that her relatives were forced to attend due to legalized segregation that existed for the previous generations of college graduates. In one case, Madea, Candice's grandmother, had to relocate her entire family to a city located 300 miles away, because that was the nearest HBCU institution offering graduate programs. She did not build resentment towards mainstream institutions, but secretly wished she could have experienced some the benefits of the major universities. Therefore, when Candice received her undergraduate degree from Baylor University, and her master's degree from Southern Methodist University, it was a surreal moment. Candice's nicknames quickly became "Miss Baylor" and "Miss SMU." Her mother was so proud of this accomplishment that she keeps her undergraduate degree at her home; she has it framed and mounted in her living room for all who enter her home to view.

Candice continued to pursue her doctorate at University of Southern California. It required more emotional and financial support than her other degrees. Candice's mother and mother-in-law would frequently purchase school clothes for her children, and make sure that they had everything they needed. Candice's mother lived in Wisconsin; however, she would call her every morning, mail care packages that included clothes, toys, and cards, and send loving emails to show her support.

Candice enjoyed working on her doctorate, and she also felt compelled to help solve problems in her community. For example, after learning about an educational model in class, she took that knowledge to create an academic program, *Poetic Diamonds*, which addresses K-12 level needs in her community; focusing on enhancing academically challenged and underserved students' written and oral communication skills. She began transferring the education she was learning in her program and improving her community. Candice also developed *The Cutting Edge Youth Summit*, a student conference that helped minority students in the areas of mentorship, leadership, and scholarship. As Candice learned more about the effects of class, education, and gender, she began a pen pal initiative to write letters of support to women on death row called the *Death Penalty Anthology* project. Her community is impressed by all that she has accomplished at a young age. They continue to support her and they feel she will be able to contribute more when she completes her doctoral and certificate programs.

Case #3

Making a community contribution is also what inspires Chandra Harkins, a playwright and business owner residing in Memphis, TN. From her teens into her adulthood, she described herself as "different" from the other women she grew up with. However, during her adult life, she went from describing herself as different, to realizing a community description of herself as "standard bearer." With a mother who stressed education as a road to independence and away from the limitations of the small town of Columbus, Mississippi, Chandra successfully became a first generation college student as well as the first in her family to obtain an advanced degree. Her mother's concerns were both practical and rooted in her own experiences. While the senior Mrs. Harkins exchanged her college dreams for the role of wife and mother, she consistently drilled and prepared Chandra for both a life outside of Columbus and for the future she once imagined for herself. Mrs. Harkins, along with her husband fully prepared Chandra for her future at the University; they were so invested in fact that they had contingency plans in place in case Chandra became pregnant or faced any other obstacles. Chandra describes her mother's involvement as instrumental both physically and emotionally. Her mother called her daily, sent care packages of food and clothing, gave advice to help her maintain a balanced life, and served not only as a mother, but as an ally as well. She ensured Chandra's success by encouraging her to study, to party but to protect herself from STIs and pregnancy by carrying her own condoms, to not become too invested in the men around her, and to maintain a focus on her goal.

In her words, Chandra found that in the process of earning her undergraduate degree, her mother was "living it with me and living it through me." Chandra went on to explain,

> *She always talked about what she would do if she were in my situation ... and she was so influential in my life I accepted that, and you know, that's what I did. I did pretty much what she told me to do.*

When Chandra announced her plans to attend graduate school to her mother, she was delighted to hear her mother's full encouragement and support, as well as the revelation that her mother had already envisioned this as a part of Chandra's life in a prophetic dream. She told Chandra "I've already seen this. I've already seen you with your blue outfit on like the college president's (referring to graduation regalia)."

Chandra's education and academic endeavors have become community property and especially the property of her mother through her mother's mentorship, prayer, support and encouragement of Chandra in obtaining her education. It also earned Chandra an esteemed role in her family. Her mother regularly consults Chandra on major decisions, summons Chandra's research skills, and maintains a meticulous understanding of Chandra's credentials, professional standing, and business endeavors. She takes pride in Chandra's achievements, protects Chandra's time and space as a businesswoman, and works to promote all of her company's activities.

Not only was Chandra's education an asset that her mother invested in and received benefits from, but Chandra's immediate family and community were influenced by her obtaining her degrees as well. Although Chandra has made efforts to be discreet about her academic endeavors, she is very aware of how significant her education is. She describes Columbus as a place that is very traditional, with limited opportunities. Her education has not only exposed her to a new world, environment, and parts of herself, but also allowed her to be an advocate for her mother, a mentor to her nephew, and a standard bearer for the larger community of Columbus. In terms of the community she encountered in college and graduate school, she has found that her education has had an impact on the Memphis community as well.

Only 24 percent of the residents of Memphis, Tennessee, the city in which Chandra attended college and continues to reside, have college degrees. By having both an undergraduate and graduate degree, she stands out as a well-educated woman whose business endeavors work to bring positive attention to the city and provide high quality entertainment and exposure to its residents.

Chandra's position as a college educated African American woman from a small town in Mississippi and still residing in the South underscores what her education means to the elder women in the community. These women who faced segregation, denial of education, disrupted educations and limited opportunities are delighted to bear witness to Chandra's and other women's success. Chandra's mother and her friends see her education as the fulfillment of what could have been, and now IS. In this way, as a first generation college student, Chandra and her peers have become the "standard bearers" for women in their community. She felt pressure to make her family proud and to disprove the naysayers, yet her success was already ensured through her mother's support, dedication, prayer, mentorship, encouragement and vision for Chandra's future. Her next step is to complete her graduate certificate in African American Literature, and teach collegiate English in addition to her work as a playwright and businesswoman. She eventually plans to pursue her doctorate as well.

Case # 4

As Chandra begins her journey towards her doctorate, Whitney Peoples is nearing the end of her time as a graduate student. Soon to be awarded her doctorate in Women's Studies, Whitney Peoples, a fourth year doctoral student at Emory University, attributes her success in the degree earning process squarely to her family and community. She explains that her community of mothers, consisting of her biological mother (Mrs. Peoples) and her co-mothers/biological aunts affectionately known as "Mama Cookie" and "Mommy Mae-Mae" as well as her grandmother instilled early on an expectation that she and her sister would attend college and obtain a professional level education. Her grandmother, who was an African American educator who held a graduate degree, was a rarity in Texas. This cross-generational value for education was impressed upon Whitney at an early age, and she explained her mother's bewilderment with some of her academic choices as well as the tensions she faced when embarking upon her unique educational path.

Whitney attended Agnes Scott College, a small women's Liberal Arts College in Atlanta, Georgia, to complete her undergraduate education. This proved to be the first of many decisions that allowed her to stake her independence yet strike a balance between the expectations of a community heavily invested in her education and her own knowledge and desire of what was best for her. Hailing from a family of well-educated women, Whitney's mothers expressed "skepticism" about her choice of a women's college in the South. She explains, "They would have rather seen me at a Seven Sisters school" Whitney's choices were scrutinized again, yet ultimately supported when she chose to leave law school during her first year, and instead pursue a Master's degree in Women's Studies. Whitney explained that her mother was able to be much more supportive when she made the decision to earn a doctorate in Women's Studies. Whitney understood the value of the doctorate in terms of professionalism, respectability, employment and earning power, and her mother understood its value in terms of the opportunities it would grant Whitney.

Whitney explains that mothering for her occurred in a multitude of ways. When she entered Emory University, she did so just after sustaining an injury, which required her to use a wheelchair and other disability accommodations. The progress of her injury required very basic care, and Whitney's mother immediately stepped fully into her role as nurturer and caretaker. She ferried Whitney around campus, helped her care for herself physically, and simultaneously assisted Whitney in the navigation of the process of beginning the school year.

Whitney describes her mother's work as consistently hands-on throughout the academic process. Whitney explained that the physical care work of mothering is a never-ending process. When she visits her hometown of Fort Worth, she explained, she gets a visual inspection from her mother, and if she is not looking "appropriate" her mother immediately begins making hair appointments or plans to go shopping. Her mother engages in mothering not only when Whitney returns home, but will also travel to Atlanta to care for Whitney. Comprehensive examinations are notoriously stressful and demanding times for students in graduate school. In Whitney's case, her mother visited her at school, and stayed with her during the exam process. She also served as a witness to Whitney's work when Whitney defended her dissertation proposal, recording the entire presentation. In this era of new technologies, this writer has witnessed Whitney's mother's use of tools such as Facebook to remind Whitney to stay focused on her studies, and express pride at her daughter's various academic milestones, such as conference presentations, the publication of articles, and the completion of various steps in her selected program.

The "other mothers" in Whitney's community also have provided her with spiritual, mental, emotional and financial support. Whitney describes the "Mae-Mae Mail" that her aunt sends: small inspirational cards and tokens of affection such as gift cards serve to remind Whitney that she is cared for and loved, that her mothers are thinking of her, and that they are confident in her ability to succeed.

Attending a graduate program in the same city that she completed her undergraduate education gave Whitney access to another community as well. She has created a new community comprised of many of her undergraduate friends, along with members of her new department. This community has also invested in and taken ownership of Whitney's academic achievements. Along with her mothers, her friends have shared in Whitney's degree attainment by providing her with a social outlet, supporting her at presentations and practice talks, and serving as a bridge between her new community in Atlanta, and her community of origin in Fort Worth, Texas.

Reflecting on the communal ownership of her accomplishments, Whitney explains that as varied as the investments are, the claims are exhibited in an overwhelmingly uniform way. She shares that her friends and mothers use the term "our degree," "our Ph.D." and her biological mother has ventured to tell Whitney, in regards to the time required to complete the doctorate, "we will finish in five years." The community's pride in Whitney's pending accomplishment is reflected in her listing in her friends' email address books, where she find nearly all of her friends and family have her listed as "Dr. Whitney." In small but tangible ways, the community is expressing its pride, support, and encouragement, urging Whitney towards completion of her doctorate.

Looking forward to her graduation, one of Whitney's other mothers has plans to cut and resize her own deceased husband's doctoral gown. Although Whitney expresses understandable trepidation regarding wearing her uncle's gown, she appreciates the sentiment of her aunt's family pride in her accomplishment.

Case #5

From graduate students to college presidents this story of African American communal support is enduring. Chancellor Erma Johnson Hadley calls herself "the little girl from Leggett, Texas." She was raised in this small southeast Texas town, where racism was visible and unmasked. Her mother poured into Hadley qualities that encouraged her to become a strong person despite her experiences of racism and sexism. Erma Johnson Hadley is known as the first African-American from Leggett, Texas to graduate from college. Her mother and community adopted her success as their own. They continued to inspire her to achieve the dream, and now she serves as the Chancellor of Tarrant County College in Tarrant County, Fort Worth, Texas.

As Chancellor Johnson Hadley reflects on her mothers' role in her educational success, she notes that her mother could not always assist her with homework but she set high expectations. Her mother always demanded that her "homework was to be neat, and presentable." When Chancellor Johnson Hadley told her mom that she wanted to go college she remembers her response, "I don't know anything about college. Erma Jean, we need to find someone who can show you how to get into college." As a result, her Home Economics teacher, Mrs. Gibson, helped her through the college admission process. This communal support for Johnson Hadley would continue through her college career.

Attending Prairie View A&M was very exciting and challenging. Although, her mother and community provided as much financial help as they could render, Johnson Hadley had to work while she attended college. In fact, because attending college was such a financial sacrifice she made it a goal to graduate in three years. Due to her hard work, she did complete her BA within this self-imposed time frame. Her community applauded her for these accomplishments and she quickly became a role model for children of color in Leggett, TX. "If anyone had a question they would say, 'Ask Erma Jean she goes to college she knows the answer!'" Despite financial difficulties, Erma Johnson Hadley overcame these obstacles and graduated from college.

After graduating from Prairie View A&M, and teaching high school for four years, she decided to pursue her master's degree in Ohio's Bowling Green State University. Although her mother did not contribute to her education financially, she did offer her emotional support during those years in graduate school.

Johnson Hadley remembers her mother's pride when she obtained her degree at graduation. "My mother had never flown before.... But she flew, so that she could attend my graduation.... After the graduation my mother said that should would be more careful about the way she spoke because her daughter had a master's degree and she was proud of that." Johnson Hadley's mother, like the mothers in the previous cases, allowed her daughter's accomplishments to guide her own behavior. Becoming aware of how she spoke and used language was a conscientious decision that Mrs. Johnson made as a direct result of her daughters higher education, exemplifying the community property notion of the advanced degree.

The multigenerational aspect of educational achievement and ownership is expressed in the experiences of Chancellor Erma Johnson Hadley's mothering of her own daughter, Ardenia. She attended Spelman College, in Atlanta, Georgia. Although, Johnson Hadley did not get a chance to enjoy the student life aspect at Prairie View A&M she witnessed her daughter's student life experiences. For example, Ardenia participated in student government every year of her undergraduate career, an extracurricular activity that was not afforded to her mother, due to financial constraints and the need to graduate as quickly as possible. Also, Chancellor Erma Johnson Hadley and her husband, Bill, would attend Parents' Weekend every year. "Anything that included parents, we were there at

Spelman showing our daughter support. I told my daughter that her job was to be a scholar... Each summer my daughter would share her experiences with me. From attending summer camps to being a White House intern, my daughter has enjoyed her college career inside and outside the classroom."

Chancellor Erma Johnson Hadley did not end her academic guidance and mentoring with her own daughter. She continues to serve as a role model for over 100,000 students at Tarrant County College. Her successes compliment her mother and community that supported her on her journey. This support continues to flow through her daughter, Ardenia Johnson Gould, and her many experiences and accomplishments as a budding academic.

DISCUSSION

From the experiences of these five women, clear themes of care work emerge. That is to say that the work of caring, providing tangible items of care and intangible items of care are a part of the practice of mothering and investment into daughters seeking higher education. It is enacted cross-generationally, communally and can be framed as activism. The end result of this care work is not one sided, however. Mothers, community members and daughters reap the benefits of the labor of mothering.

One important theme is that mothering is a continual, cross generational process. Another theme that emerged is that despite the respondents' mothers' inability to mother their daughters in vivo, they are still able to do so from afar. This form of agency, of mothering and using the power of emotional and spiritual support for one's children from afar, suggests that the contemporary mothering practices examined here are consistent with historical mothering practices in which African American women engaged (Collins 2000: 176; Conaway 6; Hunter 62).

The interviews reveal that mothering is not a process that occurs solely from birth mothers, but from mother figures as well. Patricia Hill Collins writes extensively on the practice of community mothering and "other-mothers" when she theorizes Black motherhood as a form of activism (Collins 2000: 178). In the case of Black women's minuscule representation in academia (according to the National Center for Education Statistics, they earned about 6.5 percent of doctoral degrees conferred in 2008-09 [USDoE]) the work of preparing Black women for higher education can be interpreted as activism. Rhetorical activism, which involves actually creating and modeling survivalist parenting practices similar to the methods of nineteenth-century journalist and "race woman" Mary Ann Shadd Cary,[1] is one of the direct corollaries of activist mothering. It is a practice in which many of the interviewees enacted (Conaway 6).

Finally, communal ownership comes not simply out of competitive "bragging rights" that may occur when children are young, but from actual investments into their adult children's academic experiences. The communal ownership, for these mothers, is best exemplified by the fruits they reaped from their daughters' education. Chancellor Johnson-Hadley's mother chose to make an effort to represent herself more strongly in the way she spoke, Chandra Harkin's mother now has a well educated advocate for her health challenges and daily personal business that must be handled. Candice Bledsoe's mother proudly displays her daughter's degree in her home and continues to share Candice's classwork with visitors and friends. Giovanni's mother has received word from a close friend that her own parenting practices were informed by Mrs. Dortch's. The mothers referenced are also able to hold their daughters up as examples of what can be accomplished as they go about their daily lives. Their daughters are tangible templates to younger women they mentor, younger family members, church members and friends.

Intergenerational Process

In the cases of Giovanni, Candice and Chancellor Hadley, mothering is a process that spans at least three generations as all three women have children. In Chancellor Hadley's case, we were actually able to gain an understanding and witness an investment in the next generation's undergraduate degree through her interaction with her daughter Ardenia, who attended Spelman College. Both Giovanni and Candice experience mothering from their own mothers in the sense of material, moral and emotional support through phone calls, social media, care packages and financial gifts. They also experience physical support through childcare, meal preparation, and assistance with other household duties, which allows them time to pursue their studies. In this way, not only are Candice and Giovanni being mothered, but their children are also mothered extensively by their grandmothers. Giovanni and Candice have also extended their mothering by exposing their own children to the academy in that they bear witness their mothers studying, teaching, writing, reading and being fulfilled through such work. They are also making these goals also appear tangible to their own children and defying the mother or academic dichotomy, which is very important as women are still pressed by the question of "having it all." Giovanni and Candice engage in mothering communally by volunteering in and creating events that nurture the broader community. Finally, Chandra's narrative also expresses cross-generational mothering. Her mother as well as other community mothers use Chandra's accomplishments as an exemplar for their granddaughters of how to take advantage of the opportunities available for young women in the modern era.

All of the women interviewed had to leave "home" in order to attend school. Both Chandra and Chancellor Hadley were first generation college students. They hailed from small isolated rural communities that were steeped in the traditions and poverty of the south. Both had mothers who were married and had ended their educations prematurely to as they undertook traditional gender roles of wife and mother. Their mothers fully supported and encouraged them in their pursuit of education, and both completed advanced degrees. Their mothers encouraged both women with advice, prayer, counseling, emotional support, and reminders to care for themselves regardless of their own educational attainment. Chancellor Hadley worked during her undergraduate program and sought employment immediately after graduating but was continually encouraged by her mother when she decided to pursue an advanced degree. Both Chandra Harkins and Chancellor Hadley experienced high esteem from their local neighborhood, town, and church communities of origin as not only first generation college students but also from the distinction of being among the first in the black community.

Mothering as a Communal Process

Chancellor Hadley, Giovanni, Candice and Whitney's interviews reveal that mothering is a communal process. They all experienced the support of people in the community, educators as well as extended family as they pursued their advanced degrees. From the communal decision to keep Giovanni's children with their grandparents, to Mrs. Renette Bledsoe, Candice's mother-in-law, entering her home to assist with household tasks, to the "Mae-Mae Mail" Whitney received it is revealed that mothering is a community process. Community can and does contribute in decision making, support, advice, encouragement and even guidance, this practice is an embodiment of Patricia Hill Collins' concept of othermothers (*Black Feminist* 180). In these case studies we find that the maintenance of traditional Africana[2] mothering and othermothering practices have helped insure a high level of success for the interviewees (Collins, *Black Feminist* 7; Conaway 11).

It is important to note that while this chapter focuses on mothering, all of the interviewees experienced childhood within two parent heterosexual families, which are included in their definition of community. Giovanni, Candice, Whitney, and Chandra expressed that their community included their fathers and male community members who actively "fathered" them as well, by expressing concern, offering guidance, encouraging them to stay focused, and making occasional visits. For example, Candice's father, the late Rev. Alvin C. Lucas, was instrumental in her becoming an avid reader and motivated her to write poetry, a passion that later fueled her graduate pursuits in English and education. Giovanni's father regularly called her to monitor her progress, offer encouragement and words of advice, and provided child care when she attended academic conferences to present her research. In the cases presented, the care-work aspect of motherhood becomes a practice that is enacted not only by mothers, but by fathers, aunts, in-laws, grandparents, former teachers, mentors and friends.

Communal Ownership of Education

Communal ownership occurs on the smallest up to the largest levels. Mothers recognize their daughters' education as valuable assets to the family and larger community. They commandeer the services of their daughters for research, information, writing, teaching, and community service. They seek their own self improvement as their daughters become educated. Candice's experiences in the once segregated hallways of Baylor and Southern Methodist University was seen as valuable amongst her family and community because she had access to resources both human and material that previous generations of her family had been unable to access. As Mrs. Hadley explained, when she was in her community of origin, the general statement was "go ask Erma, she goes to college." Chandra's education has allowed her to become an esteemed member of her community of origin and earned her a trusted space in her mother's life as her medical advocate and general manager of her personal affairs. Giovanni's pursuit of higher education has allowed her to help her mother envision her *own* post retirement path. Whitney has added to her familial legacy of high expectations, education, and community care, and is prepared to mentor, mother and motivate future generations.

IMPLICATIONS

This essay serves to share with the reader the complexities of mothering, care labor and investment that some African American mothers and daughters experience when a daughter matriculates into academia. Although the communal ownership of daughters' degrees is significant in and of itself, there are four specific implications that can be drawn from the experiences discussed here. From the interviews, we are able to conclude that the process of communal ownership facilitates the amelioration of the "problem" of Black motherhood and historically locates Black mothering practices. It also serves to exemplify the cyclical nature of community ownership and benefits, as well as the prestige granting power of Black mothering.

Black motherhood has consistently been challenged and problematized in the broader sociopolitical discourse. From the right to "own" their birth children during enslavement as explained by Hortense Spillers, to the modern day blame-game that attributes social problems to poor Black mothers, Black motherhood is under constant attack (Bryant 1; Collins, "The Meaning" 4;

Gumbs 1; Spillers 59). This attack exemplifies the conundrum of Black motherhood in the United States. In a nation where enslaved Black "mammies" were expected to care for white children, then suddenly, upon a few generations of freedom, were subsequently framed as ineffective at mothering their own children, a certain paradox of parenting has occurred. Through communal ownership Black mothers reassert their legitimacy and value as mothers by directly appropriating the larger society's values and privilege onto themselves through their daughters' educations. They are able to counter the public narrative and establish themselves as legitimate mothers using their daughters' achievements as "evidence."

In addition to the "right" to mother, African American mothers often feel compelled to prove they can be "good" mothers. This work builds upon the body nineteenth century evidence supporting the *effectiveness* of Black mothering and frames mothering work as activism (Conaway 8; Littlefield 57; McDonald 775). Mothering that is continually aware and focused on fighting oppression, activist mothering, is the type of work in which the mothers discussed above were/are engaged. Collins explains, "Black daughters must learn how to survive in interlocking structures of race, class and gender oppression while rejecting and transcending those very same structures" ("The Meaning" 7). This type of activism is necessary for Black women to secure their educations and compete in larger society as discussed by Audrey Watkins' expression of her views on education as a practice of social justice (14). These narratives demonstrate that while raising daughters that were educationally prepared for graduate school, these mothers also raised daughters that were politically prepared to engage in their own forms of activism.

Communal ownership is not an isolated practice; while providing mothers and other-mothers with prestige, it also serves as a larger investment into the communities from which the recipients emerge. Communal ownership exemplifies *reflexive historical practice and praxis* of Africana and African American mothering. For example, at least three of the five "daughters" profiled above participate in community, activist and rhetorical mothering practices by hosting and volunteering to work at events for parents and children in their respective communities. Candice hosts an annual event, the

Cutting Edge Youth Summit in Dallas, Texas, while Chandra and Giovanni host the *Mic Check Hip Hop Youth Seminar* and *Youth Writing Workshop* respectively in Memphis, Tennessee. Communal (othermothering) and individual investment in individual daughters is repaid to the community through service, creating a legacy of mothering as activist practice both rhetorically and as a form of social justice.

Finally, community ownership as a mothering practice is not only a claiming of rights and effectiveness but also a claim to a privileged and prestigious status that the larger society values. When daughters achieve the highest levels of education offered by mainstream society, (especially when they have been routinely denied to previous generations) communal ownership allows mothers/grandmothers to reclaim power from social institutions that would/have previously denied such prestige while simultaneously "proving" the effectiveness of historical Africana mothering practices.

The proverb from Dr. Kwegyir-Aggrey that opens this chapter is resoundingly true. Not only does educating a woman educate a nation, it reaches back and brings our past generations into the future. The communal ownership of their daughters' degrees allows mothers (and others) to emerge fulfilled as well.

NOTES

[1]Mary Ann Shadd Cary (1823-1893), an African American journalist, expatriate and self-proclaimed "race woman" used editorials to urge the "new generation" of African Americans to set up homes and families in ways that were supportive of middle-class African-American values. She sought to establish a standard for Black families that would earn the respect of whites and prove socially beneficial for the future freedmen. Her work on how to parent and form families has been considered a form of activist (other-)mothering.

[2]The authors refer to Africana mothering practices as those practices of mothering originating specifically from the sociopolitical position of African descended people in the Diaspora. The practices are neither comprehensively situated nor directly derived from Af-

rican continental practices, but serve as indicative of the practices engaged in by African descended people in North America and the Caribbean, born out of their need for survival.

WORKS CITED

Battle-Waters, Kimberly. *Sheila's Shop: Working-Class African American Women Talk about Life, Love, Race and Hair*. New York: Rowman &Littlefield Publishers, 2004. Print.

Bryant, Valerie. "The Social Construction of 'Manymothering' Representations among African-American Women." *Psychoanalysis and Psychotherapy* 16.2 (1999): 235-260. Print.

Collins, Patricia Hill. *Black Feminist Thought: Knowledge, Consciousness, and the Politics of Empowerment*. 2nd ed. New York; Routledge, 2000. Print.

Collins, Patricia Hill. "The Meaning of Motherhood in Black Culture and Black Mother/Daughter Relationships." *SAGE* 4.2 (1987): 3-10. Print.

Conaway, Carol B. "Rhetorically Constructed Africana Mothering in the Antebellum: The Racial Uplift Tradition of Mary Ann Shadd Cary." *The Journal of Pan African Studies* 2.1 (2007): 4-18. Print.

Few, April L., Dionne P. Stephens, and Marlo Rouse-Arnett. "Sister-to-Sister Talk: Transcending Boundaries and Challenges in Qualitative Research with Black Women." *Family Relations* 52.3 (2004): 205-215. Print.

Gumbs, Alexis Pauline. "'We Can Learn to Mother Ourselves': A Dialogically Produced Audience and Black Feminist Publishing 1979 to the Present." *Gender Forum: An Internet Journal for Gender Studies* 22 (2008) Web.

Guy-Sheftall, Beverly. *Words of Fire: An Anthology of African-American Feminist Thought*. New York: The New Press, 1995. Print.

Houston, Marsha. "Writing for My Life: Community Cognizant Scholarship on African American Women and Communication." *International Journal of Intercultural Relations* 24 (2000): 673-686. Web. 12 Apr. 2011.

Hunter, Tera W. *To 'Joy my Freedom': Southern Black Women's*

Lives and Labors after the Civil War. Cambridge, MA: Harvard University Press, 1997. Print.

Littlefield, Marci Bounds. "Black Women, Mothering and Protest in 19th Century American Society." *The Journal of Pan African Studies* 2 (2007): 53-61. Print.

McDonald, Katrina Bell. "Black Activist Mothering: A Historical Intersection of Race, Gender and Class." *Gender and Society* 11 (1997): 773-795. Print.

Spillers, Hortense J. "Mama's Baby, Papa's Maybe: An American Grammar Book." *Black Feminist Reader*. Eds. Joy James and T. Denean Sharpley-Whiting. Malden, MA: Blackwell Publishers, 2000. 57-87. Print.

United States Department of Education (USDoE), National Center for Education Statistics. "Fast Facts: Degrees Conferred by Sex and Race." Web. Accessed 7 April 2012.

Watkins, Audrey P. *Sisters of Hope, Looking Back, Stepping Forward: The Educational Experiences of African-American Women*. New York: Peter Lang Publishing, 2009.

2.
Teaching for Change

Notes from a Broke Queer Hustling Mama

VANESSA L. MARR

SNAPSHOT #1: A BOOTS/TRAPPED EXISTENCE

The recurring dream usually begins and ends the same way: I am floating in a tank that continues to fill with water. There is no escape hatch—only an opening that is beyond my reach. Something is trying to pull me under but miraculously I resist whatever forces are waging war against my weighted body. My arms are flailing as though they are trying to fly, but they too are pulled downward. I can feel my heart racing as seconds feel like hours. Desperate to stay alive, I kick forcefully in hopes of breaking free. After much struggle I then find myself floating upward toward the surface. As I approach the opening and begin to lift my head through—anticipating the sweet gulps of air that will soon reward me—a deluge sweeps me back under and I am forced in the depths for another attempt at survival.

I start the fall semester exhausted from another restless night. Rolling off the donated mattress that has served as my bed for the past four months, I slowly make my way from the living room (which doubles as my sleeping quarters) to the bathroom. I stopped thinking about getting a couch when I realized that even a used one is beyond my means. My stretches to relieve aching muscles produce nothing. In the bathroom I take a long look in the mirror; the dark circles under weary eyes demand closer inspection. I feel like shit—the eyes don't lie. In spite of this crude assessment, I force myself to smile. My crooked teeth grin back through the reflection, a reminder that I should have had braces years ago but could never afford to. They are the reason why I often look serious in photographs or prefer to be behind the camera—I am too self-conscious to produce full-frontal smiles for all to see. As bristles lather enamel I think about those studies that correlate physical attractiveness and higher teacher evaluations, wondering if students are grading me—a full-figured bald Black dyke—with their eyes. My mind then shifts to faculty discussions of collegiality and worry if I appear unfriendly to full-timers who could later use their observations against me when a lecturer position opens up. *She may not be a good fit for us.* I begin to brush harder, ignoring the subtle taste of blood between the gums. If I can't make them straighter, I can at least make them *whiter.* Near the end I smear the thick toothpaste foam across my lips and try to reconstruct the smile that has eluded me all these years. I look rabid but the frothy cosmetic procedure covers the gaps and overbite perfectly. The silliness of the act helps me to forget about my sore back and I am ready to face the day.

Before I leave for work, I call to check my Bridge Card[1] balance; it is the second of the month but food assistance payments are always distributed on the third. Hoping for a DHS[2] glitch, wishful thinking on my part. My chest tightens when I hear there is still only $1.25 left over from last month. I have a grand total of 19 cents in my checking account due to a computer error that deducted my electricity bill twice this month. The refrigerator is almost empty and the kids have to fend for themselves during the longer days when I'm teaching back-to-back courses. I am tempted to ask my lover—herself a Black single mother and public school teacher—for help but pride (or is it shame?) prevents me from doing so. She lives five minutes from my apartment and empathizes with my struggle, but I feel like a prostitute whenever I ask her for money. She doesn't hide her frustration whenever I skirt around the issue. The kids once told her that I was taking birthday money out of their wallets without their permission to buy groceries and toilet paper, and her response was a blend of shock and annoyance—pilfering cash from children is something a "good" mother should *never* do. Unwilling to stir up another thorny conversation about power dynamics and class dichotomies,

I convince myself that such a request would be unnecessary. There is enough peanut butter, bread and milk to hold them over; the macaroni and cheese I made three days before can serve as backup.

I begin to consider other ways I could bring in immediate income such as hocking my paternal grandmother's ring and posting photos of household items to sell online. I search the classifieds for weekend temp jobs that could accommodate my current teaching schedule. Sometimes I don't make a lunch during the lean semesters so the kids have more to eat—that strategy has worked well enough. If they call during class tonight complaining of hunger, I will stop by the grocery store and use my state-issued $1.25 to pick up something for them to snack on before bedtime. I begin to wonder whether they would call me at all since they have been instructed to reach me during class time *only* in the event of an emergency. I imagine them trying to do their homework with grumbling stomachs and avoiding the phone altogether because they know how important it is for "mama to focus at school so she can graduate and get a very good job someday." They know the drill well; I gave them the first lesson years before when they were in diapers. *Not now, sweetie—Mama's trying to focus on this paper, Okay?* It's the same line I tell myself when the shutoff notices start piling up or the credit collectors are asking to speak to me. *I'm trying to graduate. I'm trying to teach. I'm trying to get a very good job. I'm trying....*

Before I walk out the door, my daughter hands me a note from her elementary school's food services department: Her lunch account is $2.00 in arrears and payment is to be made as soon as possible. Hearing my voice shift in a tone usually reserved for punishment, she's quick to explain the pizza sticks that she chose instead of the blander items usually set aside for free-lunch students. "I didn't know I wasn't supposed to get those," she says apologetically. "I was too hungry to pay attention and I wanted to get through the line. But I liked getting the same stuff other kids were getting. Why can't I get pizza sticks, too?"

"Because Mom's *broke*—she can't buy *those* kinds of lunches!" my teenage son belts out from his bedroom. He's been a free-lunch kid since kindergarten and knows how to navigate the lunchroom. I felt sorry for him during those early years because students had to verbally identify themselves as either "full," "reduced," or "free" lunch: kids with money were "full" whereas welfare brats were "free" and were also branded as such in terms of discipline and academics. As a high-school student in Ann Arbor, however, he can use an electronic keypad to punch in a code in order to discreetly (and mercifully) move through the line quickly without his well-off peers knowing just how much of a failure his mother is on paper.

"Yeah, I'm broke—for now...Why you think I do what I do?" I shoot back as I walk out the door. It takes everything inside me to sound convincing.

Despite my persistent worrying, I have designated my forty-minute commute from Ann Arbor to my university teaching gig in Detroit as don't-think-about-money time. The issue is always drilling in the back of my mind and I try to push those thoughts as far back as possible to maintain focus on the bigger picture: another college degree and the hopes of securing gainful employment. I purposefully ignore the "Check Engine" light that wants to direct my attention to the screeches and rattles emitting from under my car's dusty hood—definite (and costly) repairs that must be made. Watching the landscape transform as I drive past hilly subdivisions and manicured lawns to fire-scarred neighborhoods and abandoned warehouses provides me with lessons in gratitude. *I may sleep on an old mattress in a small apartment with two kids and drive a car that's falling apart, but at least I live in an affluent college town. I live within walking distance from a grocery store chain, a coffee shop, and a decent library. As far as I know, my children are safe and I can leave them home alone for hours if necessary. They attend "good" schools that will improve their chances of success later in life. I have no reason to complain.* As I am nearing the Detroit border, my cell phone begins to vibrate in my jacket pocket. The caller ID flashes an 1-800 number that is unfamiliar. I answer, but there is no response. I assume there is a delay in the connection. "Hello? Helloooo?" I call into the silence. I wait for the click that signals a live line. Finally, an automated voice greets me and instructs me to please wait to hear an important message from my credit card company. No doubt, this important message has something to do with money I don't have but is owed to someone on the other end of the connection. *"Hello?"* I ask, hoping the politeness in my voice will alter the purpose of the call. A soft feminine midwestern voice responds, "Good morning. May I speak to *a* Vanessa Marr?" Whenever a caller addresses me with an indefinite article attached to my name, I know it is a creditor hounding for payment. She is not looking for A Vanessa Marr—she wants THE Vanessa Marr who has skipped another payment.

Although I have handled these types of telephone calls for years, I still fumble around for the right words. Bill collectors are never interested in the sob stories told to them by their debtors—their objective is to demand or arrange for payment, not to discern fact from fiction regarding their clients' tales of hardship. "But I'm not like the others," I want so desperately to explain and pierce through their apathy. "You see, I'm trying to make a better life for my kids and me. I'm a graduate student trying to support a family on loans and stipends. I'm trying to teach college students to succeed in the 'real world.' I'm trying to get off welfare. I just need someone to cut me a break. *I'm trying....*" Instead, I give my standard response using my best "standard" English: "Oh, yeah ... that last payment. Yes, I knew when it was due but I don't get paid until next week. I know there will be a late fee assessed, but I have no choice. Yes, I'll be sure to send in the full amount next week. Thank you for contacting me ... You have a good day, too." The soft feminine caller from the credit card company seems satisfied with my promise to pay, and leaves me to finish my commute. I didn't have the heart to tell her that I have given that same promise to several other collectors, offering to deduct from the same paycheck that is already completely spent. Would it have mattered if I had told her the truth? Once a deadbeat, always a deadbeat. *But I'm trying....* The despair that clutters the Detroit skyline appears uncomfortably closer after the call. In a fit of frustration I slam my hands on the steering wheel and begin to scream at god, at the car, and at myself. The tantrum leaves me trembling and makes my throat hurt.

I'm breaking in a new pair of old shoes this morning. A recent purchase at St. Vincent's thrift store in Ann Arbor, my brown suede laced men's loafers are about a size too big and devoid of cushioning. Unable to afford clothes at a full-price retailer, I try to look for professional attire for pennies on the dollar. Despite its reputation of affluence, Ann Arbor is prime shopping for cash-strapped people such as myself; thrift stores are not as heavily stigmatized in these parts because trendy-yet-frugal college students frequent them in search of the latest in avant-garde couture. When I discovered my brown suedes at St. Vincent's, I thought I had hit the jackpot: a designer brand from Italy for only $3. I imagine their previous owner to be a retired prof—some bearded white guy sporting a wool jacket, tailored slacks, and brushed brown suede shoes. But they are literally and figuratively shoes too big for me to fill. They hurt like hell, especially when I walk across the gravel-covered parking lot across the highway from the building where I teach speech and business communication courses. By the time I make it to the door, the bottoms of my feet are throbbing. It is then that I begin to limp in order to provide some relief. Perhaps I am being punished for trying to wear shoes clearly not designed for Black working-class women in academia. Worse, I feel I am being punished for encroaching a space clearly not designed for me. While studying the sisterly wisdom of Gloria Anzaldúa, Barbara Christian and bell hooks, I often discover firsthand the ways in which the ivory tower is systematically structured to render women of color invisible and silent at even the most "diverse" institutions of higher learning. It is during the drives between part-time teaching assignments, during the faculty meetings that do not welcome my presence or my vote, and during contract negotiations with administrators who do not put my lack of a livable wage or health insurance on their bargaining table when I feel as though I matter least.

As I slowly make my way to the elevator, one of my current students, Stacy[3], seems to be approaching me. "Hey, Professor Marr! What's up?" She chirps at me but brushes by as though she is running to someone else's class. While I smile at her during this brief exchange, I'm secretly relieved that she didn't want a long conversation. Not only am I eager go to my office and sit down before my morning session begins, but it also annoys me when students refer to me as "Professor" and I rather avoid them than have to wrestle with the title. I prefer to be called simply by my first name since contingent faculty have no designation. It separates me from many of the full-timers who can purchase their comfortable shoes at full-price if they so choose.

Before limping into the adjunct office, I stop by the main office to collect my mail. The department secretary greets me and informs me that Jenny just called and left yet another message for me about my bank loan. I'm late with that payment, too. "Is it a collection call?" she asks. "God, I hate those!" She knows I could use some sympathy. I hate returning Jenny's calls. While most creditors contact me on my cell phone to protect my privacy and preserve my dignity, Jenny likes to play hardball by calling me at work where I can't hide—public humiliation is her preferred modus operandi. When I finally make it to my office, I almost overlook the torn piece of notebook paper sitting on my desk—a message in large letters instructing me to CALL JENNY RE: LOAN PAYMENT. Evidently she called the main office the day before. To add insult to injury, Jenny also sends a terse e-mail message to my inbox while I am preparing for my classes. I am to phone her immediately to address my delinquent account since previous efforts to reach me have gone unanswered. Determined to complete my preps and nurse my tantrum-induced sore throat, I choose to respond to Jenny via e-mail. I quickly thank her for sending a reminder and make an actual promise to mail out a money order next payday. She may keep harassing the front office if I don't pony up, so I readjust my budget for a $300 payment to the bank; some other creditors will get nothing as a result but I'll try to work on those accounts later. *Later* always sounds reassuring. I'm anxious to get to class in order to feel like a productive citizen once again.

SNAPSHOT #2: RESILIENCE AS RESISTANCE IN THE URBAN CLASSROOM

One month into the winter semester I am sitting in the Washtenaw County DHS office a few hours before my late afternoon class at another campus slightly closer to home. Every six months I submit my income and employment information to remain eligible for the food stamps that help keep my family afloat. Instead of receiving the usual letter confirming membership on the dole, however, I am notified of imminent cancellation due to an income increase—a $5,000 summer research grant—the previous year. Assuming that the department mistakenly regarded the grant to be permanent income, I make several frantic attempts to contact my caseworker the day before my visit. No answer. I want to leave a voice-mail message and explain the mix-up, but her mailbox is full and cannot accept one more client's plea for an appointment. Knowing it will be a long wait, I stuff a stack of ungraded essays in my tote and head out the door. By time I make it to the center, there are at least 100 people waiting to be seen. I take a number, find a seat, and try to focus on grading reader response essays for the next two hours. To avoid eyestrain, I look up to glance at the faces of the people seated closest to me. The young Black mother trying to keep her newborn and toddler boys quiet. An older White man balancing his oxygen tank against an empty chair. I return to the business of grading, though my eyes keep running across the same line. When my number is finally called, I jump up and rush to the counter. I ask to see the caseworker to review my status and to request a hearing.

"Do you have an appointment?" the clerk asks tersely through his bullet-proof glass barrier.

"No … I couldn't get through to her voicemail." I respond, trying to sound as desperate as I felt.

"Sorry—no one gets in without an appointment. That's the policy. If your caseworker isn't answering her phone, you can call the manager's line." He writes the phone number down a small piece of paper and slides it through the narrow opening between the glass and the counter. I am ordered to return to my seat. Hoping for a live connection, I dial the numbers. No answer. Again. I hang up and redial at least a dozen times in hopes of irritating somebody—anybody—enough to pick up a phone. Still nothing. Frustrated to the point of tears, I leave for campus and try to prepare a lesson in my throbbing head.

By the time I walk into the classroom, I am physically and emotionally drained but look forward to teaching nevertheless. It is there where I can truly be myself and move about comfortably in my own skin—crooked teeth, bald head and all—even while wearing uncomfortable shoes. I can leave my financial burdens at the door and kick back with other college students struggling to get ahead through education. I joke with one student in particular, Raymund, a White sophomore who is exploring postmodern theory in his spare time. "Good luck with that, chiiile," I needle him. Raymund and the rest of the class begin to laugh. My attempted switch to Black vernacular provides the punch line as a means of resisting dominant discourse while my body makes the moves to match: hands resting on hips, eyes rolling back, mouth smacking loudly. Through most of the semester we have been practicing effective presentation skills and the benefits of employing "good" speaking techniques, though I question whether doing so guarantees positive results. My humorous comment to Raymund is intended to generate critical analysis: Is this guarantee offered to *all* people who employ academic English? What if someone doesn't have the "right" body size, skin color, gender or upbringing? Does "proper" speech matter in such cases? In this space I can facilitate discussions on White privilege by using education as a springboard.

Social class is often acknowledged but rarely discussed within the context of multiple identities in academic settings often due to the discomfort the topic produces among privileged participants. Though not intended to condemn individuals of elevated social status, discussions regarding class privilege in social structures and institutions are designed to get to the heart of the issue—unloading the cultural baggage that comes with hierarchical systems created to uphold certain populations while marginalizing others. The urban classroom (which, in my case, is being taught by a working-class instructor) can make these issues more salient. My stories of hardship intertwine with those of my students. Students who can't relate are invited to share their cultural assumptions regarding class. Gina, whose parents immigrated to the States from Poland when she was seven, vents during a heated discussion on universal health care: "I don't see why *we* have to pay for other people to see a doctor just because they're too lazy to get a job that provides health insurance. Just look around campus at these bums panhandling and digging through trash cans.... We're supposed to pay for *their* health insurance? My dad came to this country, learned English, worked his butt off, and became successful! Why can't other people do that?!" After a few of her classmates respond in support of or in opposition to her assertions, I comment by saying that this nation's history includes 500 years of oppression against people of color—start with the Native Americans and Mexicans who had their land stolen from them, as well as Africans who were brought to this country against their will. There are systems still in place designed to oppress these and other groups—be it through immigration "reform," mandatory sentencing, zoning ordinances, and the like—that make it damn near impossible to get ahead. For certain groups, working one's butt off isn't enough—it *never was* enough. I want to go further by saying, "Just look at *me,*" but I hold back this time. Although Gina and her supporters are not swayed by my argument or the discussion in general, I hope they at least gain some perspective. That would be a step in the right direction—facilitating dialogue to promote social change beyond the classroom. Near the end of class my cell phone begins to vibrate—another 1-800 number from another debt collector flashes on the caller ID. I put the phone on mute and ignore the call to make the most out of a teachable moment.

"Do you ever speak to the panhandlers on our campus? Do you ever offer them food? Do you ever hear their stories?" I ask the class. The students appear surprised to hear me to suggest such a thing. Reggie, a Black criminal justice major, chimes in: "That's crazy! You know they just want money for crack. I've been living here all my life—that's just how it is, man." The class agrees. I immediately share my story about a panhandler I met outside my office building when I first started studying and teaching in Detroit. I didn't have a quarter to give him but had a little more on my student card, enough to get him a sandwich and chips. He introduced himself as Jerome and I shared my first name while we shook hands. On the way to the sub shop he told me about his battles with alcohol addiction and the steps he's been taking in his life to get his act together. Assuming I was an undergrad, he encouraged me to finish college so I can get a good job. I didn't want to tell him that I was in grad school partly because I couldn't find a good job anywhere, so I played to his assumptions. He was especially appreciative of my generosity, but I was more appreciative of his company. I didn't have to engage in dry academic banter or keep up appearances to validate my existence with this man—it was okay to keep it real and to put my guard down. When I finally disclosed that I was an instructor on campus, he was thrilled that I would take time to talk with him. "That should be the other way around," I told him. "This was the best conversation I had all day ... I'm glad I met you. Take care of yourself, Jerome." My students try to understand why I would talk to a complete stranger who asks for change and picks around garbage. "What better way to know the world around you?" I respond. "We're all connected in some way regardless of our position in life." I desperately try to believe that is true. While it is possible to make these connections through reflexive writing, personal encounters are problematic when one party feels threatened by another. It is through sharing one's story with another in an inclusive space that leads to transformation and liberation, even amid threats to cancel food stamps while the caseworker is nowhere to be found.

The chance encounter with Jerome deeply planted the pedagogical seeds necessary for me to reconsider my approach to teaching in relation to my own intersecting identities, those that are more often in conflict with the institutional ideal than not. When I began graduate school, I searched for a way to best articulate the isolation and alienation I was experiencing in a learning environment that privileges White and middle-class cultures. I was desperate to find a way to bring my Blackness, my queerness, and my working-class ghetto-ness from the margins without feeling that I didn't belong in a college classroom in the first place. Given the conversations I have had with students from similar backgrounds who were experiencing similar struggles, I knew I had to do more to decentralize my role as instructor and increase my focus on the financial, educational, and emotional needs of students who were trying to make their way through the sometimes unforgiving terrain of higher education. Living the life of the mind while leaving my body and soul detached could never be an option for me. Grounded in the Black feminist tradition, this formation of a "queer hustling mama" pedagogy provides a space for me to combine personal experience, dedication to community, and commitment to caring as a cornerstone in order to "transform current positions of powerlessness" among oppressed students and instructors that centers on—but can also extend beyond—people of color (Omolade 38).

As a result, I work to integrate practical solutions to situations that are most relevant to my students and their everyday lives. If someone cannot afford textbooks for my courses, I either distribute loaners (donated by students from previous semesters) or make sure electronic copies of the readings are available for download to help keep down costs. If my teaching schedule coincides with lunch or dinner, I encourage students to coordinate potlucks or, if I can afford to do so, purchase my own light snacks to share. If a single mother does not have childcare, she knows her children are always welcome to sit in and participate—they can "co-lecture" with me depending on their age and comfort level. Students who need emergency transportation can call me before class to see if I'm along their route. Because I am an out lesbian, students who are struggling with issues regarding their sexuality especially seek my company and know where to find me when they need a listening ear, some words of wisdom, or a simple hug. Because I am still in school myself, students who are struggling with the financial and emotional aspects of college see me to learn how to navigate the financial aid red tape or to understand the importance of self-care when they are spread too thin between family, work, and academic obligations. Although I am not "required" to work beyond my teaching duties and office hours, I use these opportunities to nurture and build community to my advantage. I do not engage in these acts of compassion as a means of portraying myself as the self-sacrificing mammy hell-bent on burning out; rather, I am establishing what bell hooks characterizes as "homeplace," a site of resistance traditionally created within gatherings inside church basements and at kitchen tables to combat systems of racial oppression (42). Not only does the classroom serve as a source of empowerment for my students and me to act on our own behalf, but it also provides a safe space to discuss social inequalities in education and to engage on a personal level. When I explain to students what it means to be an adjunct instructor, many are shocked to hear that I do not have health insurance or that my income qualifies me for welfare benefits. They are curious to know how that can happen and why a college education doesn't automatically lead to material success. Some want to know how they can help, to which I often respond: "Just spread the word that we exist and that we are struggling. When you hear that cuts to higher education are justifiable because supposedly all professors make too much money, remember us. Remember me. Then act accordingly." As students see me hustling to make learning matter, they see me hustling to make our lives matter as well. We are lifting as we climb together, one weary step at a time. *Remember us. Remember me.*

SNAPSHOT #3: GROWING HOMEPLACE BEYOND THE CLASSROOM

While attending the annual Allied Media Conference at my home campus one summer, I am fortunate to come across the Single Mamis of Color caucus. It is a refreshing sight: a gathering of about 15 Black and Brown women—some with playful small children in tow—sitting under a large tree to have a working lunch. Although I have passed by this tree countless times while hurrying between classes and hurrying home, it never looked so alive before. These women, themselves a blend of working-class graduate students and queer-identified community activists, have traveled with their babies from as far away as California and New York to sit under this tree in Detroit to share their stories and to connect with others like them. They talk of how they are treated on their campuses, about how it is difficult to find support among faculty who frown on them because they need childcare at academic conferences or need to negotiate teaching schedules in order to meet their sons and daughters at the bus stop. They talk of the struggles of being involved in their respective radical activist communities that don't know how to (or don't want to) accommodate young children at their meetings. They talk of the challenges of balancing their lives as mamas and lovers, organizing political protests between romantic dates and bedtime stories. They talk of the freedoms they experience through their blogs, poems and performances. As I join in the discussion and begin to share my own journey, I want to soak the ground and the tree with my tears. A woman sitting nearby wraps her arm around me; the warmth of her sideway embrace makes me feel at home even though I am supposed to be hosting. We all agree that the AMC is a good place where *hermanas* can build an intentional, sustainable community while defining *mami'hood* through collective action. There is healing in numbers. We then get to work bringing our concerns, ideas and dreams into the discussion: creating childcare collectives at academic and political conferences, integrating cultural constructions of motherhood in our curricula, forming neighborhood small groups to share resources and strengthen kinship circles, and so on.

With each suggestion come stories of how the women's personal and political lives would be affected for the better if others play some small part. I begin to think about how I could provide a short-term solution when one of the participants asks where she could be able to purchase affordable food with her Lone Star Card, Texas's version of food stamps. "There's a grocery store within walking distance from campus," I say. "Some of the stuff is on the pricey side compared to the suburbs, but I'll be happy to chip in with my Bridge Card." Other women join in, offering to use their state-issued cards to purchase groceries for those who packed little food to make for lighter travel. After the meeting a few of us walk across the highway to the supermarket to pick up items to cover simple meals for the remaining two days of the conference. Upon the request of my newfound cohort, I slip two pounds of cheddar cheese, a pack of tortillas, a small box of rice, a half-gallon of milk, and three cans of pinto beans into my shopping cart. I run my card through the checkout reader and wait outside for the rest of the group. We find a bench on campus and begin to distribute our bounty, making sure that each participant has enough food to feed her family for a night or two. We briefly continue the conversation of turning ideas into action while bridging theory and practice. As I am putting beans and rice into bags, I begin to understand the practical implications of a more engaged form of education activism that can nurture, feed and sustain a community.

Two years after that life-changing gathering under the tree, I am back on my home campus to teach a junior-level communication theory class. I let students know that I have completely revised the course in order to convert it into one that centers on service-learning in Detroit. As we start to go over the syllabus, I immediately direct them near the top of the first page where I include in boldface one of my favorite quotations by Gloria Anzaldúa as a way to set the appropriate tone of experiential learning in general:

> Throw away abstraction and the academic learning, the rules, the map and compass. Feel your way without blind-

ers. To touch more people, the personal realities and the social must be evoked—not through rhetoric but through blood and pus and sweat. (173)

A nervous laughter hangs in the air. We talk about what the statement means in relation to traditional forms of instruction. The students, many of whom are studying public relations, are murmuring amongst themselves. I jokingly promise not to subject them to anything cruel and unusual, but I will expect them to get their hands dirty—both literally and figuratively. While we study the theoretical foundations of human communication, we will also work with a neighborhood farming collective on the far-east side to collaborate with its members on projects ranging from gardening to community event planning. Although some of the students wonder aloud how they are going to find time to juggle the assignments in addition to the six to eight hours of service scheduled between attending lectures and writing papers, most of the class expresses excitement and looks forward to applying what they are learning outside the classroom. I hope that is the case for all of them.

As part of their final projects, a large group of students chooses to volunteer at the neighborhood festival co-sponsored by our serving-learning partners. I sign up to work the children's game area. For seven hours on that hot Saturday we haul bags of ice, pitch tents, paint faces, grill hot dogs, and teach children how to play baseball. I watch from a short distance as students listen to people in the community share stories about their streets, schools, and churches. I too am listening and learning from them—for the first time in a long time I feel at home. When we meet in class the following week, I invite students to give mini-presentations of their field experiences. One student, a Black working mother and Detroit resident, shares with us her initial struggles with interacting with some of the festival attendants because the only time she travels to that part of the city is to drop up and pick up her children at the private school located nearby. She continues by saying that the project made her open her eyes to what was going on in her community, so much so that she plans on working with another festival co-sponsor to serve as a mentor for young women and girls at the conclusion of the course. Several students nod in agreement, eagerly wanting to discuss other possibilities to "do theory" in a manner that is real to them.

POSTSCRIPT

I am reading an e-mail message sent from one of my former students who had asked me to be a reference on her Teach for America application earlier in the year. After weeks of nail biting, she is notified of her acceptance into the competitive program where she will be trained to teach inner-city youth in the South. The news makes me smile—this was once a student who was determined to study accounting in order to land a "good" corporate job but was redirected along the way. In her e-mail she partially credits my dedication in the classroom as one of the reasons why she wants to pursue the profession herself. Tears fill my eyes as I think about the agonizing moments when I wanted to walk away from graduate school and from teaching altogether because I was sick of being tired all the damn time. I wanted to stop struggling for air as I slept, worrying about the next bill and car repair requiring my immediate attention. With this letter, however, I am drawn back to my love of teaching—the thrill of introducing students to new ways of seeing and engaging in the world. I find wholeness through my work in the classroom and in the communities that nurture my spirit. I realize that though I am broke, I refuse to be *broken*. As I wipe away tears, I find a renewed sense of hope just as the phone begins to ring. Another 1-800 number flashes across the screen. I clear my throat, take a deep breath, and answer the call.

NOTES

[1] A replacement for federally issued food stamps, the Bridge Card is currency for Michigan's food and cash assistance program participants.
[2] Michigan Department of Human Services
[3] All names have been changed unless otherwise noted.

WORKS CITED

Christian, Barbara. "The Race for Theory." *Feminist Studies* 14.1 (Spring 1988): 67-79. Print.

hooks, bell. *Yearning: Race, Gender, and Cultural Politics*. Boston: South End Press, 1990. Print.

Omolade, Barbara. "A Black Feminist Pedagogy." *Women's Studies Quarterly* 21.3/4 (1993): 31-38. Print.

WORKS CONSULTED

Anzaldúa, Gloria. "Speaking in Tongues: A Letter to 3rd World Women Writers." *This Bridge Called My Back: Writings by Radical Women of Color.* 2nd ed. Eds. Cherrie Moraga and Gloria Anzaldúa. New York: Kitchen Table: Women of Color Press, 1983.165-174. Print.

Collins, Patricia Hill. *Black Feminist Thought: Knowledge, Consciousness, and the Politics of Empowerment.* 2nd ed. New York: Routledge, 2000. Print.

Ellis, Carolyn. *The Ethnographic I: A Methodological Novel about Autoethnography.* Walnut Creek, CA: AltaMira, 2004. Print.

Haymes, Stephen Nathan. *Race, Culture, and the City: A Pedagogy for Black Urban Struggle.* Albany, NY: SUNY Press, 1995. Print.

hooks, bell. *Teaching to Transgress: Education as the Practice of Freedom.* New York: Routledge, 1994. Print.

3.
"I Am My Child's First Teacher"

Black Motherhood and Homeschooling as Activism Within and Beyond the Academy

MARCELLE M. HADDIX AND LATOYA L. SAWYER

THE CONCEPT OF MOTHERHOOD has been central to the traditions and philosophies of people of African descent. While historically the concept of Black motherhood has been praised and even glorified in the African American community, "the ideas that mothers should live lives of sacrifice has come to be seen as the norm" (Christian 1985: 234). In her work on Black feminist thought, Patricia Hill Collins discusses how Black women keep in tact the controlling image of a strong, devoted, self-sacrificing Black mother to maintain norms of racial solidarity. She goes further by stating that "glorifying the strong Black mother represents Black men's attempts to replace negative White male interpretations with positive Black male ones" (175). This remains particularly problematic and is challenged by the three themes of Black feminist thought put forth by Collins:

- the importance of defining and valuing one's consciousness of one's own self-defined standpoint,
- Black women's experience at the intersection of multiple structures of domination, and
- the importance of recognizing Black women's culture, including themes of motherhood, sisterhood, and creative expression.

In essence, only Black women can define and redefine Black motherhood. The boundaries that define Black motherhood are ever changing and fluid within this framework where, for example, the tradition of othermothering is of central importance. Othermothering is the assistance delivered to biological mothers, or bloodmothers, in the care of their children that stems from Black women's need to collectively nurture one another's children for survival. The tradition of othermothering in the U.S. is traced back to slavery where othermothering was a survival mechanism and a vehicle for educational and cultural knowledge for Black women. As Collins writes, organized, resilient, women-centered networks of bloodmothers and othermothers are key in understanding Black motherhood and its potential for activism and social change and movement.

Definitions of Black motherhood continue to evolve and are reconceptualized within Hip-hop feminist thought. Hip-hop feminist thought continues in the tradition of othermothering that empowers Black women. While adhering to this Black feminist core agenda, Hip-hop feminism privileges the women, men and children of Hip-hop culture and the working-class, poor, and emerging middle-classes– those in or from the street/ 'hood that often go overlooked and/ or misunderstood by other forms of feminism (Peoples 22). Hip-hop feminist thought draws heavily from a Hip-hop state of mind; "one that freely samples, mixes, and remixes" (Pough 79) and allows for new and varied means of accomplishing its goals.

The twenty-first century Black mother in an increasingly global and capitalistic economy, where the number of new prisons are on the rise and jobs and public schools are declining, must engage in collective hustle in order for her and her family to survive. Hustle, the intense work ethic that is a part of Black and Hip-hop culture, reflects a "by any means necessary" approach to survival and prosperity. Black mothers of the Hip-hop generation draw on the tradition of othermothering and utilize contemporary tools, such as new media, in order to organize and form the women-centered networks necessary for the advocacy and activism. These Black mothers are the children of parents from the Civil Rights generation, generally women born between 1965 and 1984 (Neal). Also referred to as the "post soul" generation (Neal), these Black mothers have cultivated the political, social, and cultural experiences within the African American community post the Black Power Movement and the Civil Rights Movement. These Black mothers have come of age during times marked by the realities of systematic rollbacks of Civil Rights gains, the ravages of drug culture in urban areas, and the rise of the prison industrial complex that followed it.

Beverly Guy-Sheftall argued that she was not as convinced "that young Black feminists are carrying on the legacy left by nineteenth-century abolitionists, antilynching crusaders, club women, Civil Rights organizers, Black nationalist revolutionaries, and 1970s Black feminists" (1093). Contrary to her argument, in this chapter, we discuss how our involvement in a homeschooling community informs our interrelated roles as Black mothers and as activist scholars. We underscore Collins' argument in that there is a need to make connections between trends within Hip-hop feminism and new grassroots feminist organizations within African American communities and infusing churches, recreational activities, and civil-rights organizations of Black civil society with a feminist sensibility. As she argues, the themes of feminism as articulated by this next generation of Black feminists need to be heard within African American communities and should inform Black women's community work. Our experiences represent one example of how Black mothers are working to create quality, just and emancipatory education for their children, and, as we will discuss here, there are particular limitations and realities that determine who decides to and who is able to homeschool at any given moment and in any given context. But, it stands to illustrate the ways that Black feminism is reconceptualized and refueled by the efforts of a new generation of feminists.

In this chapter, we rely on Black and Hip-hop feminist theories (Collins; Peoples; Pough) as frameworks to privilege the counterstories (Solórzano and Yosso) of Black mothers in African American homeschooling communities as we navigate within and beyond master narratives that position Black parents as absent, uninvolved, unengaged, and/or not caring about their children's educative experiences. In this chapter, we re-frame and leverage the role of today's Black mothers in the education of their children, examining Black motherhood as a form of activism and a catalyst for educational change. In the following sections, we employ autoethnographic methods (Camangian; Alexander) to share our stories about how our identities as Black mothers to Black boys informs our work within the academy. We share our personal experiences and tell stories of navigating an urban school district in the United States and making deliberate choices to homeschool our sons as a result of the overwhelming miseducation of African American male students (Holzman). In an effort to spotlight African American homeschooling in the twenty-first century as a contemporary Black/Hip-hop feminist movement within the African American community, we discuss the paradoxes inherent in working within the academy yet, as aspiring and early career Black women scholars, educating our own children outside of traditional academic contexts.

TAKING BACK OUR CHILDREN'S EDUCATION: MARCELLE'S STORY

In February 2009, I participated in a community forum on the state of education in the city of Syracuse, New York. My involvement was first as a parent who had a troubling experience with the school district, but also as a literacy scholar and English teacher educator from Syracuse University. As I listened to the stories from other community members, parents expressed frustration that "Black boys don't even go to school" and "our African American boys don't know how to write." One parent said, "You are your child's first teacher. The schools don't teach the children anything about history. They need to know their history." Parents and other community members discussed the importance of the Black community taking back the education of our children. We talked about the need for mentors and the importance of nurturing parent involvement in schools.

Some in attendance were unaware of the failure of the local schools to educate all children. Few were aware of the local school data that reported a hovering 50 percent graduation rate for all students and 25 percent graduation rate for African American male students. To investigate this community concern further, I interviewed school leaders and community members to understand the local history of school failure for African American youth. Many of the problems concerned community members' critique of the ineffectiveness of the majority White, female teacher force and the lack of present, consistent, and effective parent-teacher relationships. While some problems had been identified, fewer solutions were presented. There was, however, the deep frustration with the current state of education for African American children by several community members and parents, so in response, I co-founded a parent group, MOYO (Mothers Offering Youth Opportunity), to begin to explore the reasons for and to identify solutions for the achievement gap for African American males. Though the group focused on supporting mothers of color, group meetings were often attended by a diverse group of community members, male and female, concerned with changing educational outcomes from their children. From 2009-2010, the group sponsored six community meetings to discuss Dr. Jawanza Kunjufu's book, *Countering the Conspiracy to Destroy Black Boys*. In 1982, Dr. Jawanza Kunjufu spawned a national debate about his indictment of the United States for what he called the genocide—the deliberate and systematic destruction—of the Black male. Kunjufu argued then, as he still does, that solving the problems of Black boys now may eliminate the problems of future men. Reasons he cited for what he identified as the "fourth grade failure syndrome" for Black boys included low teacher expectations, adolescent boys "no longer cute," lack of parental involvement, peer pressure, and the lack of male teachers and role models (see also Noguera).

On a Saturday in March 2010, MOYO sponsored a community reads event, "Saving Our Black Boys," to determine solutions for what was going on in the city. Parents and community members invested time to initiate an action-oriented movement to improve the academic achievement of African American males. The questions framing our work together that day were: What are some of the key factors affecting the academic and social success of Black boys, and what can we do to improve upon the current educational experiences of our Black boys? Inspired by Paulo Freire's framework for cultural circles as a site for transformation and social change, participants worked in small groups to brainstorm responses to these questions guided by the reading of Dr. Kunjufu's book and according to the key reasons he cited for the academic failure of African American boys.

My work with the community reads event was initially as a concerned parent and as a literacy researcher and university professor with resources and "capital" to serve the needs of my community. In time, I began to identify as an emerging community activist desiring real change in our schools and in the lives of the children and families that lived in my community. My participation in the community meetings informed and shifted my role and impacted my relationship to my research interests. I knew that I wanted to design and conduct research that privileged the voices of individuals who are often marginalized and that is rooted in the community. As a Black woman scholar, and more importantly, as a Black mother who is not simply interested in but vigilant about the urgent need to change the current educational system for Black children and adolescent youth, my passion and activism often supersedes a goal of advancing knowledge for the field of literacy research. Instead, my research agenda prioritized working to transgress (hooks) the boundaries and limits of the current educational system for some families and eradicating the detrimental effects of the lack of freedom that many families feel in providing educational opportunities for their children. The research questions were no longer my own and they did not just originate from my own personal experiences; instead, they stemmed from our collective inquiry into the issues facing our children.

One of the solutions that day was to embark upon a parent movement to "Take Back Our Children's Education." Many parents, fed up with what some called the "persistent miseducation and failure of African American youth," discussed the possibility of forming their own schools and the vitality of African American homeschooling. During those community meetings, I met several families who had removed their children from the public school system and had taken on homeschooling as an immediate solution. I had never considered homeschooling to be a real possibility or an option, mainly because I held certain misguided assumptions and stereotypes about homeschooling. Yet, nationally, homeschooling is on the rise in minority communities (CNN.com). Many families cite their dissatisfaction and distrust of the public school system to educate their children as a reason for homeschooling. I learned from the other parents in my community about homeschooling and became a part of an African American Homeschoolers Network.

Deciding to pull my own child out of the very system that I purport to want to help transform was a decision laced with paradoxes. My mission and conviction as a literacy activist-scholar and teacher educator is to improve the educational experiences for all children, particularly children from marginalized communities, and I value the role of parents as critical stakeholders in this change. What does such movement do to address the failing standards of public school systems when many highly-motivated, engaged, and resourceful parents leave the system? Was my decision only serving me and my family? How is public school education for children of color transformed when key stakeholders are no longer involved? Inherent in the final question is a misconception about parents who decide to homeschool. Different from dominant narratives about homeschooling parents, including their disengagement and lack of involvement with mainstream educational initiatives, I found that members of the African American Homeschoolers Network were even more involved with their local public schools. For example, one parent attended regular school board meetings to advocate the larger concerns of families from her community. Another parent sought ways to collaborate with her local school to provide enrichment experiences for both traditionally schooled and homeschooled children. I grappled with these complex realities and determined that there were ways for me to accomplish many goals simultaneously. Homeschooling my own child did not mean that I would lessen my commitment to preparing a new generation of teachers to effectively teach in diverse school settings. It did not mean that I would stop initiating and engaging in literacy reform efforts in my local schools.

Yet, deciding to pull my own child out of the school system and educate him "at home" was a scary decision, even for a literacy scholar and teacher educator. How would I homeschool my son and work full-time as a literacy scholar and teacher educator? I am a non-tenured assistant professor at a research institution which signifies certain scholarly and professional expectations if I want to earn promotion and tenure. I am preparing the new generation of teachers to teach other people's children, yet at the same time, I felt that I was neglecting the quality of the teaching and learning experience that I wanted for my own child. Being realistic about the multiple identities that I occupy, I had to determine a way to find balance between being a researcher, a teacher educator, a community activist, and now a homeschooling parent.

My decision to homeschool is possible because it involves an equal partnership between my husband and I, and we have cultivated a support community through a local African American Homeschoolers Network. My husband's prominent role in the homeschooling of our son is not the typical scenario in homeschooling families, but it demonstrates the promise of having more Black male role models in the lives of all children. Even within our group, the network is comprised of several Black mothers who have similar stories and reasons for homeschooling—they want quality education for their children and are fed up with the dysfunction and miseducation ever present in their public school district. The group meets regularly at a local library to support one another and pool instructional and curricular resources. Whenever possible, the group sponsors enrichment classes for children and extra-curricular outings for families. For me, homeschooling is possible because of the support of "othermothers" (and fathers) in this community.

IT TAKES A NETWORK TO HOMESCHOOL A CHILD: LATOYA'S STORY

My first experience with homeschooling was ten years ago when I decided not to enroll my oldest daughter in kindergarten. At that time, I was a stay-at-home mother with my five-year-old daughter, Nyelah, and my one-year-old son, Khalif. I taught phonics, math and art between loads of laundry, making meals, and potty training. The next year, I enrolled my daughter in first grade at a local private school. She was well prepared and shot to the head of her class. All of her teachers remarked that she was such an eager learner. I, of course, wanted the very same love of learning for Khalif, and my children that came along after, however; I decided to homeschool them when Khalif and my younger son, Hakeem, did not demonstrate this same enthusiasm and I realized their school learning environments were problematic. This time, however, I was homeschooling as a full-time doctoral student, wife, and mother of four. This in itself challenged the notion that mothers must all be self-sacrificing in order to adequately fulfill their role. In my attempt to manage these three roles, I ultimately strove to nurture my family, myself, and my community. These efforts required the support of many othermothers in real and virtual spaces.

A friend and fellow homeschooler invited me to the Facebook group Homeschool with Freedom (HWF) in January 2011. I was excited to find a homeschool group on Facebook, especially one that acknowledged and welcomed my cultural heritage as an African American woman. HWF is a closed group on Facebook for Homeschool parents from across the African Diaspora. The people in the group represent a wide range of ideological, religious, and political views. The group's 194 members are predominantly female. African Americans and women are among the top users of social media sites, in part due to wireless and mobile Internet connections (Smith; Sutphen). With this increase in Internet access, it is also likely that there are also a range of socioeconomic statuses represented within the group as well.

Individual member profiles show that members of the group represent different parts of the United States and the Caribbean. Members represent the North, South, East and West coasts, as well as the mid-West. For two months I read other posts and investigated links to resources, however; I did not post comments. For the majority of the homeschool parents in this group homeschooling is not just about teaching reading, writing, and arithmatic. These Black homeschoolers have made the lifestyle choice to homeschool in order to give their children a well-rounded education that is culturally relevant, and epistemologically nonviolent.

While this approach is arguably not for everyone, and alone does not help to educate all Black children, I contend that in the twenty-first century with the high stakes involved with the school-to-prison pipeline, Black families' approaches to educational activism cannot be "either/ or," but must instead be a "both/ and" approach. I equate the homeschool work that Marcelle, myself, and other Black parents engage in as similar to abolition and Underground Railroad efforts during slavery. In the midst of developing an abolition movement and pressuring the State to end the violent and oppressive institution of slavery, Harriet Tubman, Rev. Jermain Loguen and others helped individuals and groups to escape from their plantations. They did not wait for change. So, too, as with many of us who have the ability to homeschool, we work to transform the unjust educational practices and institutions, we work collectively and with others to demand the State provide quality education to *all* students and we work to "emancipate" as many children from the school-to-prison pipeline as we can—starting with our own.

As homeschooling depends on forming networks and communities for socialization as well as to avoid isolation, this Facebook page is a way for homeschool parents that might otherwise be in the minority in their actual neighborhood or city to interact with others in a space where they are in the majority. The primary functions of the group are to share educational resources as it relates to home schooling, including links to websites to purchase materials from commercial vendors and from each other on sites like eBay, and for parents to network.

On March 9, 2011 I posted a question to the group in hopes of receiving at least one answer. This brief exchange between TT and I (LS) is just a sample of the community building practices that take place on HWF Facebook page. The passage below shows me (LS) asking for advice from other homeschool mothers who are also balancing homeschooling with responsibilities outside of the home.

> LS: Is anyone else home schooling elementary school age children while working or a f/t student themselves? We're making it through this academic year, but I'm looking for tips, resources, and other support to help keep me going. This is tough.

The first response comes from TT. Here she offers her own experiences as an example of how to manage the challenges of mothering, homeschooling, and working outside of the home. As typical in online spaces and computer-mediated communication, TT uses e-English characterized by abbreviations, acronyms, distorted words, and more relaxed grammatical rules.

> TT: i work but not full-time. i teach fitness classes and african dance so my kids travel with me every where i go. this is one of the reasons that i am so fluid in my style of teaching. books on cd while in the car. keeping myself present ... in the moment to look at learning opps. wasting no time on time monsters such as tv, online time, unnecessary talking on the phone. staying on top of house cleaning DAILY but not worrying about it if things get out of hand. taking advantage of breaks by actually resting so that i get rejuvenated. appreciating that it is tougher to work while hsing [home schooling]. i would rather do this any day than send my kids to school. (last comment is not an indictment against schools b/c lots of my friends' kids go to school but i appreciate hsing MORE for me and family for reasons i am sure many of you already know). it is more about the mind set sister.

TT's response relies on a shared knowledge when she says she would rather "hs" (homeschool) than send her children to traditional school. Implied in this statement is the knowledge that most homeschool parents on the site believe that traditional school enacts and reinforces undesirable dominant discourses and epistemologies. TT is careful not to condemn schooling overall, and clarifies that it is not the choice for her and her family. She also calls me, LS, "sister." TT and I have never met face-to-face, so her reference to me as "sister" is a familial term of identity and endearment. This identity is based on gender, race, and our shared homeschooling agenda. TT offers more encouragement in her follow-up post.

> TT: the other thing i think about is that no matter how hard life seems with working, homeschooling and family life, my life is 1000 times easier than my ancestors ... be they slaves, hunter gathers or whoever ... folks back in the old day had to ... WORK HARD. Our times seem hard but when we really study life in the recent and distant past, I am living like a queen! it is all the mindset. it is hard but maybe we are being built up like they had to be. only we don't raise our food and animals and build our own homes

and make our own clothes but instead we homeschool and work at the same time.

Here TT connects contemporary challenges of Black women to history of struggle of Black women. She asserts that her hard-times pale in comparison to her "ancestors" who were possible "slaves, hunter gatherers or whoever." This reinforces the notion that her choice to homeschool and her determination are rooted in a deeper cultural struggle. While she says the folks "back in the day" had to struggle and make certain sacrifices, she acknowledges that she has the agency, power, and ability to make the choice to "hs." The repetition of the word "mindset" places emphasis on the importance of having a particular way of seeing and understanding the world and situations. TT then makes a significant shift when she uses the pronoun "we" to describe the Black "hsers" on the page. Three lines prior to the use of "we," she uses pronouns "I" and "my" to describe herself. In these lines she compares the struggles of Black "hsers" to that of the ancestors and frames those struggles as edifying. She suggests that "we are being built up" like they had to be. In this comparison, homeschooling and working at the same time is equivalent to other acts of survival, such as the raising of food and animals, and building homes from "back in the day." TT frames homeschooling as a form of self-sufficiency and activism. This is an example of how Black women can and are carving out spaces online and building communities of support to edify one another and combat systems of oppression when necessary, such as school systems that they do not believe are adequately educating their children.

TOWARD REMIX-ING BLACK MOTHER/SCHOLAR/ACTIVIST IDENTITIES

The different roles that we occupy within and beyond the academy are interwoven and interdependent. Our involvement in homeschooling communities informs our interrelated roles as a Black mothers, an activist/scholars, and a critical educators. For example, Marcelle's identity as a homeschooling parent directly informs the ways that she prepares new teachers to work in increasingly diverse schools and communities where it is paramount that they have an understanding and appreciation for the importance of parent voice. This is an eminent concern given that she is preparing a mostly White, middle class, female teaching force for the realities of working with and effectively teaching a student population that is viewed as "other people's children" (Delpit). The overwhelming emphasis on the preparation of White, middle class, female teachers for working with an increasingly racially and linguistically diverse student population (Sleeter) inadvertently suggests that one way to mitigate the educational failure of Black children is via the White female. Marcelle's decision to homeschool her son exemplifies the tradition of Black motherhood as activism—taking back her son's education and reinscribing a powerful image of Black women as othermothers for their own and other people's children. Her teacher education students witness a counternarrative of Black parental involvement in their children's education, different from the representation of Black parents as absent, uninvolved, and non-caring. Instead, Black mothers, from within and outside school systems, are powerful social actors in contemporary education reform movements.

LaToya's participation in the virtual homeschooling community demonstrates the twenty-first century potential for new grassroots Black/Hip-hop feminist movements toward change and transformation in the Black community. This is one example of a new revolution that draws on new media and digital literacies; in this way, the othermothering community transcends physical boundaries and limits. Via digital forms and networks like Facebook, Black mothers within the broader global community can organize and mobilize to reform the educational experiences for all Black children. In this way, the legacy of Black feminist traditions are carried on and extended in new ways, different from yet similar to the work of Black women in the nineteenth and twentieth centuries. While navigating her academic and professional journey, LaToya relies on the innovations of new Black and Hip-hop feminist movements to support her identities as a homeschooling parent and as an emergent scholar. These innovations come primarily in the form of new and social media, such as Facebook and Twitter. Black social media communities are comprised largely of Black women and men of the Hip-hop generation and is a contemporary medium for activism in Black communities because it 1) "broadcasts" and "publishes" stories of importance to communities of color faster and more frequently than traditional media; 2) is a site of various communities of practice (Wenger) where Hip-hop feminist scholar-activists and community members can come together to discuss, theorize, and strategize feminist solutions to an array of issues affecting women, men, and children of color locally, nationally, and transnationally; and 3) is used to galvanize critical masses and communicate calls to action, protest, and petition in real time in both virtual and non-virtual spaces. In many ways, "the 18th and 19th century tradition of petition (Thomas Paine & David Walker) has been revived through social media" (Tillet).

As Black women scholars, educating our own children outside of traditional academic contexts has not been without challenges and is inherently paradoxical to our own academic journeys and histories. We both are products of public school educations, and we both have navigated within traditional school systems. Both from working class backgrounds, our parents, even if they wanted to, did not have the time or resources to decide to homeschool. They sacrificed for us in myriad ways, however. Because we work to ensure democratic and liberatory education within school settings we desire to send our children to quality public schools, but our work also makes us more aware of the oppressive conditions that exist in our local schools. Yet, the decision to homeschool our children, in addition to our many professional and personal obligations and commitments, is another representation of the ways that we as Black women live lives of sacrifice (Collins). Homeschooling has been an empowering experience for us as Black women, and it is one way that we challenge the negative images of Black mother that persist in our society. In this way, Black motherhood is reconceptualized as a powerful form of political activism and resistance.

WORKS CITED

Alexander, B. K. "Performance Ethnography: The Reenacting

and Inciting of Culture." *The Sage Handbook of Qualitative Research*. Eds. Denzin, Norman and Yvonne Lincoln. 3rd ed. Thousand Oaks, CA: Sage, 2005. 411-41. Print.

Camangian, Patrick. "Starting with Self: Teaching Autoethnography to Foster Critically Caring Literacies." *Research in the Teaching of English* 45 2 (2010): 179-204. Print.

CNN.com. "Homeschooling on the Rise, but Why?" Ed. Fredricka, Whitfield, 2010. Print.

Collins, Patricia Hill. *Black Feminist Thought: Knowledge, Consciousness, and the Politics of Empowerment.* 1991. 2nd ed. New York: Routledge, 2000. Print.

Delpit, Lisa. *Other People's Children: Cultural Conflict in the Classroom.* New York: New Press, 1995. Print.

Freire, Paulo. *Pedagogy of the Oppressed.* New York: Continuum, 1970/1982. Print.

Guy-Sheftall, Beverly. "Response from a 'Second Waver' to Kimberly Springer's 'Third Wave Black Feminism?'" *Signs* 27.4 (2002): 1091-4. Print.

Holzman, Michael. *Yes We Can: The 2010 Schott 50 State Report on Black Males in Public Education.* Cambridge, MA: Schott Foundation for Publication Education, 2010. Print.

hooks, bell. *Teaching to Transgress: Education as the Practice of Freedom.* New York: Routledge, 1994. Print.

Kunjufu, Jawanza. *Countering the Conspiracy to Destroy Black Boys.* Chicago, IL: African American Images, 1982. Print.

Neal, Mark Anthony. *Soul Babies: Black Popular Culture and the Post-Soul Aesthetic.* New York: Routledge, 2002. Print.

Noguera, Pedro A. *The Trouble with Black Boys ... And Other Reflections on Race, Equity, and the Future of Public Education.* San Francisco, CA: Jossey-Bass, 2008. Print.

Peoples, Whitney A. "'Under Construction': Identifying Foundations of Hip-Hop Feminism and Exploring Bridges between Black Second-Wave and Hip-Hop Feminisms." *Meridians* (2008): 19-52. Print.

Pough, Gwendolyn D. "What It Do, Shorty?: Women, Hip-Hop, and a Feminist Agenda." *Black Women, Gender, and Families* 1.2 (2007): 78-99. Print.

Sleeter, Christine E. "Preparing Teachers for Culturally Diverse

Schools: Research and the Overwhelming Presence of Whiteness." *Journal of Teacher Education* 52.2 (2001): 94-106. Print.

Smith, Aaron. *Home Broadband 2010*. Washington, DC: Pew Research Center's Internet & American Life Project, 2010. Web.

Solórzano, Daniel G, and Tara J. Yosso. "Critical Race Methodology: Counter-Storytelling as an Analytical Framework for Education Research." *Qualitative Inquiry* 8.1 (2002): 23-44. Print.

Sutphen, David. *New Study Shows Blacks Closing the Digital Divide with Whites*. theGrio.com. 2010. Web.

Tillet, Salamishah. "The Eighteenth and Nineteenth Century Tradition of Petition." Paper presented at Black Thought 2.0 Conference, Duke University. Twitter, April 2012. Web.

Wenger, Etienne. *Communities of Practice: Learning, Meaning, and Identity*. Cambridge University Press, 1998. Print.

4.
Resisting with Child

Black Women's Embodied Negotiations of Motherhood in the Academy

SEKILE NZINGA-JOHNSON

"DON'T GET PREGNANT before getting tenure!" "Have one, no more!" Sound familiar?

I too, recall hearing this professional "advice" during my own graduate education. A Black female faculty mentor of mine said to me on the first day of my doctoral program, "Congrats on getting engaged, but don't you go have any babies while you're in this program!" I was six months pregnant before I shared my pregnancy with her. I was excited about my pregnancy but was afraid that I would lose much needed mentoring and support because I had actively chosen not to comply with her directions. Later in my doctoral studies, I was in a meeting with a white female faculty mentor and was discussing the possibility of publishing one of my papers. Unprompted she advised, "Be sure not to get pregnant before you complete your dissertation proposal." I was happily three months pregnant at the time. In both instances, I was both offended and shocked. I was an adult and therefore was not expecting instruction about my personal life within a professional setting. The aforementioned examples are not offered as justification for my own personal ax grinding but do serve as testimonial evidence of common sanctions given to female graduate students and junior faculty by their colleagues and mentors within the academy. Such well meaning, albeit conformist and gendered advice, is often relayed by academics regardless of their social location, academic field, rank or institutional affiliation. Some might offer a counter argument by suggesting that academic mentors and peers are simply attempting to decrease the documented career risk of underrepresented and vulnerable scholars, including women of color like myself. Yet, these impositions hold significant cultural meaning for all bodies in the academy but may hold particular meaning for women of color academics as they make decisions about family and careers. Black women, in particular, must negotiate the simultaneity of the academy's patriarchal and gendered practices of managing women's reproduction along with the U.S.'s racialized practices of controlling Black women's bodies and sexuality.

The purpose of this study was to gain an understanding of Black women's decision-making and negotiations of parenting and professing at the beginning of their careers within the professional context of the academy. The goal is to better understand the role academic culture has in shaping academic women's parenting and reproductive decisions. By interrogating both the implicit and explicit messages academic culture communicates to Black academic women, we may be able to discern and confront these interactive and normalized forms of corporeal control.

BACKGROUND AND SIGNIFICANCE

The academy represents a contradictory location, which is responsible for both producing and perpetuating much of the racialized gendered cultural messages that can often impede Black women's and mothers' success within the U.S. and yet it is also an institution that can serve as a vehicle for their upward mobility. The compounded intersectional disadvantage that women of color experience as they navigate becoming or being academic mothers has been alluded to but has largely been absent in the recent discourse on mothering in the academy (Williams 2012). Volumes published on gender equity research such as Susan Bracken, Jeannie Allen and Diane Dean's *The Balancing Act: Gendered Perspectives in Faculty Roles and Work Lives* and well received anthologies such as Elrena Evans and Caroline Grant's *Mama PhD: Women Write about Motherhood and Academic Life* and Rachel Hile Basset's *Parenting and Professing: Balancing Family Work with an Academic Career* all offer much needed analysis and testimony in the pursuit of shattering the silence surrounding academic mothers' existences within the academy (Leonard and Malina 30). Feminist scholar, Carmen Armenti has offered a rich analysis of the interplay between gender, power, and organizational culture on academic women's reproductive choices (211-231). However the majority of academic-mothering narratives and academic-mothering scholarship offer limited intersectional analysis of the complexity of academic women of colors' parenting decisions and career issues.

As unwelcome outsiders within the academy, many Black women enter the profession with a keen awareness of their gendered and racially marked bodies. Gabriella Gutierrez y Muhs, Yolanda Flores Neiman, Carmen Gonzalez and Angela Harris's timely volume, *Presumed Incompetent: The Intersections of Race and Class for Women in Academia,* highlights the professional issues, struggles and triumphs of women of color within academia in the twenty-first century. However, pregnancy and subsequent motherhood call attention to Black women's racialized gender and activate a host of additional cultural meanings within this professional context. Their bodies, with or without child, are most often read as intrusive, (hyper)sexualized, out of control, and yet invisible (Hammonds 93). Yet, Robin Silbergleid suggests a pregnant belly serves to legitimize heteronormative family structures and thus is a welcome sight within the academy (134). Susan Bordo complicates Silbergleid's position by asserting "the pregnant body is simultaneously a (hetero)normative female body—a body that is most outwardly marked as female by extension feminine—and also the female body at its most excessive and unruly, intruding visibly into a space, the university, that is historically rendered bodies invisible in the privileging the mind" (132). I would like to extend Bordo's insight by suggesting that her analysis invites new questions about academic mothering. We might then ask how do Black women, whose bodies are marked by their racialized gender and rendered unruly and visibly intruding into space, navigate the academy?

Specifically, it is important to situate Black women's active yet complexly constrained reproductive choices within the discourse on mothering and the academy. I begin by offering a brief discussion of the politics of Black women's reproduction within the U.S. and then link this history to contemporary Black academic women's circumstance. I then review the current literature on mothering in the academy and locate the compounded intersectional barriers faced by women of color academics within this current, and as I argued in this volume's Introduction, limited body of scholarship. Finally, through interviews, I privilege Black academic mothers' voices who are at the beginning of their professional journeys and where they are first met with the impositions of the profession. The participants' collective voices reveal that as academic-mothers they embody living contradictions through defiantly claiming an embodied intellectual space and place within a profession that many have deemed as belonging to a sacred few.

POLICING BLACK WOMEN'S REPRODUCTION AND SEXUALITY

The control of Black women's reproduction, motherhood and sexuality delineates a particularly dark trajectory within American economic and social history. Dorothy Roberts' groundbreaking book, *Killing the Black Body*, expertly chronicles the vast ways Black women's bodies have been manipulated on behalf of U.S. economic and political interests by controlling their reproduction and the African American population as a whole. From forced reproduction during slavery to population control through birth control and sterilization, Roberts' deftly documents how Black women's bodies have been consistently monitored and managed by a patriarchal and racialized state. Contemporary Black women continue to battle for reproductive autonomy and rights to their bodies. For example, a recent anti-abortion billboard campaign sponsored by "Life Always" and "That's Abortion," utilized a racist shaming campaign to challenge Black women's reproductive freedom by suggesting that the high rate of abortions among Black women serves as an indictment of their complicity in the genocide of the Black population in the U.S. These racialized attacks allege the widespread incompetence of Black women with regard to their ability to make independent decisions concerning their bodies and reproduction. These ideologies historicize the contemporary thoughts, attitudes and behaviors of contemporary Americans, including those who are college and university professors. Thus, academics' purportedly benign messages about managing motherhood cannot simply be framed as pertaining solely to career success but also are connected to long histories of "knowing what's best" for hypersexual and "poor choice" making Black women. Unsupportive and indoctrinated, and even feminist, colleagues, like the one mentioned in Patricia Lessane Williams' essay (this volume), do little to transform the institutions we inhabit when they embrace the ideologies of exclusion that define academia.

Thus, the assumed liberal academy provides fruitful terrain upon which to examine the functions and impact of the work based reproductive control of academic women. I am not suggesting this form of control is comparable to the forced medical practices of sterilization and mandated birth control underwent by untold masses of poor, disabled and women and girls of color (Davis 217); rather, I argue the academy may enact a more subtle coercive manifestation of corporeal control or a "psychological sterilization" for many women, which has particular implications for women of color who desire biological or legal motherhood. Many Black academic women, like most academic women, feel compelled to comply with these cultural mandates of the profession. Yet a growing minority of "others" have chosen to take uncharted course of becoming mother-academics as they navigate the choppy gendered and racialized waters of academe.

WALLS, PIPELINES AND OTHER BARRIERS FACING ACADEMIC MOTHERS

Exploring women's interests in mothering runs the danger of being interpreted as pronatalist. Feminists have long since identified the limitations of compulsory motherhood and celebrated education as an emancipatory vehicle to counter women's economic dependence on men. Advances in reproductive technologies have also granted many women, particularly middle class Western women, greater power over their reproductive decisions (Davis 203). Black feminists and other feminists of color, as well as several contributors to this volume, have consistently argued that motherhood is not limited by biology and can include social aspects of mothering and motherwork such as othermothering (Collins, "Shifting" 49) and community mothering (James 45). Additionally, queer scholars have also challenged the hegemony of heteronormativity by privileging child-free, non-biological family formations, and other queer family configurations in discourses on the family (Epstein 7-14). Nonetheless, the emerging data on academic women suggests that many desire to become mothers but feel constrained by their careers (Kemkes-Grottenhaler 213-226; Krakauer and Chen 65-70).

"Professional" advice of discouraging child bearing is illegal according the *Pregnancy Discrimination Act* of 1978 (Title VII). Yet, despite legislative inroads, these messages impart a persistent cultural mandate that women's bodies, while tolerated, must not become unruly with the physicality of pregnancy and motherhood and should fit neatly within the confines of the patriarchal norms of academia. Not surprisingly, recently Nicholas Wolfinger, Mary Ann Mason and Marc Goulden using census data found women academics are the least likely to become mothers when compared to highly educated women in other professions (1652-70). Women faculty who desire children practice in what Robert Drago and Carol Colbeck describe as "bias avoidance" strategies because they fear pregnancy and motherhood may further mark their already alien gendered bodies (1222). Academic women who enter the job market are often faced with hiding their pregnancies or mothering status during their interview process. Pregnancy, like race, announces the body as present, disobedient, and sexualized. Thus not becoming pregnant or cloaking a pregnancy can be viewed as a survival strategy for navigating a highly gendered workplace environment.

Those disobedient women who dare not to heed the university's persistent disembodied, self-sacrificing, labor intensive norms by becoming pregnant and/or mothers run the risk of later judgment. The emergence of what has been called "second generation" discrimination litigations offers us evidence of academic women's resistance against these patterns of covert forms of discrimination (AAUW 13). The physical condition of the pregnant body has been interpreted as passive, unreliable, unintelligent, feminine and uncommitted to their careers. For example, research conducted by Jane Halpert and Julia Burg revealed that respondents rated professional women who were pregnant as incompetent when compared to non-pregnant women and reported that they tended to receive negative performance evaluations (241). Academic women are aware that their gendered bodies are read by students and peers and ultimately learn that pregnancy and motherhood are penalties their careers cannot afford (Ward and Wolf-Wendel 191).

Those academic women who become mothers may attempt to "avoid bias" by presenting themselves as unchanged by their motherhood or by any other caregiving responsibilities for that matter. This is most evidenced by the scarce and hesitant use of work-life balance policies by women academics found in analyses of family leave usage (Drago and Colbeck 1222; Wolfinger, Mason and Goulden 1652). However, the performance of being "just one of the boys," as Martha Ellis Crone articulated, has short-term benefits at best (160). Of course, privileging non-reproductive ways of being are valid existences for women. Yet, if one's existence entails a performance of detachment for individualist professional gain it may be an ineffective means of establishing gender equity within the workplace. This "survival" strategy also does not benefit academicians who may not desire children but do indeed desire relational connections and time away from the workplace without penalty. Despite the long history of feminist activism within the academy is clear that many women (and men) continue to face great dilemmas of career-life balance (Mason, Goulden and Wolfinger 9). Apathy and inaction reinforce the status quo and place all bodies and all desire for work-life balance at further risk.

Many scholars have attempted to explain the stifling of academic mothers' careers. Faye Crosby, Joan Williams and Monica Biernat used the term "the maternal wall" to define the economic and professional ghettos that academic women face once they become mothers (675-682). Mary Ann Mason, Marc Goulden and Nicholas Wolfinger's research identified "the leaky pipeline" as the widespread pattern of career disruption faced by many academic mothers, particularly those with young children, at every point of the professional trajectory for academics. Their work suggests some women are forced to retreat to the domestic sphere under the cloak of "choice" or "opting out" (Stadtman Tucker 1). This appears to be a pattern for those academic women with more economic privilege and has been overstated in the press (Williams, *Reshaping* 14; Stone 4). For example, Sheila Gregory's study of Black women who leave the academy found that many chose other employment opportunities that offered better work climate and which afforded them greater chances of being promoted based on their intellectual and professional contributions. The need to both economically provide for their families and maintain self-respect was critical to their well being (141). These "choices" carry dimensions of free will but also of constraint because they represent the forced yet stabilizing economic decisions many women make in order to make a life for themselves and to provide for their families.

Joan Williams asserts that gendered structural barriers such as the "maternal wall" and "the leaking pipeline" operate in ways that unjustly penalize academic women who mother (*Reshaping* 17). Williams and Biernat further argue that these workplace barriers are mobilized against working mothers because there remains an unresolvable contradiction between the expectation of the ideal (and /masculine/disembodied/objective/rational) worker and the expectation of the ideal (and /feminine/embodied/subjective/emotional) mother (675). Indeed, rank and file workers, including academics, must often suppress their connections to family, community, culture and any other evidence of their corporeal existence in order to be touted as "ideal workers" within capitalist rational economic models of productivity. However, the maternal wall has generally been conceptualized and researched independent of women's social locations. Williams' work has begun to explore the nature of women of color's workplace experiences and has suggested that they may face "double jeopardy" when confronted with the maternal wall. The mutually constitutive barriers of race and gender are captured by a woman who participated in a focus group conducted by Williams and her colleagues with the Center for WorkLife Law as she explained the possibilities of the maternal wall for women of color:

> I think gender biases work differently for women of different groups-race/ethnicity, immigration status, class of family of origin, and language. It's not just heightened for "other" women. For example, the stereotype that women of certain groups have "too many babies" affects perceptions of which women take time for family leave. (*Reshaping* 10)

Thus women of color mothers may not only face the economic and career penalty due to pregnancy and motherhood, but their motherhood is complicated by racialized gender stereotypes as well.

Although Black women's working conditions within the academy involve context specific challenges, working outside the home is a familiar role for many Black women and Black mothers. Thus, Black academic women who choose to become mothers embody an axis of contradiction within the binary of "ideal worker/ideal mother" framework used by most scholars who study academic motherhood. The metaphor of the "ideal worker" narrowly considers gender exclusive of its interaction with race, class and other social factors. Black women's mothering and work have never had the privilege to be dichotomized. In addition, Patricia Hill Collins also has suggested that economic providing has historically been part of Black women's conceptions of "good mothering" ("Shifting" 49). This serves as a counter point to the binary of "ideal mother" and "ideal worker" metaphors because good mothering has been connected to economic provision for many Black women. As stated earlier, resolving the "Ideal mother/ideal worker" conflict by "opting out" is also a rare privilege for many working women, including woman of color. Thus, the "ideal worker/ideal mother" framework is helpful in understanding some of the forces at play for working mothers but does not fully explain the structural factors associated with the majority of working women's career and family issues.

Finally, the rise in "maternal wall" based discrimination litigation among academic women evidences the disturbing nuanced trend in gender based discrimination within the work place (AAUW 1). Current data suggests that only six percent of discrimination cases are brought to trial and only one third of them are won on the basis of race, ethnicity, disability or gender (Nielsen, Nelson and Lancaster 175-201); however, pregnancy discrimination cases have a significantly higher success rate of 50 percent (AAUW 9). This trend in litigation runs the risk of privileging women who articulate pregnancy and motherhood as the sole issue in their discrimination and potentially undermines any intersectional discrimination claims that might be put forth by women of color who are pregnant and/or mothers/caregivers.

Collectively, the aforementioned issues, histories, and sociocultural understandings outline a series of interactive barriers that Black women and other women of color face upon entry into the academy and consider motherhood. It behooves us to then examine Black women's decisions, choices and the journeys as academic mothers within this context.

METHODS

What does this disembodied professional environment mean for women of color? Why would Black women who are already marginalized by gender and race choose to become mothers under these oppressive work place conditions? How do Black women academics' negotiate their mothering within the academy?

The voices and themes herein are drawn from semi-structured interviews and email surveys from an ongoing project with 20 Black academic women who are in the early stages of their academic and mothering careers. The respondents were doctoral students or junior professors from large predominantly white research institutions in the northeast United States. Most interviews took place in person and lasted one to two hours. A few respondents submitted their responses via email. A basic interview outline was used to guide the interviews. A systematic, constant comparison approach to developing grounded theory (Strauss and Corbin 61) was applied to the analysis and interpretation of the data as presented in the transcribed interviews.

The themes and variations about the mother academics' experiences were integrated with an interdisciplinary review of scholarly literature. Collaboration with an external researcher was established in order to assure that issues of validity and reliability were met. Specifically, transcripts were given to an outside researcher who read all transcripts and interview summaries to identify possible themes and areas for further exploration (Thurmond 254). However, the final concepts and design of this study emerged from the data collected. The following sections offers three dominant themes or categories that emerged concerning the respondents' experiences as mother-academics: Dual Journey, Eyes Wide Open; and Competency Questioned.

DUAL JOURNEY

An important factor for the majority of participants was their active decision to become mothers and to become academics. They described the co-occurrence of these life events as reclamation of their rights to educational and reproductive freedom. Many participants stated that they were aware of the rules for women but refused to have their bodies controlled by the culture of the academy. The majority of the respondents also stated that their personal and professional goals were clear and realistic. At the time of the interviews they were all actively moving towards tenure or the completion of their doctorates with support and encouragement from their families and communities. More than half of the participants said they received direct messages from other faculty and their mentors to delay or forego mothering. Thus, for these women choosing to mother and being an intellectual concurrently was a conscious choice to disobey the rules. For example, an African American doctoral candidate and new mother reported, "Yes I knew what I was getting into but I wanted to live my life on my own terms." Another shared,

> *I had another female professor say to me, "How are you going to finish with two children?" Interestingly enough, this professor is a feminist scholar. I've sometimes wondered if in some such scholars' minds feminism excludes the experiences of marriage and motherhood. I resist labels, but I am clear that the oppression of women is something I abhor and challenge consistently. Can't I be opposed to the oppression of women and still desire a bond with a man and children?*

For some, mothering as well as being an academic is defined as an act of resistance against a system that has yet to accept their intellectual capabilities or personal and adult choices. The respondents' personification of the Black academic-mother defies both the popularized inferential racialized representations of the incapable "bad Black mother" as well as the unintelligent "other." Neither of these representations seemingly have a rightful place in the "esteemed" academy. Dorothy Roberts decried that "Black mothers have borne the weight of a century's worth of disgrace that has been manufactured in popular culture and the academy"(21). Thus their ironic presence in the academy has often been viewed as undeserving, unwelcome, alien and illegitimate (Harris and Gonzalez 3). Respondents reported not being dissuaded by the disembodied culture of the academy and referenced Black women's long history as balancing work and family as well as dealing with workplace hostility. "My grandmother had six children and worked for twelve hours a day. I pull strength from her." They arrive in this relatively new workplace with a history of resistance that has informed their journey to and through the academy.

Their very presence disrupts what it means to be an intellectual; a counter location to the expected white, male, hetero, grey haired, and relationally unattached stereotype. Their presence in the academy also brings the fictional picture of not conventionally good enough mothers into the fore" and disrupts the binaries of "good mother/bad mother" and "ideal worker/ideal mother."

EYES WIDE OPEN

All interviews began by asking respondents if they were fully aware of what lies ahead for them professionally within the academy. They unanimously responded affirmatively that they were keenly aware of the simultaneous hypervisibility and invisibility of their bodies as academics. Many of the interviewees reported that (mis)readings of their bodies extended across the academic environment, in their classrooms, prying into meetings, in their interactions with colleagues as well as in their early review processes towards promotion and tenure. Several respondents reported that they believed their multiply marked existence had great implications for their professional trajectory. Vesta, an assistant professor stated," I know my ways of thinking and being are not welcome here. I feel it. But I am clear about why I am here." Another respondent, Sheila shared, " Yes, I'm the only one. However, I am determined that I will make my way through this place unscathed and on course." Their testimonies reveal that they are claiming their stake within the academy despite the circumstance of their objectified legacy of speculation, interrogation, and misinterpretation.

CAREFULLY VETTED

Yolanda Covington-Ward (this volume) maintains that the phantoms of many racialized and gendered stereotypes follow Black women into the academy. Several respondents echo her assertion and contend that these phantoms not only follow them into the academy, but also inform their procreative decisions. The majority of the women interviewed reported cautiously vetting their procreative desires as they also weighed the challenges of establishing intellectual authority within the academy. Those who consider pregnancy with its accompanying, ever present, protruding abdomen confront the long held sexualized and racialized gender stereotypes that may be projected upon them by their colleagues and students. A doctoral candidate shared:

> *Almost all the Black women in my grad program had babies while in the program. Almost none of my white peers did. So when I became pregnant, I was very quiet about. Although I had planned this pregnancy, I felt overexposed—like I did something wrong. Like I was telling the world—"yeah, I have sex."*

Others reported feeling the pressure to further "avoid bias" in an attempt to not have their competency questioned and may also choose not to trigger any unearthed and unspoken racism and sexism. The testimony of a Black female doctoral student, illustrates this dilemma in choosing to disclose her second pregnancy. " We wanted to have the children while we were young. However, I was so uncomfortable telling my grad advisor. She has already warned me not to have children while in the program. I had already broken the rules once." These testimonies suggest an awareness that is grounded in their understanding of their marginalized reality yet also demonstrate their desire to mother despite the resistance with which they were confronted.

Each woman revealed an active thought process in making the

decision despite the direct messages they received from peers, professors, and mentors as well as indirect messages they received from the masculinist and alienating culture of the academy. Mothering as an academic for them was an act of defiance against a system that does not respect nor make space for their existence. As one respondent celebrated, "I knew we could do it, we saw others doing it and it was inspiring." bell hooks suggests that marginality can be a site of resistance and strength and several of the respondents turned towards other women of color academic mothers, particularly graduate students and junior faculty, for support, validation, and camaraderie (15).

COMPETENCY QUESTIONED

Robin Silbergleid's asserts, "we are all bodies, even if we are hired for our minds" (143). Yet it remains unclear whether "twofers" such as women of color academics are indeed hired or desired for their minds or their institution's diversity fulfillment. One respondent who was an assistant professor and new mother, counters Silbergleid's claim by reporting, "I exist in a highly toxic and alienating climate of institutionalized injustice, I am not sure why they hired me." Lisa's comment suggests that she must negotiate her hyper visible body and any subsequent pregnancy and motherhood within a workplace that does not honor her presence. Those academic women who are already multiply marked by race, ethnicity, and other social categories must consider whether they desire this additional chapter of potential diminishment to be superimposed upon their hyper exposed bodies. Like Lisa, Black women academics who chose to mother must consider these precarious choices within the constraints of withering diversity policies and "use at your own risk" work-life policies, which doubly threaten their professional success. Allison Griffen contends that the bodies of heterosexual pregnant women are "at home in the academy" (206).

Yet, Pam, a doctoral student shares, "I tried to hide my pregnancy, make myself more invisible than I already was." The perception that a pregnant abdomen within the academy is of no threat to the status quo, disregards the material conditions of those whose existence is already unwelcome and vulnerable. Many other respondents were well aware of how the risk of mothering heightens the potential of having their commitment to their careers further discredited. Another participant recalls her treatment from a professor whom she was working for as a graduate assistant:

> *He didn't talk about it, so I couldn't talk about it. I felt disempowered already and the pregnancy seemed to only give him further authority to disregard me, treat me as if I am not focused and therefore am not serious about being a scholar.* (June, graduate assistant)

Vanessa Dickerson and Michael Bennet, in their work on Black women's embodiment, contend "all too often the black female body is looked upon or made the object of the gaze. The body is still perceived as unworthy, if not worthless" (197) and therefore unwelcomed—especially in the university.

Several respondents who were interviewed reported that once they become pregnant and/or mothers they were also touted as the chief architects of their own professional demise. Their decisions are often framed as poor personal choices instead of penalties from noncompliance with the unwritten sets of guidelines and was reminiscent of the racialized and gendered rhetoric spoken about mothers who receive public assistance. In an interview, one respondent who was denied tenure from a research university, shared the following, "I was discussing my situation with a senior (white female) colleague of mine and she said, 'You know, I waited to have my children until after I was tenured." Her hopes had been that her colleagues would not hold her cultural "transgression" against her, though she now had to accept, even with her high level of productivity, as many women do that she was being punished for being "irresponsible." Such a culture forces women to resist self-inflicting narratives around their reproductive choices and competency.

CONCLUSIONS

Maria Balderrama, Mary Texeira and Elsa Valdez urge us "to continue [to] name the traditions of exclusion in academia" and that "humanizing the academy begins in understanding the ideology grounding its everyday practices" (211-212). This preliminary research project provides a picture of the experiences of Black academic women who decide to become mothers early in their careers. Results reveal Black academic mothers have a host of mutually constituted cultural issues that they confront within the academic workplace.

Black women like many women of color have had their reproductive choices managed by others for far too long. I argue, based on the academic women's voice herein, that reproductive freedom continues to be locations for feminist intervention both outside and within the academy. Yes, we must adamantly resist notions of compulsory motherhood and heteronormative models of family formations. However, we must search a balance between our valid critiques of pronatalist ideologies and our urgent necessity to validate the embodied and situated conditions of the majority of women in the world. These data, despite overarching themes of trepidation, reveal that the mother-academics herein are subversively confronting the norms of the academy and have refused to be obedient and splinter themselves. Their embodied professional lives serve as counter narratives despite the unsupportiveness that they face.

Aside from the individual acts of subversion noted herein, the sheer lack of numbers soberly reminds us that Black women remain professionally and economically vulnerable as academics (USDoE). As mentioned earlier, family policy researchers have offered a multitude of policy-based solutions; however, they continue to be plagued by institutional resistance and worker trepidation. These policies require collective support from the professoriate so that the work of keeping our profession diverse does not fall solely on academic women's informal supports.

Professional women of color may have greater social capital due to their advanced education but as Vanessa Marr and Stacia Brown share (this volume), and scores of academic mothers of color can attest, their families' material conditions and their own disenfranchised positions within their institutions deserve our attention. Much more work is needed to track the interactive effects of structural barriers, which continue to limit professional mothers' career trajectories.

In closing, Black mother academics are just one critical and urgent location to initiate a wide scale cultural shift in the notions of "work-life" balance within the academic workplace. Academics must collectively become what Robert Drago and Carol Colbeck term as "bias resisters" (18). There is a dire need to build alliances and name and oppose the discriminatory and exclusionary practices of the academy; otherwise, all bodies will be penalized. All academics in their multiplicities deserve fulfilled lives without having to deny their embodied existence as intellectuals. The "bias avoidance" tactics of not acknowledging one's life desires outside of work may serve as individualist survival strategies for many, however, these strategies do little to address the collective freedoms of workers and institutional transformation.

WORKS CITED

American Association of University Women (AAUW) Educational Foundation and the American Association of University Women (AAUW) Legal Advocacy Fund. *Tenure Denied*. 2007. Web.

Armenti, C. "May Babies and Post-tenure Babies: Maternal Decisions of Women Professors." *Review of Higher Education* 27 (2004): 211-231. Print.

Balderrama, Maria, Mary Texeira and Elsa Valdez. "Una Lucha de Frontera (A Struggle of Borders): Women of Color in the Academy." *From Oppression to Grace: Women of Color and Their Dilemmas Within the Academy*. Eds. Theodorea Regina Berry and Nathalie D. Mizelle. Virginia: Stylus. 2006. 209-232. Print.

Bordo, Susan. *Unbearable Weight: Feminism, Western Culture and the Body*. Berkeley: University of California Press, 1993. Print.

Bracken, Susan, Jeannie Allen, and Diane Dean. *The Balancing Act: Gendered Perspectives in Faculty Roles and Work Lives*. Virginia: Stylus, 2006. Print.

Collins, Patricia Hill. "Shifting the Center: Race, Class, and Feminist Theorizing about Motherhood." *Mothering: Ideology, Experience and Agency*. Ed. Evelyn Nakano Glenn, Grace Chang, and Linda Forcey. New York: Routledge, 1994. 45-65. Print.

Collins, Patricia Hill. "The Meaning of Motherhood in Black Culture and Black Mother/Daughter Relationships." *SAGE Journal* 4.2 (1987): 2-10. Print.

Covington-Ward, Yolanda. "Fighting Phantoms: Mammy, Matriarch, and Other Ghosts Haunting Black Mothers in the Academy." *Laboring Positions: Black Women, Mothering and the Academy*. Ed. Sekile Nzinga-Johnson. Bradford, ON: Demeter Press, 2013. 236-256. Print.

Crone, Martha Ellis. "One of the Boys." Evans, Elrena and Caroline Grant. *Mama PhD: Women Write about Motherhood and Academic Life*. New Jersey: Rutgers 2008. Print.

Crosby, Faye J., Joan C. Williams and Monica Biernat. "The Maternal Wall." *Journal of Social Issues* 60.4 (2004): 675-682. Print.

Davis, Angela. *Women, Race and Class*. Toronto: Random House, 1981. Print.

Dickerson, Vanessa and Michael Bennet. Eds. *Recovering the Black Female Body: Self Representations of African American Women*. New Brunswick: Rutgers University Press 2001. Print.

Doane, Janice and Devon Hodges. *From Klein to Kristeva: Psychoanalytic Feminism and the Search for the "Good Enough" Mother*. Ann Arbor: University of Michigan. 1993. Print.

Drago, Robert and Carol L. Colbeck. "The Avoidance of Bias Against Caregiving: The Case of Academic Faculty." *American Behavioral Scientist* 49 (May 2006): 1222-1247. Print.

Drago, Robert and Carol Colbeck. "The Mapping Project: Exploring the Terrain of U.S. Colleges and Universities for Faculty and Families." Final Report to the Alfred P. Sloan Foundation. University Park, PA: Pennsylvania State University, 2003. Web.

Epstein, Rachel. "Queer Parenting in the New Millennium: Resisting Normal." *Canadian Woman Studies* 24.2,3 (2005): 7-14. Print.

Evans, Elrena and Caroline Grant. *Mama PhD: Women Write about Motherhood and Academic Life*. New Brunswick, NJ: Rutgers 2008. Print.

Gregory, Sheila T. *Black Women in the Academy: The Secret to Success and Achievement*. Lanham: University Press of America, 1999. Print.

Griffen, Allison. "At Home at Work: Confining and Defining Pregnancy in the Academy." Ed. *The Teacher's Body: Embodiment, Authority and Identity in the Academy*. Diane Freedman and Martha Stoddard Holmes. New York: State University of New York Press 2003. 199-208. Print.

Halpert, Jane and Julia Burg. "Mixed Messages: Co-worker Responses to the Pregnant Employee." *Journal of Business and Psychology* 12.2 (1997): 241-253. Print.

Hammonds, Evelynn M. "Toward a Genealogy of Black Female Sexuality: The Problematic of Silence." *Feminist Theory and the Body: A Reader.* Ed. Janet Price and Margit Schildrick. New York: Routledge, 1999. 93-104. Print.

Harris, Angela and Carmen Gonzalez. "Introduction." *Presumed Incompetent: Intersections of Race and Class for Women in Academia.* Ed. Gabriella Gutierrez y Muhs, Yolanda Flores Niemann, Carmen G. Gonzalez. Boulder: University of Colorado Press, 2012. 1-19. Print.

hooks, bell. "Marginality as a Site of Resistance." *Out There: Marginalization and Contemporary Cultures.* Eds. Russell Ferguson, Martha Gever, Trinh T. Minh-ha and Cornell West. Cambridge, MIT Press, 1990: 341-343. Print.

James, Stanlie M. "Mothering: A possible Black feminist Link to Social Transformation." *Theorizing Black Feminisms: The Visionary Pragmatism of Black Women.* Eds. Stanlie M. James and Abena P.A. Busia. London: Routledge, 1993. 44-52. Print.

Kemkes-Grottenthaler, Ariane. "Postponing or Rejecting Parenthood? Results of a Survey Among Female Academic Professionals." *Journal of Biosocial Sciences* 35 (2003): 213-226.

Krakauer, Lianne and Charles P. Chen. "Gender Barriers in the Legal Profession: Implications for Career Development of Female Law Students." *Journal of Employment Counseling* 40 (2003): 65-70. Print.

Leonard, Paulilne, and Danusia Malina. "Caught Between Two Worlds: Mothers as Academics." *Changing the Subject.* Eds. Cathy Lubelska, Jocey Quinn and Sue Davies. Bristol: Taylor & Francis Publishers, 1994. 29-41. Print.

Mason, Mary Ann, Marc Goulden and Nicholas Wolfinger. "Babies Matter: Pushing the Gender Equity Revolution Forward." *The Balancing Act: Gendered Perspectives in Faculty Roles and Work Lives.* Eds. Susan Bracken, Jeanie Allen and Diane Dean. Virginia: Stylus, 2006. 9-27. Print.

Nielsen, Laura, Robert Nelson, and Ryan Lancaster. "Employment Discrimination Litigation in the Post Civil Rights United States." *Journal of Empirical Legal Studies* 7.2 (June 2010):

175-201. Print.

Nzinga-Johnson, Sekile. "Introduction: Black Women, Mothering and the Academy Extending the Boundaries." *Laboring Positions: Black Women, Mothering and the Academy*. Ed. Sekile Nzinga-Johnson. Bradford, ON: Demeter Press, 2013. 1-31.

Roberts, Dorothy. *Killing the Black Body: Race, Reproduction, and the Meaning of Liberty*. New York: Random House, 1998. Print.

Silbergleid, Robin. "An Introduction to Gender Studies: Pregnancy, Parenting and Authority in the University." *NWSA Journal* 21.1 (Spring 2009): 131-150. Print.

Stadtman Tucker, Judith. "The Opposite of Choice." *The Mothers Movement Online*. September/October 2007. Web.

Stone, Pamela. *Opting Out? Why Women Really Quit Careers and Head Home*. Berkeley:University of California Press, 2007. Print.

Strauss, Anslam and Juliet Corbin. *Basics of Qualitative Research: Grounded Theory Procedures and Techniques*. Newberry Park, CA: Sage, 1998. Print.

Thurmond, Veronica. "The Point of Triangulation." *Journal of Nursing Scholarship* 33.3 (2001): 253-258. Print.

United States Department of Education (USDoE), National Center for Education Statistics. "Fast Facts: Degrees Conferred by Sex and Race." Web. Retrieved April 7 2013.

Ward, Kelly and Lisa Wolf-Wendel. *Academic Motherhood: How Faculty Manage Work and Family*. Brunswick, NJ: Rutgers, 2012. Print.

Williams, Joan C. "Double Jeopardy? How Gender Bias Differs by Race." Paper presented at the National Academies' Conference Seeking Solutions: Maximizing American Talent by Advancing Women of Color in Academia. June 7-8, 2012, Washington, DC. Web.

Williams, Joan C. *Reshaping the Work-Family Debate: Why Men and Class Matter*. Cambridge: Harvard University Press, 2010. Print.

Wolfinger, Nicholas, Mary Ann Mason and Marc Goulden. "Alone in the Ivory Tower: How Birth Events Vary among Fast-Track Professionals." *Journal of Family Issues* 31.12 (December 2010): 1652-1670. Print.

5.
"I'm Not Your Mama; Do Your Work"

The Black Female Academic as Surrogate Mother

TOKEYA C. GRAHAM

"MOM! MOM!" As I round the corner, I hear a familiar voice calling out. *"Mom! Mama Graham! Wait up!"*

One of my students runs to catch up as I reluctantly slow down. Outwardly I'm calm, but I am furious on the inside—Mom? Mama Graham? Oh no, he didn't!

"Excuse me, _____. You can't call me Mom. It's just not appropriate. You have to refer to me as Professor Graham ... okay?"[1]

Moving closer to my office, I pause and take a reflective breath. I can't believe I have to tell him not to call me 'Mom.' I shake my head to clear my thoughts. Even though I am upset, this does not come as a surprise. This is not the first time this has happened to me and I am sure it will not be the last.[1]

FROM AT HOME MOTHER TO COMMUNITY COLLEGE PROFESSOR ... MAMA

Prior to becoming a professor, I was a stay at home mother. In this role, I was recognized by my relationships with my children—solely. At times, I resented being singularly defined by my maternal accomplishments and longed for my own identity. I decided to further my education in preparation for my eventual return to the workforce. I knew that potential future employers would question my at-home time and wonder what I had been doing for all of those so called "non-working" years. Well, *mothering*, of course. But, sadly, mothering is not often valued as "real" work.

When I returned to college, I was not defined by my role as a mother; I was a student first. In those newly shaped moments, I relished the freedom that my peripheral participation in the academy allowed. This new identity validated my scholastic capabilities, not the capacity of my womb. In graduate school, I decided that I wanted to become a professor because I gained new appreciation for my intellectual acuity and felt I would be a wonderful educator. Within three months of graduation, I was hired at a college that was a perfect fit for me and for my family. I had been accepted within the halls of the academy and felt powerful beyond description. What I did not realize then was that in my new role as a community college professor, I would be called upon to operate as a surrogate "mama" to many of my Black students. Early on, I had no idea of the many ways that race, gender and class would complicate my professorship. I had no way of knowing that these components of my identity would be problematic for some, yet provide comfort for others. I could not predict that my students would have expectations of me that were outside of the scope of my paid responsibilities.

I work at a downtown urban campus and I began my community college teaching career knowing that a great number of the students might need support outside of the classroom. I had once been a student at the same institution and knew some of their struggles firsthand. However, I was excited about teaching at my alma mater and hoped to return to have a positive impact on the students. This desire to be a change agent was part of the initial appeal of teaching at a community college: "many [faculty] expressed a social justice commitment to teaching at the community college level, believing they can teach and inspire the students who typically begin their academic careers at community colleges. As one explained, 'We allow the students who otherwise would be segregated from the academic situation access.... It's really [a] way of contributing to social justice'" (Wolf-Wendel, Ward and Twombly 264-65). In my experience, this is very true; I am often professor/advocate in order to obtain the best for and from my students.

Teaching at a community college presents different challenges because the open admission policies result in a wide spectrum of students who range from being fresh out of high school to those who have not been in a classroom in decades. Recent data suggests that "more students than ever are going to community colleges – and their numbers account for nearly half of all the college undergraduates in the country. Nationwide enrollment at community colleges grew by 15 percent from the fall of 2008 to the fall of 2010 with an all-time high of 12.4 million students that year on 1,167 campuses, according to the American Association of Community Colleges" (Adams 14-17). Additionally with the economic downturn, more people are returning to school in the hopes of securing new skills to make them more employable.

Community colleges also have many students who are ill-prepared to pursue advanced studies. These students "generally, contend with more academic risk than their four-year peers. [They] are more likely, for example, to be financially independent, single parents, attend college part-time, and work full-time" (Greene 515). Statistically, over half of all community college students require some level of academic intervention. Academic intervention can range from receiving tutoring to taking preparatory courses. Because of the broad range of academic services, many students find that community colleges best suit their educational needs.

OTHERMOTHERING, THE PURSUIT OF EDUCATION AND THE IMPLICATIONS OF BLACKNESS

Unfortunately, whatever ails the majority population will impact minority communities that much more. Thusly, it should come as no surprise that Black community college students face greater challenges and "are almost twice as likely as their White peers to enroll in at least one developmental course where they and other developmental students were 39 percent less likely than their prepared counterparts to persist and earn a degree or certificate" (Greene 514). From the outset, Black students are often positioned to fail—academically, financially and socially. They may languish in remedial or preparatory courses for many semesters often with little academic advancement. These developmental courses can drain students' financial aid and limit their ability to complete their degrees.

These challenges come as no surprise because throughout history, Black people have faced structural obstacles in pursuit of education.

However, some were able to create alternate education systems by circumventing oppressive societal and economic class structures. One of the successful roads of educational attainment included the practice of "othermothering." Othermothering describes a role that many enslaved women played as their community's first (and mostly only) teachers: "the practice of othermothering allowed Black women to educate and socialize children in their own ways and traditions in order to uplift the Black community" (Guiffrida 716). This practice set a foundation for Black women's roles as academic providers/caretakers.

While Othermothering benefitted some enslaved children, most slave mothers did not have the knowledge to properly educate them. Other means would to be needed to introduce formal education to Black communities. As the country moved through Reconstruction and beyond, most Blacks still received inadequate educations, if any at all. During the early twentieth century and throughout the Jim Crow era, segregation resulted in substandard educational institutions for Blacks. Even after *Brown v. the Board of Education* legalized the integration of public education, schools remained largely segregated due to geographical locations, socioeconomic divisions and extralegal practices. This residue of over 400 years of disenfranchisement from the educational arena continues to plague Black students:

> Consistent attacks on affirmative action; funding inequities for public institutions that annually offer college opportunity to more than a quarter million African American students;...and infrequent policy analyses will continually manufacture insufficient access and equity barriers for those who could ultimately benefit from college participation. While it is important to acknowledge and honor historical advance, contemporary times call for new policy efforts to solve persistent problems. (Harper, Patton and Wooden 410)

Some may feel that Blacks have overcome as a race, but how do current legislative and public policies reflect this reality? Blacks tend to be disproportionately poorer, less educated and the most incarcerated in this country. Any and all of these realities affect the population of students I teach.

It must be stated that not all Black students need academic support, but they are still considered at risk due to their marked status. Many higher education institutions (like other academic environments) employ discriminatory practices that push Black students to the margins of learning centers. Lowered expectations, culturally insensitive comments and actions are all examples of institutionalized discrimination which negatively impact Black students. These factors may also explain why they are more likely to seek Black faculty out for assistance and why many of the students at my institution look to me as a "surrogate mama." Although I want to assist Black students on their paths to success, it can be overwhelming to add additional mentoring responsibilities to an already difficult job. Considering this, I teeter awkwardly between the needs of my students, the expectations of my cultural community, the assumptions about my gendered responsibility and the guidelines of my institution.

MENTORING 101: MEETING BLACK STUDENTS' NEEDS OR HOW TO BURN OUT EARLY

The current reality is that if a Black professor is not available to serve as "translator" or "guide," then many Black students can get lost in the halls of the academy. Having Black faculty mentor Black students is often vital to their academic success. One might wonder how mentoring a Black student differs from any other mentoring done by a Black faculty member (particularly a Black female professor). I offer that in groups where mass oppression (i.e. slavery or Jim Crow) has occurred there is a level of bonding between survivors/descendants of survivors. This shared cultural legacy can lead to feelings of connection and kinship. Additionally, these connections can be beneficial to the students: "[they] expressed that African American faculty tended to demonstrate more positive beliefs in their academic abilities and provided students with more motivation to succeed" (Guiffrida 712). This motivation is often the only encouragement Black students receive. Experiencing the interactive effects of racism, classism and/or sexism taints the academic environment which further isolates Black students.

Unfortunately, despite the benefits to Black students, juggling many mentoring relationships can interfere with long term career success and satisfaction for Black female faculty. Career burnout is very real even if one only considers the amount of time it takes to cultivate these relationships. At the college where I am employed, I am one of only two Black professors (both female) in a department that has almost 50 full-time faculty. By virtue of this, we have heightened visibility to all of the Black students, not just the ones who are enrolled in our courses. These students seek us out to discuss everything from academic to personal issues. The sheer volume of students who look to us for guidance is staggering; if I am not careful, I might spend a whole day in my office counseling and advising students long after my teaching is completed.

At times, mentoring can be misread as mothering which is problematic. The expectation for Black female faculty to provide academic "mothering" is due to the combination of our gendered and racialized identities. Because we are Black *and* female, the task of mothering is inferred with the suggestion that it is for the students' best interests. But what of my own interests? Is it ethically prudent to position the needs of some of my students above others? I grapple with this question almost daily. An important point of note: I am not suggesting that *all* Black female faculty *must* provide mentorship to Black students. That's unfair and unrealistic. I will say that Black female faculty should do what they feel they need to do for career satisfaction. What I am positing is that most often Black students seek out Black female faculty for mentorship which can be difficult to manage. Fair? Absolutely not. However, it *is* very real.

I'M NOT THEIR MAMA...

Relegating Black women academics to roles defined by motherhood in relation to our interactions with students can be a tactic to undermine our significance as intellectuals. Misguided wisdom suggests that Black women cannot be academics and that our worth is predicated on our service to others. Higher education is often thought of as men's space; anyone who is not heterosexual, middle class, white and/or male is pushed to the margins. I think it is interesting to note that Black professor as "mama" (to students and her own brood) might be more acceptable to unwelcoming colleagues. This makes sense to some, because to have a Black female professor in a subservient position which does not require one to consider her academic accomplishments is more tolerable.

In some ways, my colleagues think that my connection with Black students is based only on race or a perceived maternal draw. This fallacious thinking invalidates my pedagogical approach to cultivating a rapport with *all* of my students. Additionally, Black students sometimes mistake my concern about their work as an attempt to fill a void that they may have in their lives. However, it is not my wish to be placed in a parental role. It is too volatile, too draining and should not be one of the requirements for my employment. If I operate as a parent I may overstep boundaries in deed and in language, compromising my professional integrity. I may take students' comments personally in ways that interrupt my ability to grade or critique without bias. I recognize that some students seek out professors who will interact with them casually; however, I believe that I do myself and my students a disservice when I am unable to separate my parental role from my professional one. The hidden suggestion would be that as a Black academic, I could only control my classroom by using parental tactics that are unsuitable inside of the walls of higher education. It seems as if it would be professional suicide for me to gain the reputation as someone who "mothers" her students as opposed to teaching them. I do not want to be held responsible for something that is not my charge from the offset.

INSTITUTIONAL RESPONSIBILITY: BALANCING FACULTY AND STUDENTS' NEEDS

Institutions of higher education must recognize the complexities that working in higher education present for Black female professors and find ways to support our existence within the academy. This will only happen if Black female faculty is seen as vital to the core of the institutions in which they work. If our positions are viewed as arbitrary, then any overuse, misuse and/or abuse is not viewed as problematic. Colleges must implicitly state that past practices are unacceptable and work to support us or continue to witness further burnout. It is not the responsibility of the faculty to provide what students need outside of the classroom. Think about it—how often does the counseling staff provide academic tutoring? Yet, Black female faculty is expected to balance counseling/mentoring with teaching. Each department in the college has a defined role that should work in tandem to meet students' needs. The work on behalf of *some* students (i.e. Black) should not be done by *some* faculty (i.e., Black female professors).

So how should institutions cultivate Black student achievement? Through the implementation of focused support programs like Doorways to Success which "is an initiative designed to help African-American and Latino male students...achieve a college degree. More than 90 percent of program participants are considered economically disadvantaged and academically unprepared for college" (Workforce Diversity). These programs allow other college staff to provide mentorship and support for Black students without exploiting the labor of Black female faculty. Unfortunately, they are often in jeopardy or underfunded. They also take a lot of time, capital and commitment to operate. Sadly, once programs like these are cut, there is the continuous push to have Black female faculty mentor Black students. This creates relationships that allow students to be connected to the school in ways that are beneficial to the students and the college: students graduate from college and the college retain students. It seems very simple, but the physical, emotional and financial cost to the Black female professors is great.

The type of work I do at the community college is undervalued because it is viewed as being "natural." I teach five courses a semester (not including advising and committee work) and simply do not have the time to dedicate more service hours to meet all of my students' needs. I cannot claim many of these mentoring hours as compensable work and they are not truly counted towards my tenure. However, I feel pulled in the direction that puts the student and by association, the institution first. As the professor, similar to many mothers, I am relegated to the bottom of the needs pool. While I may have some personal satisfaction by mentoring

Black students, it *is* work and thusly should be recognized and compensated. Many Black students seek me out because they feel that, as a Black woman, I can understand their issues and sometimes, I just cannot. Sometimes because I am part of the system they find fault with, my vantage point is not one that echoes their sentiments—regardless of race. Paradoxically as a member of the academy, students feel as if I can do double duty; I can work *with* them and *for* them. Once again, this situation benefits the college financially. Additionally, it allows the responsibility for student success to be placed upon Black female faculty when it is the college's ultimate responsibility. I challenge higher education institutions to meet with Black students to identify their cultural, social, financial, emotional and educational needs and to provide appropriate services to meet them.

Without the college taking ownership (double meaning intended) for its responsibility to the students, I serve as an undercompensated triage agent, metaphorical wet nurse and ill-suited nanny for these students who occupy the margins. I am a small part of the wheel doing a major part of the labor. And due to this, I become complicit in my own undoing. I am allowing the academy to push me to the same margins that I encourage my students to rail against. Because I am a Black woman, it is easier to assign me to these roles. Unfortunately, these expectations come at the risk of professional burn out and career isolation. Doing double duty is disruptive and taxing. Higher education institutions must be more diligent in the ways that they seek faculty support for students. They also must be mindful that these roles cannot be defined as Black women's work.

It is imperative that institutions create inclusive spaces that meet the needs of students and faculty. It is just as important that they don't sacrifice one's voice for the other. In addition to meeting with students, administrators need to consult with Black female faculty to give voice to the frustration, isolation and/or general concerns that are involved when dealing with Black student needs. This is a point of empowerment for the faculty and does not perpetuate long held expectations about what our roles should be with Black students. When institutions continue to expect these unbalanced relationships, they promote the idea that Black women are insignificant and are "the help" no matter the titles and/or degrees they hold.

When Black people enter the halls of academe, our bodies are read as foreign and our mere presence can arouse unwarranted hostility from those in the majority. If I am to advance professionally, how can I seek guidance from colleagues who do not welcome me? If I am a student, how can I seek guidance from a professor who does not value my presence? These are complex institutional issues that must be addressed if institutional change is intended to happen. I have limited power in my own space as a professor, so how can I help students move forward if my own journey is rife with stumbles and discrimination? What am I to do if I am constantly wedged between students and administration, even as I work on behalf of both? How can I meet my students' needs, if I too, am invisible in the academy?

FINDING MY PLACE: ADVOCATING FOR SELFHOOD

As an academic, my career has been shaped by race, gender and class. Elements of motherhood further complicate my identity—personally and professionally. When students insist upon putting me in the role of surrogate or pseudo-mother, I feel an unspoken pressure to adopt an ill-fitting identity. Unfortunately, I have a perceived nurturing disposition that suggests a pseudo-parent. Being mindful of this, I check my own signals to make sure that I am not sending mixed messages. This self-preservationist tactic is beneficial to the students and to me because it prevents us from crossing boundaries that are necessary in professor-student relationships.

Perhaps, if I am honest with myself, I can admit that any misstep in my mind always feels like I am somehow adding a blemish to the shaky perception of Black professionals. Other academics who are not Black and female are allowed to be more of their full selves and carve paths that are related to the work that they do and not the roles that others would have them occupy:

> [R]acism, sexism and numerous other "isms" are systems of advantage that provide those of the "right" race and sex with opportunities with rewards that are unattainable

to other individuals and groups in society. Sometimes they work in isolation from each other, but most of the time, they operate in combination to create a system of advantages and disadvantages that enhance the life of those of the "right" race and sex while limiting the life changes of those who are not. (Wright Meyers 25)

And for me, this has been one of the greatest challenges: finding balance and my place in the academy.

In pursuit of tenure, it seems as if I cannot ignore or deny the students' sometimes invasive requests. At times, I feel powerless to establish boundaries and I fear that I may be denied promotion or other academic advancements. I have so much I have to fight for in my every day responsibilities that I cannot allow anything to minimize my professional reputation. For example: many of my colleagues allow students to call them by their first names. I do not. I teach at a community college and many of the students are my age or older. In order to differentiate our roles in the college, I am always referred to as "Professor Graham." For me, being called "Mama Graham" or "Tokeya" undermines my role on campus. Culturally, addressing any adult or authority figure by his/her first name is viewed as a sign of disrespect. I feel that as one of few Black female faculty, I must make sure that I am always addressed by my full title because I am always professor, never mama. I am always supportive, but never maternal. This is my career, not my family. And even if students feel that maternal ideologies are what propel my interactions with them, it is simply not the case. As a professor, it is my job to cultivate greatness and inspire lifelong learning. Unfortunately because I am a Black woman, the lens through which these actions are viewed is considered "mothering."

I find that I struggle the most in my own desire for placement, position and voice. As a Black woman, I have been part of all movements connected to struggle and progress. Often my issues go unaddressed and my voice is silenced. It saddens me that my greatest accomplishments are often tied to what is deemed as women's work—nurturing and caretaking. While there is dignity in both of these characteristics, I should have the *option* of using them at my workplace. I struggle with the notion that Black women academics have to minimize our professional worthiness and instead focus on how the majority culture is comfortable seeing us. I do my best work when I am free to forge my own path and decide how I want to give of myself. The way I teach is in no way connected to the way that I parent. I recognize that there is a need for mentoring in our community and I will continue to serve as a liaison between my students and my employers. I just do not want to be limited by the imposed boundaries of my gender and my race. I want to be fully actualized as an intellectual who is knowledgeable about my discipline. Ultimately, I want to bask in my own multiplicities and in my own accomplishments. In fact, it is what I want for my students as well.

NOTES

[1] It should be noted that this student is only eleven years younger than me.

WORKS CITED

Adams, Caralee. "New Popularity Challenges Nation's Community Colleges." *Education Week* 30.34 (2011): 14-17. Web. 14 Jul. 2012.

American Association of Community Colleges (AACC). n.d. Web. 15 July 2012

Guiffrida, Douglas. "Othermothering as a Framework for Understanding African American Students' Definitions of Student-Centered Faculty." *Journal of Higher Education* 76.6 (2005): 701-723. Web. 14 Jul. 2012.

Greene, Thomas G., C. Nathan Marti, and Kay McClenney. "The Effort–Outcome Gap: Differences for African American and Hispanic Community College Students in Student Engagement and Academic Achievement." *Journal of Higher Education* 79.5 (2008): 513- 539. Web. 14 Jul. 2012.

Harley, Debra A. "Maids of Academe: African-American Women Faculty at Predominately White Institutions." *Journal of African American Studies* 12 (2008): 19-36.

Harper, Shaun, Lori D. Patton and Ontario S. Wooden. "Access and Equity for African American Students in Higher Education: A Critical Race Historical Analysis of Policy Efforts." *The Journal of Higher Education* 80.4 (July/August 2009): 390-414. Print.

Wolf-Wendel, Lisa, Kelly Ward and Susan B. Twombly. "Faculty Life at Community Colleges: The Perspective of Women With Children." *Community College Review* 34.4 (2007): 255-281. Web. 14 Aug. 2012.

Workforce Diversity. "MCC Programs Cited for Effectiveness — Doorway to Success, 'WINS' Earn SUNY Awards." Workforce Diversity, Mar. 2009. Web. 15 July 2012.

Wright Myers, Lena. *A Broken Silence: Voices of African American Women in the Academy.* Wesport, CT: Bergin & Garvey, 2002. Print.

II.
TESTIMONY

6.
Black Academic and Single Mother

Colliding Statuses

ROSALYN TERBORG-PENN

FOR AFRICAN AMERICAN ACADEMIC WOMEN who are mothers, the term "superwoman" has been used over time as a negative caricature, depicting "mother-graduate student-professor-scholar" attempting, but often unable, to juggle all of these roles well. In some cases the challenge becomes proving to oneself that you can survive the tasks as well as prove the stereotype wrong. Nonetheless, African American academic mothers do not consider themselves to be super women because most working mothers outside of academia experience similar stresses when trying to be an exceptional parent and worker at the same time. Among the major barriers to success are institutionalized patriarchy and racism throughout academia on multiple levels.

Our editor has looked at several indices among Black academic women that place their experiences within a paradigm defined as "multiple marginalities." Black academic women, the editor found, embody multiple marginalities within academia despite their higher educational and so-called economic status because traditionally academia remains patriarchal/sexist, racialized, elitist, and anti-family. Although the public may assume that those with doctoral degrees earn considerable salaries, most academics are underpaid. Women often earn less than men, especially if they are not tenured. Higher paid academics exist in elite institutions, if they have full professorships or endowed chairs. Black women with these kinds of positions are few and far between. Consequently, academia remains a site of struggle and resistance for African American women who are also mothers (Sinzdak and Williams).

This essay is a memoir, which reflects the various stages in my own career as both an academic and mother, because the two colliding statuses coincided, so did the strategies I developed to transverse the barriers erected by patriarchy, sexism and anti-intellectualism. Because my professional academic experiences were for the most part in historically Black institutions, racism was not always part of the struggle equation. However balancing academic responsibilities and parenting responsibilities was a challenge. For me, motherhood in a two-parent household lasted only seven years. Single motherhood continued for twenty more years as my daughter attended elementary school, secondary school, undergraduate school and graduate school. Although my status as an educated, professional woman may have set me apart from other single, working mothers, being an African American female made me vulnerable to many of the same pitfalls other Black women share.

OVERCOMING THE "NO MATERNITY LEAVE" POLICY AT MORGAN STATE COLLEGE

Graduating from Queens College and leaving New York City to seek my fortune in the District of Columbia was not an easy goal to accomplish in the mid 1960s. Traditional middle-class parents like mine frowned upon unmarried daughters leaving town without a laudable reason such as marriage or graduate education. My parents did not understand why I had to leave New York City, when I could stay at home and attend New York University where my father had matriculated. Fortunately for me, my father wanted me to become an attorney and his father wanted me to become a physician. They believed that I should attend university to become a professional. This was a progressive view for the times, when many of my female friends' parents wanted them to find mates and marry either after high school or immediately after college (Terborg-Penn, "A Black History").

The early 1960s predated the second wave of the woman's movement, and many families with traditional viewpoints/perspectives believed that young women who wanted to strike out on their own were radical or so-called "fast" women, whose reputations would be tarnished if they left home for no "respectable reason." I finished undergraduate school in the middle of the Civil Rights Movement and on the cusp of the Woman's Movement. Consequently, I applied for master's degree programs in the discipline of U.S. History, which were located in the nation's capital. The District of Columbia was home to The Library of Congress and The National Archives, plus Howard and other universities. In addition, my mother's sister, her children and several other cousins lived there and attended Howard University. As a result, my parents could not really argue against me going to Washington, DC, because I had a family network there.

Howard University was my first choice, but I had applied for a guaranteed student loan, and one needed to provide letters of acceptance to the bank before the first of July. George Washington University (GWU) accepted me in time, but Howard University did not send their letter of acceptance until August. As a result, I enrolled in the History Master's Degree Program at GWU and left New York City on the eve of the March on Washington in 1963.

I lived and worked in the District of Columbia until I earned my MA degree and then started looking for professional jobs in the Federal Government and in local colleges. However, my thesis advisor would not write a recommendation for me. I suspect that he knew that I would have trouble finding a college teaching position in segregated Washington. Eventually I learned of an opening at Morgan State College in Baltimore. Because I had worked in community development agencies in Washington and knew someone who knew the chair of the History Department at Morgan State, I was hired in August 1969. Often in the past and in the present, who you know determines whether you get the position or not (Terborg-Penn, "Being and Thinking" 75).

At the time, Morgan was primarily a liberal arts college, a historically Black college (HBCU), with about 3,000 students and a new graduate school offering Master's degrees in disciplines such as History, English and Education. The campus was diverse with a recent history of civil rights activism. About two thirds of the students came from Maryland. The remaining third came primarily from northeastern states, and from Caribbean and African countries.

The Morgan State environment was welcoming, but teaching in Baltimore meant moving away from Washington, primarily because my new husband and I could not afford to buy a house in a nice neighborhood in the de facto segregated District of Columbia. Consequently, we decided to move to Columbia, Maryland, a new planned city located between Washington, where he worked, and Baltimore, where I worked. Segregation was banned in Columbia, so housing was open to all who could afford to rent or buy.

In my youthful transition, working at Morgan State as Instructor of History was a dream come true, because I did not have to convince my colleagues that teaching about and researching Black life was worthwhile, an obstacle I had to overcome at GWU. The absence of racism at Morgan State was refreshing. In addition, I had mentors who truly wanted me to succeed, including Dr. Benjamin Quarles, one of the historians whose works I had read as an undergraduate. I was searching for authors who wrote about Black life. Although my mentors at Morgan were men, I soon learned that some of the most influential professors on campus were Black women, an unusual reality in academia. Drs. Iva Jones in the English Department, Gladys Bradley Jones in the Education Department, and Irene Diggs in the Department of Sociology and Anthropology were radical women who spoke their minds, influenced college policies, and ultimately became my role models. However, I soon learned that one of the women had never married, and three of the four women were married to colleagues on campus, but none of them were parents. Consequently I could not look to them for advice about the hazards of being both a mother and a scholar at Morgan State (Terborg-Penn, "Being and Thinking" 75).

In the meantime, my senior male colleagues in the History Department encouraged me to go back to graduate school to earn my Ph.D. My colleagues wanted me to remain at Morgan, but I could not, they argued, if I was not tenured. At Morgan State in those years, tenure required passing your Ph.D. comprehensive exams. You qualified to become an associate professor once you earned your doctoral degree (Terborg-Penn, "Being and Thinking" 76). However, for me, affording to go to graduate school competed with buying a house. Both my husband and I worked full time and part time jobs to earn the money needed. In addition to Morgan State,

I taught at Howard Community College in Columbia, Maryland, even after we bought our house, because we were planning to start a family.

In 1971, my husband and I were ready to start our family. In inquiring about maternity leave, I learned the Morgan State maternity leave policy was based on the same one for sabbatical leave. Women faculty members were not eligible for maternity leave until seven years after teaching full time. I then realized why so many women faculty were childless, or had come to Morgan State when they were older and already had children. I did not realize until a few years later that patriarchy was alive and well at Morgan State. To succeed and move through the ranks to become a professor, women were not supposed to put motherhood alongside teaching and researching. In this sense, academia was anti-family for women, whether the sentiments were deliberate or not.

I was prepared to resign, until the Dean of Faculty, Dr. Percy Baker, suggested that I apply for "leave without pay" in order to enroll in a Ph.D. program. He knew that I had been accepted into the Ph.D. Program in History at Howard University, where I planned to begin classes while on maternity leave. Morgan President King Cheek agreed with the Dean's strategy. The college submitted my letter for leave of absence without pay to the State of Maryland, indicating that I would go to graduate school to earn the Ph.D. The administrators spoke nothing about maternity leave.

Luckily I had saved some money, a habit I learned from my parents who said saving even just a few dollars regularly was needed for a "rainy day." However, my savings were not enough to go to school full time, because my husband and I lived off of two salaries. Consequently, I would continue to teach part time at the community college to pay tuition and to afford childcare so that I could attend classes. In my husband's mind, this was my project, so it was my responsibility to take care of the baby, not his. My choices in 1972 were to be a working mother during the first year of the baby's life, a position I had hoped to avoid, or not work, stay home with the baby, and not earning the degree I needed to keep my position. Patriarchy/sexism were alive and well at home and in academia. However, I refused to be daunted. I needed to keep my teaching position by earning my doctoral degree.

EARNING MY PH.D. AT HOWARD UNIVERSITY WHILE PUBLISHING

I began my doctorate at Howard University in the history department in Fall 1972, when my daughter, Jeanna Penn, was four months old. For the first year I was a part time student coordinating childcare, teaching Introduction to Sociology, taking six hours of classes each semester, and raising my child on the days that I did not have to work. I dared anyone to call me a "super woman," because several other women I knew who were in their late twenties and early thirties were doing the same as I. Nonetheless, I remained stressed by fatigue and my husband's lack of empathy for me as a working mother and student.

My major field of study was U.S. History Before the Civil War, with a concentration in Afro-American History. I knew I wanted to write a dissertation on some aspect of Black women's lives. Little did I know that I was the first person in Howard's History Department to declare a topic about Blacks and women's history and that I would have an uphill struggle because I had to convince faculty that Black women's experience was viable (Terborg-Penn, "A Black History" 195-96).

In hindsight I realized that the 1970s was the time of major academic debates about not only whether women's lives were different than men's experiences and deserved to be studied, but also whether Black history deserved to be studied. Finding the history of Black women was indeed enacting triple jeopardy—because of class, race and gender. However, a movement was rising among a handful of African American women in academia and I became a part of the movement.

During the early 1970s, I joined my fellow students at Howard University and began attending academic conferences. In the early years, my childcare providers took care of my baby and my husband managed to return home from work to relieve them. However this occurred with some resentment on his part. Nonetheless, I managed to attend meetings held in Washington or Baltimore by The Association for the Study of African American Life and History (ASALH), and The American Historical Association (AHA). These associations became springboards for my professional development and allowed me to network with better-known individuals in the discipline. Testing my analysis required presenting my work at conferences. In 1973, the Black Studies Program at the University of Louisville held the first conference I ever attended, where the theme was "Black Women." Several of us from the History Department at Howard University submitted paper proposals and applied for travel grants. Dr. Lorraine Williams, the chair of the History Department at Howard University, saw to it that those of us who wanted to attend received funding. It was at this conference that I presented the paper, "Discrimination Against Afro-American Women in the Woman's Movement, 1830-1920," which I later published as an article. Little did I know that the article would make me become a pioneer in developing Black Women's History (Terborg-Penn, *African American Women*).

In the meantime, Lorraine Williams obtained funding for a one-hundred year study of Freedmen's Hospital of the Howard University School of Medicine, which later became Howard University Hospital. Williams appointed Dr. Thomas Holt to write the book with Cassandra Smith-Parker and me as his graduate research assistants. This was my first experience researching for a book-length study. The project was quite significant to my scholarly development, although it slowed my dissertation research. When the book was published in 1975, Smith-Parker and I shared the authorship with Thomas Holt, who gave us credit for not only collecting the research, but also helping to shape the concept and analysis. The book, *A Special Mission: The Story of Freemen's Hospital, 1862-1962*, was a small volume, but it was my first book (Holt, Smith-Parker and Terborg-Penn). Soon afterwards I passed my Ph.D. comprehensive exams, I applied for a position as assistant professor at Morgan State and was promoted. However, the college was suffering financially, so I received no increase in pay for my promotion. I was an assistant professor in name only, receiving the pay of an instructor.

In the meantime, my new academic success encouraged me to join with fellow Howard University graduate student Sharon Harley for another book project. We conceived the idea for an anthology on Black women's history for practical reasons. Like me, none of my fellow students who were college faculty could find scholarly books and articles on African American women's history short of a few biographies and documentary collections. Our first step was recruiting colleagues to write essays with historical themes for a manuscript, "The Afro-American Woman: Struggles and Images." Editing essays was not as difficult as finding a publisher to agree to read the manuscript. We began in 1974 by sending letters to numerous university presses.

Finally, by 1976, one of the Howard history faculty members, Dr. Al-Tony Gilmore, recommended us to his publisher, Kennikat Press. We had never heard of this press, but what choice did we have? Fortunately the publisher understood our vision and reviewed our manuscript. Harley and I both wrote two essays each. Harley and I had carefully selected African American authors, most of whom were graduate students working on various topics about Black women. I defended my dissertation in 1977, while the press considered the essays we had submitted. My daughter was five years old, and in the fall of that year, she entered kindergarten.

The Afro-American Woman: Struggles and Images was published in 1978, shortly after Howard University conferred my Ph.D. Historians hailed the anthology, the first to examine African American women's history in a scholarly way. Harley continued to work on her dissertation. As for me, from that point on, I was asked to serve on historical association committees, deliver lectures and write articles about various aspects of Black women's lives (Harley and Terborg-Penn).[1] Consequently, immediately after finishing my dissertation, I started applying for grants, researching and writing again. I had hired a babysitter when writing my dissertation because my husband was rarely available to take care of our child so I could write. I continued the strategy until the summer of 1979, when I became a single parent and could not afford to hire anyone to assist me with anything for about five years thereafter.

BECOMING A SINGLE PARENT

Before attempting to write this section, I consulted with my daughter, Jeanna Penn. I needed her perspective as well as my own. She began by remembering about circumstances thirty years before. Her first recollection was, "You stopped cooking and allowed the television to raise me." I reminded Jeanna that she did not like my cooking and refused to eat much of what I cooked even before her father left the household. She conceded and then reflected seriously about how hard it was for us in a neighborhood where most of the mothers stayed at home, and those who worked outside of the home had husbands. I was the first woman in the neighborhood who became a single mother, and Jeanna became the first child that she knew in her second grade class to have no father at home. However, by the time she transitioned from elementary to middle school, several parents among her classmates and friends had gone their separate ways. We were social pioneers. Jeanna acknowledged how hard it was for me not to have the support of my female peers. I know it was difficult for her as well.

From my own experience and those of others, I learned that it takes about five years for a working, single mother to recover financially from marital break-up. Although I received regular child support, it remained a fixed amount for ten years. My husband refused to give me a divorce, but paid our relatively modest mortgage. He said this arrangement insured his investment in our mutually owned property. Consequently, when mortgage payments went up, I was covered. Nonetheless, for about five years I remained on a strict budget until my salary could catch up with my expenses. The extra funds I earned supplemented my meager salary to allow Jeanna enrichment classes in summer school and intramural sports. Her father lavished her with birthday and Christmas gifts, plus took her shopping for clothing, but I was responsible for paying bills, which aside from food, housing, auto payments, insurance, phone, and utilities, included medical and dental co-payments, girl scouting expenses, children's trips to cultural activities, and visits to see family in New York City. In remembering these things over the years, Jeanna praised me for doing a good job under difficult circumstances.

Understanding the complexity and impact of parental break-ups on children was difficult for me to grasp, because the phenomenon was outside of my personal experience. My parents remained in a good relationship throughout their long marriage. However, my mother's two sisters had been widowed or divorced when in their forties. As a child, I paid little attention to the familial impact of divorce despite my knowledge of their situations. Apparently, you have to live such circumstances to understand them.

One clue came to me from the nurse in Jeanna's elementary school. In 1980 the school nurse called to tell me that Jeanna was upset. My daughter had told her that I was about to "get rid of our dog, like I had gotten rid of her father." I was aghast, and explained what I had told Jeanna. "The dog is sick. I am going to take him to the vet, but if the cost of treatment is too expensive for me to afford, I will have to put the dog to sleep." The nurse and I talked about how children see life circumstances differently than adults. Perhaps Jeanna's father told her that I had put him out and made her feel responsible. The nurse suggested counseling. However, in 1980, my health insurance required a hefty co-payment for such services. Unfortunately, I did not have funds for counseling at that time.

Luckily, the dog survived a bit longer. Nonetheless, I realized that sometimes luck, not always reason, determines outcomes. I continued to be as honest as I could be with Jeanna about what we could afford to do and what we could not. For a few more years she wanted to know when we would stop being so poor.

The precarious financial status of Black single mothers is a reality for professional as well as non-professional women workers in the 2000s just as it was in the 1970s. Meizhu Lui, director of the Closing the Gap Initiative in Oakland, California, contributed to a 2010 report, "Lifting as We Climb: Women of Color, Wealth and America's Future." She believed that the financial downturn from 2008 to 2010 compounded the problems of single Black women because unemployment has always been twice as high in Black communities than in white communities. Esther Bush, Executive Director of the Pittsburgh Urban League, reported seventy percent of African Americans in the city to be single mothers. The recession hit them especially hard, with four out of ten families headed by single mothers in Pittsburgh living in poverty (Grant).

Luckily, I had a support network that began shortly after I became a single parent. Jeanna's godparents, who lived in the District of Columbia, and my parents, helped me when needed. However, they lived in New York City. My mother's younger sister, Rosalyn Coleman, lived in Columbia, so I could count on her for moral support and in emergencies. Nonetheless, all of them had full time jobs. Jeanna liked all her family members, so she cooperated with them, but she did not like any man who entered my life. I was perplexed about this, since her father had set up a new life for himself even before he left the household.

Unlike many single academic mothers, I had the opportunity to try balancing parenting with dating. Fortunately, I entered a relationship with a professional African American man. Michael Terry lived nearby in the District of Columbia. Nonetheless balancing a social life, with parenting and my university commitments was always like walking a tight rope. Nonetheless, Michael and I maintained a relationship for many years until cancer took his life in 2004.

Despite the threats of not being able to stretch my limited income, my goal was to set standards and live by them. My mothering style was similar to my teaching style. I argued that you must work to earn what rewards you receive. This value I imparted to my daughter and to my students. In addition, I told them, if you need help, let me know and I will do the best I can do to assist you. I learned that one's students were similar to one's children. Some of my struggling students sought my assistance and completed the course with good grades, but others did not seek assistance did not do well as a result. Jeanna never wanted help with her homework, and often refused to let me see it without putting up a fight.

Fortunately Jeanna was a smart student, but we learned from a middle-school meeting called by the Principal, that she and several of her peers were under-achievers—smart students who tested well, but did not make the effort to perform above average. Jeanna and I both attended the meeting and realized that she was not alone. Consequently, I learned to let up on my verbal expectations and tried a different course. For example, I was advised to allow her to pick her punishment rather than imposing one upon her. Jeanna often picked a punishment worse than the one I would have selected. However, unlike her friends, I did not allow Jeanna to have a television or a phone in her bedroom. On the other hand, most of the house was open to her. I would leave books and pamphlets around for her to see, instead of asking her specifically to look at the items. Years later I learned that she had read many of the books I had on my library shelves, all of which were available to her.

In the meantime, I put a lock on my bedroom door to keep Jeanna from raiding my closet. Apparently all of her peers "borrowed" their mother's jewelry and clothing, an act my peers would never have considered when we were children. Jeanna felt that sometimes I seemed crazy, whereas, to me sometimes she seemed angry as she developed as an adolescent. From 1979 to 1985 I raised Jeanna with limited familial support. My parents had moved to St. Croix in the U.S. Virgin Islands in 1982. They insisted that Jeanna and I spend every Christmas holiday with them. With their financial assistance we acquiesced. Jeanna enjoyed spending time with her grandparents, and her cousins who lived on the same property. After two years I could not see why my small amount of discretionary funds were designated to pay for these trips. I began to feel trapped. Then in 1985 my parents decided to return to the states and move to Columbia, Maryland.

Their move was great for Jeanna, but stressful for me. She loved my mother's cooking and my father's jazz collection. She visited them regularly and sometimes stayed with them when I was out of town. At thirteen, Jeanna had the family she coveted, as my brother and his family visited my parents from South Carolina periodically. My parent's nieces and nephews from the Baltimore-Washington area visited them too. However, my parents still viewed me as their child under their control, making it difficult for me raising an adolescent daughter.

JUGGLING COLLIDING STATUSES — RESEARCHING, TEACHING, AND MOTHERING

As I juggled providing time and attention to my daughter, my parents and my partner Michael, during the 1980s and 1990s my life was contrasted between stress and professional success, which exacerbated my Type One Diabetes. To me everyone wanted my attention simultaneously. Fortunately, by the mid 1980s my health insurance provided counseling services at a more moderate co-payment rate and my salary had caught up to my expenses. Both Jeanna and I went into counseling. Venting did help me unload stress, but the professionals could never seem to provide the best strategies. I had to work them out myself, plus Jeanna resented being in counseling.

The worse period was 1987, the year Jeanna was fifteen, and one day we literally came to blows. My parents came to the rescue by talking to Jeanna in a calm, but forceful manner. She seemed to be crying for help. However, her father remained aloof and above the fray. Our mother-daughter relationship slowly improved thereafter.

Teaching was my balm because most students respected me and gave me positive feedback. Researching and writing helped me to earn a Ford Foundation Minority Fellowship in the early 1980s, which stroked my ego. I also won a Bunting Institute Fellowship from Radcliffe College, then a Smithsonian Institution Faculty Fellowship, both during various summers in the mid to late 1980s. However, I never had a large enough block of time to revise my dissertation into another book until the 1990s, because a heavy teaching and administrative schedule divided my time at Morgan, and family responsibilities limited my time at home. Nonetheless, I published numerous articles and gave lectures. Friends and family called me a "workaholic," but academic work kept me sane, plus I needed the extra money to provide the professional development I required to be successful and the cultural lifestyle Jeanna and I hoped to maintain.

On the professional level, my Black female colleagues often discussed the costs of moving up in the profession, which seemed to be higher for us than for African American men or white men and women with similar credentials in the academy. The gap was not merely perceptional. In her article, "Racialized Gender/Gendered Racism," social scientist Stanlie M. James commented about the gendered "Black tax" that African American women pay because of the added disadvantage of being not only Black, but also female. The "Black tax" applies to all working African American women in one way or the other, she argued, even if they are single mothers. James and others developed this theory after examining the negative assumptions that policymakers have applied to Black women as citizens, and provided the statistical data to prove it (James 388-89).

Throughout the 1980s I had developed a role as scholar-activist, primarily because I taught at an HBCU. Many of us were compelled to challenge "benign neglect" in state funding and program approval, plus negative views from mainstream institutions about so-called unprepared Black students. I was applauded and honored for my work as a pioneer in developing African American Women's History, and by the mid 1980s, in developing African Diaspora Women's History too. However, my colleagues in mainstream academia seemed to herald me more as an activist who promoted Black women historians than as a scholar of Black Women's History. I often felt marginalized by their elitism.

During these crucial years in my career development, I had to acknowledge that being a scholar was also difficult because I was a single mother and, in 1986, I had become the Coordinator of Graduate Programs in History at Morgan State University. I administered two graduate programs, plus taught three, three-credit courses each semester. To make things worse, I had limited travel funds to attend conferences outside of the region. Nonetheless, I was the Principle Investigator for a National Endowment for the Humanities funded research conference, "Women in the African Diaspora: An Interdisciplinary Perspective," sponsored by the Association of Black Women Historians, an organization I had co-founded. Writing a theoretical essay about African Feminism and co-editing the anthology that resulted from the conference seemed to enhance my reputation as a scholar-activist, rather than as a serious scholar, although my published articles are sited continually by other scholars. However my colleagues at Morgan State felt differently and by the end of the 1980s I was promoted to Full Professor of History (Terborg-Penn, Harley and Rushing).

Some of my friends in mainstream institutions suggested that I needed to finish my monograph on Black women and the Woman Suffrage Movement in order to earn more respect in the broader profession. I agreed, but needed a block of time away from Morgan State so that I could work without distractions. Since writing my dissertation, I had done additional research focusing on African American women who had been woman suffragists, and published several articles focusing upon them. I had found significant information during my first sabbatical leave from Morgan State during the 1978-79 academic year. However, my heavy teaching load, administrative duties, and service to the profession left me little time to write a book.

The year 1990 was a turning point for both me and for Jeanna. She graduated from high school, enrolled at Morgan State and moved into the dormitory. Although I did not see nor hear from her for the first six weeks of her first semester, soon thereafter I saw Jeanna and her friends on a regular basis. After declaring a major in Speech for a brief period, she switched to African American History, explaining that she grew up reading my history books and felt confident about understanding the field. Jeanna was nineteen years of age and had matured significantly in one year. Having her own space away from mine was good for both of us. Nonetheless, I did not apply for grants and sabbatical leave again until her senior year, because I was always on call to assist with her social, intellectual and medical concerns. Jeanna Penn graduated with honors and a BA degree in May of 1994, making me a very proud mother.

In July 1994, my responsibilities for the past academic year ended and I began my sabbatical leave with a fellowship at the Smithsonian Institution. My goal was to write my long awaiting book. During my sojourn at the Smithsonian, I re-wrote my manuscript. In 1995 I submitted it to Indiana University Press. The reviewers supported my work and the press offered me a contract. *African American Women in the Struggle for the Vote, 1850-1920* was published in 1998, and the following year it won the ABWH book prize.

FROM PARENTING MY CHILD TO PARENTING MY MOTHER

Caregiving of elder parents for middle-aged adults was a significant late twentieth century dilemma, which continued into the twenty-first century for many women in my generation. As senior adults live longer than they did the generation before, dementia became prevalent and the health dangers for over worked family caregivers common (Mace and Rabins 288). The burden of adult children taking care of aging parents was especially immobilizing for many African American women who were already over-burdened single parents.

Shortly before Jeanna began college, my parents needed my assistance as my father's health began declining in the late 1980s. My father, Jacques Terborg, Sr., did not suffer from dementia, but his physical health declined, as I helped him and my mother provide care for nearly a decade before he passed away at the age of 88 in 1997. Although Jeanna had moved to the District of Columbia and enrolled in the History Master's Degree program at Howard University, she was devastated by his death. I was too, but glad that he had not suffered for more than twenty-four hours. He had lived long and well—the longest living person at that point on both sides of my family.

In the meantime, my mother's mental health began to deteriorate, and I was once again distracted from my professional activities. Nonetheless, Jeanna and my Aunt Rosalyn helped me with my mother's ultimate decline into dementia. Neither my brother, who resides in South Carolina, nor his daughters provided meaningful assistance. After earning her certification in documentary filmmaking from George Washington University, Jeanna moved to Los Angeles in 2001 to pursue a career in film writing. However, she returned to Maryland periodically to visit me, and to help with her ailing father and grandmother.

Nonetheless, I suffered the emotional and financial toll over time for becoming my mother's surrogate parent. I needed to refinance her condominium and become a co-owner. In the process, I made all of the needed repairs, which she seemed not to believe were needed, ordered her medications, transported her to doctors and labs, and made sure that her bills were paid and her taxes filed.

Reluctantly, my mother, Jeanne Terborg moved to an assisted living residence in 2003 as her dementia developed into Alzheimer's disease. Unlike many African American women elders, Jeanne's retirement income, her Social Security benefits, plus her savings enabled me to pay for most of her assisted living expenses. However, for the nearly five years in assisted living, her monthly costs increased twenty-five percent yearly, and I eventually had to move her from the corporate owned facility she rented to a more modest, privately owned one. My fear was that my mother would outlive her resources and have to move to a Medicare approved facility. However, Jeanne passed away at the age of 91 in 2007, and the stress from my juggling of colliding statuses subsided. Compared to most single, working African American women, my plight was minimal. Nonetheless, I faced the emotional toll of loss, and the task of settling her affairs, a chore that continued into 2009.

Throughout my forty years of university teaching, my life experience proved to me over and over again that women must work harder to accomplish professional goals. Our society teaches males and females that women's domestic work in families never ends, while men are normally excused from assuming such responsibilities. Although I had retired from full time teaching in 2006, I continued to supervise my dissertation students until 2009, and to assist Jeanna with her wedding, and emergencies that she had in assisting with her father's health problems.

COMMONALITIES AND DIFFERENCES BETWEEN DIVERSE, AFRICAN AMERICAN WORKING MOTHERS

The burden of responsibility for personal and family survival has been higher for African American single mothers than any other group, even as they experience multiple marginalities. One of the documented reasons is institutional racism. Another reason is the often illogical "fear" non-African Americans have of Black people, a fear that has been cultivated in American culture since emancipation.

University of Maryland Law Professor Taunya Lovell Banks recalled an incident, when she and two other Black law professors visited a colleague in a luxury condominium in Philadelphia. The lawyers were professionally dressed and riding the elevator. At two different stops, the white women who stood outside of the elevator door when it opened would not enter the elevator, revealing their discomfort at seeing three Black women standing together. Banks and her colleagues realized after the second time that despite their academic positions and their professional attire, gender and class did not insulate them from the fear that whites have of African Americans (Banks 98-99).

Despite higher education and the advantages that middle-class status bring to most professional Black single mothers, their life experiences often mirror those of working-class women in similar households. Societal assumptions about, and fears of, Black people have determined our position in the workplace so that African American women have to work harder yet receive less to earn positions that other women and men obtain more readily.

According to the *Pittsburgh Post-Gazette*, an economic research group released a report in March 2010 about the grave financial challenges single Black women faced in the United States (Grant). The study, which collected data in 2008 before the nationwide financial downturn, revealed not surprising data that on average women earn less and have fewer assets than men of the same race. However, the disparities for single African American women were overwhelmingly greater than those for any other group of females and males during prime working years. Many Black women reported that they could not take unpaid sick days or make repairs to vehicles or dwellings without going into debt. The shocking conclusion was the amount of median wealth reported by the study for single Black women in 2008: $5 (cash in the bank, stocks, bonds and real estate—minus debt). For white women in their working prime, the median wealth recorded was $42,600. The report revealed a bleak picture for single African American women ages 18 to 64. The median household wealth for single women living in households with other wage earners was only $100; however, the median household income for single Hispanic women was $120 (Grant).

Although the wealth study news reports focused on the impoverished Black women working in service industries with no benefits, similar characteristics describe the reality of many junior, single African American mothers in academia—last hired for non-permanent positions, under paid, over worked, first fired. Perhaps Black academic women do not qualify as impoverished, but I suspect that many are not far from the crisis that will put them there, such as the high instances of sub-prime mortgages offered and taken by single Black women in the mid-2000s.

As Sekile Nzinga-Johnson has argued in her introduction, class, higher education, and professional employment cannot always shield academic mothers from racism and sexism in the workplace and in public life. Black academic women, despite their access to better employment, find themselves in the same paradigm as working-class Black women in the service sectors of the economy who experience multiple marginalities. In the case of academic women who are both Black and single mothers, marginalities increase, because traditions change very slowly in academic institutions. Despite higher educational and so-called better economic status, the patriarchal/sexist, racialized, elitist, and anti-family traditions cancel out academic advantages for single Black women with doctorate degrees, assuring multiple marginalities for them. For many single Black academic mothers, luck, not reason, often brings us to the place where we can feel safe to practice our craft and raise our children without fear of professional dislocation, stress, and even poverty.

NOTES

[1] See, for references to the impact of the book, Wilson; James, Foster and Guy-Sheftall (xiv, xxv fn5, xxvii fn 14).

WORKS CITED

Banks, Taunya Lovell. "Two Life Stories: Reflections of One Black Woman Law Professor." *Critical Race Feminism: A Reader*. Ed. Adrien Katherine Wing. New York: New York University Press, 1997. 96-100. Print.

Grant, Tim . "Study Finds Median Wealth for Single Black Women at $5." *Pittsburgh Post-Gazette* 19 March 2010. Print.

Harley, Sharon and Rosalyn Terborg-Penn, eds. *The Afro-American Woman: Struggles and Images*. Port Washington, NY: Kennikat Press, 1978. Print.

Holt, Thomas, Cassandra Smith-Parker and Rosalyn Terborg-Penn. *A Special Mission: The Story of Freedom's Hospital, 1862-1962*. Washington: Academic Affairs Division, Howard University, 1975. Print.

James, Stanlie M. "Racialized Gender/Gendered Racism: Reflections on Black Feminist Human Rights Theorizing." *Still Brave: The Evolution of Black Women's Studies*. Ed. Stanlie M. James, Frances Smith Foster and Beverly Guy-Sheftall. New York: The

Feminist Press, 2009. 383-391. Print.

Stanlie M. James, Frances Smith Foster and Beverly Guy-Sheftall. "Introduction." *Still Brave: The Evolution of Black Women's Studies.* Ed. Stanlie M. James, Frances Smith Foster and Beverly Guy-Sheftall. New York: The Feminist Press, 2009. xi-xxviII. Print.

Mace, Nancy L. and Peter V. Rabins. *The 36-Hour Day: A Family Guide to Caring for Persons with Alzheimer's Disease.* New York: Warner Books, 1991. Print.

Sinzdak, Jean and Erica Williams. "African American Women Work More, Earn Less: New Census Data Show Economic and Educational Status of African American Women Still Lags Far Behind White Women." The Institute for Women's Policy Research, March 29, 2005. Web.

Terborg-Penn, Rosalyn. "A Black History Journey: Encountering Herbert Aptheker along the Way." *Nature, Society and Thought: A Journal of Dialectical and Historical Materialism* 10.1,2 (1997): 189-200. Print.

Terborg-Penn, Rosalyn. *African American Women in the Struggle for the Vote, 1850-1920.* Bloomington: The Indiana University Press, 1998. Print.

Terborg-Penn, Rosalyn. "Being and Thinking Outside of the Box: A Black Woman's Experience in Academia." *Telling Histories: Black Women Historians in the Ivory Tower.* Ed. Deborah Gray White. Chapel Hill: The University of North Carolina Press, 2008. 72-84. Print.

Terborg-Penn, Rosalyn. "Discrimination Against Afro-American Women in the Woman's Movement, 1830-1920." *The Afro-American Woman: Struggles and Images.* Ed. Sharon Harley and Rosalyn Terborg-Penn. Port Washington, NY: Kennikat Press, 1978.

Terborg-Penn, Rosalyn, Sharon Harley and Andrea Benton Rushing, eds. "Introduction." *Women in Africa and the African Diaspora.* Washington: Howard University Press, 1987. xi-xxi. Print.

Wilson, Francille Rusan "'This Past was Waiting for Me When I Came': The Contextualization of Black Women's History" (Review Essay). *Feminist Studies* 22.2 (Summer 1996): 347-51. Print.

7.
And There Went My Adventurer's Spirit

Motherhood and Fieldwork Post-9/11

PATRICIA WILLIAMS LESSANE

GROWING UP ON THE SOUTH SIDE of Chicago in the 1970s, I benefitted from the "village" experience of being mothered and reared by the other women who lived on my block. I was an "old folks'" child because my parents were forty years old when I was born, and already had three teenagers by that time. My experience as the child of older parents—privy to adult conversation, solitary play time, and hours spent reading the newspaper and literature—influenced my love of school, veracious appetite for words and books, and pursuit of academic excellence. When my father died suddenly when I was six years old, my mother Annie Ruth embraced her dual role as mother and father to me and was determined I would grow up whole and self-sufficient. My mother's courage and strength during that trying time, coupled with the love I received from other women on my block, provided much needed nurturing and a sense of safety. Without being asked, these women "stood in the gap" and provided additional support and balance to my rearing. And like many black mothers, Annie Ruth demonstrated mountain-moving strength, unyielding faith, and belief in the impossible. Though she had little more than a sixth-grade formal education, she encouraged me to dream big and instilled in me the belief that everything is possible with hard work and determination. Her words and her example of motherhood—part warrior and part guardian angel—have influenced the way I see the world and the role I play in it. Indeed, her tireless hard work and love are models for the way I mother my own children.

My mother was and still is my first love. Warrior, conjurer, and medicine woman, she taught me the importance of love, humility, strength, and grace under fire. She is the mother I still long to be. Admittedly, I did not always yearn to be a mother; but sometime during college, when I fell head over heels in love with Black women writers, something beautiful, magical, and spiritual happened to me. I began to really see myself as an artist—loving, fearless, and worldly. I had always recognized the power of words. From the time I was very little, I had known I wanted to be a writer. Reading books and writing poems and short stories were two of my other first great loves. My mother was the consummate storyteller. She often could be found "holding court" with her friends and relatives, mesmerizing us all with tales laced with comedy, conjure, and comeuppance for southern and northern Whites alike. One of my mother's most elaborate stories was about her very own Lazarus experience—when she was miraculously raised from the dead. I never tired of hearing my mother recount the story of how, at the age of twelve, she had been pronounced dead by doctors after a drawn-out bout of bleeding ulcers. As her mother and siblings had wept for her in the hospital hallway, she had begun to cough and proceeded to ask for water as she lay on the hospital stretcher. "Everybody gathered 'round me," she would say. "It was a miracle that I had survived!"

My mother indulged my own stories and encouraged me to capture my dreams and imaginings on paper. However, I did not begin regularly tending to my love of storytelling until my early twenties, when unharnessed written expression was crucial for me as an individual, a woman coming into my own. It was then I began dreaming of motherhood. I imagined giving birth to a tribe of warrior children who would be both poets and provocateurs. I envisioned myself traveling the world with my children, nursing them under trees in exotic places as I conducted fieldwork. It is no surprise that the anthropological methodologies of ethnography appeals to me. In many ways, conducting participant observation and field interviews nurture my love of storytelling. Collecting and documenting the life stories of my informants—the cadence, the spirit, and the voices of the people I encounter—come alive when I recount my field experiences.

I look back fondly at my courageousness, imagination, romance with words, and overall joie de vie. However, about halfway through my graduate program, reality clipped my wings and curtailed my ability to dream, to fly. I found myself in a state of limbo. My hunger for knowledge, adventure, and happiness as a new mother were somehow usurped by the violent realities of the day. Rather unexpectedly, the world became a very dangerous place where, in my mind, mothering and doing fieldwork were mutually exclusive. Overnight, my desire to protect my child trumped the idea of traversing the globe documenting the stories of other people's lives.

In thinking about the theme of Black Motherhood in the Academy, I was initially reminded of my experiences as a graduate student and new mother on 9/11, and how nursing my first child while witnessing the terrorist attacks on television would eventually affect my scholarship, fieldwork, and experiences in both realms. I recall being seized with fear for my friends and family, and ultimately for my child. If such a vicious attack could occur on U.S. soil, what dangers lay in store for us if/when we as Americans traveled abroad for fieldwork? Like many Americans, I spent my days and nights enthralled with what had happened—what was the death toll? What had the authorities learned about the final hours of the victims? Who were the victims? Who were the perpetrators?

I sunk into a depression. It became increasingly difficult for me to think about my evolving philosophical ideas about motherhood, the academy, and my day-to-day experiences as a mother vis-à-vis the post-9/11 cultural and political climate in the United States without examining how my own mother nurtured and raised me. Her example of motherhood, along with her wisdom and help she gave, truly influenced the way I currently navigate the different arenas of my life and negotiate space in each to always be true to myself and my dreams. Furthermore, while the horrific events of 9/11 altered my approach to my work in the academy and dampened my adventurer's spirit, my mother's diagnosis of and subsequent death from lung cancer in 2003 increased my appreciation for mothering as an important component of self-actualization and self-determination, and agency, as well as a key trope of feminist discourse. My position is not rooted in an essentialist view of "womanhood as motherhood," but rather in the belief that because feminism addresses liberation and agency, it is possible to learn valuable lessons for both within examples of healthy mothering within our own experiences and of other women's experiences that further historicize the institution of motherhood.

My goal in these few pages is to contextualize my journey as a mother, feminist, graduate student post-9/11, and motherless child within a Black Feminist framework as a way to examine how the dichotomies of "scholar," "teacher," and "mother" become intricately complex when traumatic events disrupt the experience of each. If our experience as women within the academy is shaped by socially proscribed notions of gender and sexuality and our scholarship is influenced by our politicized experiences (on the margins of society and the academy) within those frameworks, then it stands to reason our experiences as mothers within the academy embodies the dialectic between both. Furthermore, our dual experiences as scholars and mothers in the academy are further complicated by the realities of individual and collective traumas. In my case in particular, my role as a new mother in the wake of 9/11 and my mother's death from cancer influenced my work as an anthropologist.

COMING OF AGE AT "BLACK WOMEN IN THE ACADEMY: IN DEFENSE OF OUR NAME"

In 1994, I was one of hundreds of African-American women—students, scholars, and lay people—who attended the transformative conference "Black Women in the Academy: In Defense of Our Name" held at MIT. As a graduate student in the Master of Arts in Liberal Studies program at Dartmouth College, I had thrown myself headfirst into the world of scholarship by Black feminists such as Hazel Carby, Barbara Smith, Patricia Hill Collins, Kimberlé Crenshaw, and Angela Davis, so I was overwhelmed with the thought of attending a conference where so many of these "uber" Black women scholars would be present. It was truly an amazing event, and I was able to see scholar-activism at work; these women not only talked the talk, but also walked the walk of liberation and self-determination. As I sat enthralled by their presence, I became baptized by their words; I was transformed. It was then I determined my work as an educator and scholar had to be meaningful and rooted in a Black feminist framework that not only liberated all women of color, but one that sought to uplift the African-American community particularly. Yet, a shocking response by a noted feminist scholar to a question posed by a fellow graduate student quickly checked my euphoria. Her question: "What advice would you give a graduate student raising a child while trying to complete graduate training?" The response: "Don't have any children. You can't do scholarship and raise children at the same time."

My colleagues and I sat stunned. Though we were young women, without "chick nor child," we imagined motherhood in our future. We mulled over the comments during lunch and dinner and surmised that while motherhood may not have been a priority for that generation of Black feminist scholars, it was for us. Furthermore, each of us saw motherhood as inextricably tied to our feminism—if we were ever to move beyond the current realities of sexism, classism, and racism, we had to start that struggle in our homes as mothers of warrior girls and compassionate boys. We could and would have it all—the family and the career—and we kept our pledge as each of us went on to have wonderful careers and families. We were encouraged by Patricia Hill Collins who reminds us that:

> The insistence on Black female self-definition reframes the entire dialogue from one of determining the technical accuracy of an image to one stressing the power dynamics underlying the very process of definition itself. Black feminists have questioned not only what has been said about Black women, by the credibility and the intentions of those possessing the power to define. When Black women define themselves, they clearly reject the taken-for-granted assumption that those in positions granting them the authority to describe and analyze reality are entitled to do so. Regardless of the actual of Black women's self-definitions, the act of insisting on Black female self-definition validates Black women's power as human subjects. (S17)

Nevertheless, those words at the conference haunted me as I

attempted to balance completing my doctoral work in Anthropology and being fully present in the lives of my husband and family. Nonetheless, I pressed on, believing my hard work and commitment to both areas of my life would eventually pay off, providing me with the amazing life of which I had always dreamed.

CHARTING MY COURSE

By 1998, I had entered the doctoral program at University of Illinois at Chicago and my dream of traveling the world conducting ethnographic research was within reach. To my great fortune, several of my professors had young families, including my graduate advisor, Dr. Alaka Wali, who was married and had also raised her children while in graduate school. Alaka quickly moved from simply being a graduate advisor and mentor to a model of the type of scholar, wife, and mother I was determined to become. I inhaled her stories of fieldwork in Peru, Harlem, and other parts of the world, along with the love and pride she had for her two teenage children.

Then, in 2001, my son sprang from my body, a living, thriving being who ushered me into the sacred sisterhood of mothers. Surrounded by my mother, nurses, doctor, and my supportive husband, I entered a new stage in my life as a woman and as a feminist. And again, while I do not embrace an essentialist view of motherhood as it relates to female identity, I do recognize and appreciate how the unique experience embodies the two. Furthermore, as a third-wave womanist, I embrace the fluid nature of feminism and its power to liberate women, families, and entire societies from the dangers of sexism, homophobia, racism, classism, ageism, violence, and heterosexism.

Becoming a mother has afforded me the greatest opportunity to define myself as a woman and feminist by reifying those values embraced by feminism, and Black feminist thought in particular. I agree with Patricia Hill Collin's assessment of the importance of self-definition in Black feminist discourse in that "Black women create their own standards for evaluating Afro-American womanhood and value their creations..." (S18). Additionally, my coming-of-age during the post–Civil Rights and Women's Movement eras of the

1980s and 1990s has equipped me with a global perspective about the threats to womanhood and female self-determination worldwide. This perspective and my experiences as a Black woman and mother have influenced the way I interact with other people, and particularly how I nurture and rear my children. Through regular travel and thoughtful conversations with my children about race, gender, and class, as well as contemporary issues facing women and global people of color, I have been able to demonstrate to them just how inextricably tied my philosophical ideals are to my life as a Black woman in the world today.

Soon after my son was born, I completed my required coursework, passed my comprehensives, and began writing my dissertation proposal. Like most graduate students, I was excited about the impact my work could have in the Academy, but I was also feeling the emotional and physical angst associated with the "liminal personae" (Turner 95) of graduate school I was embodying. Victor Turner has described the liminal state of ritual initiation as the time when the initiate exists virtually between two worlds—that of the uninitiated and the initiated. In *Ritual Process*, Turner writes:

> Liminal entities, such as neophytes' initiation or puberty rites, may be represented as possessing nothing. They may be disguised as monsters, wear only a strip of clothing, or even go naked, to demonstrate that as liminal beings they have no status, property, insignia, secular clothing indicating rank or role, position in a kinship system—in short, nothing that may distinguish them from their fellow neophytes or initiates. Their behavior is normally passive or humble; they must obey their instructors implicitly, and accept arbitrary punishment without complaint. (95)

In many ways, the graduate school experience mirrors that of the uninitiated—we move through a series of academic, mental, physical, and emotional tests in order to achieve acceptance into the community of our wise elders. Yet in the end, our endurance or dedication to the process in and of itself does not determine our initiation, but rather our performance as decided by the wise and experienced academic "priesthood" who have undergone similar rituals of graduate school matriculation. While contemplating how to navigate the course before me, I often regarded my vulnerability as a new mother in graduate school. Although many of my mentors were parenting young children, would my decision to become a parent before my career had even started, be held against me?

Furthermore, I was trying desperately to do *everything* the "right" way like many new mothers I knew. Days moved slowly; between nursing and napping, I squeezed in time for reading and writing my proposal. I longed to control some aspect of my life, for it seemed I was in a perpetual holding place, trying hard to move upstream toward completion of my degree, only to be pulled back downstream by the realities of liminality. Often times, I found it challenging to be completely in the moment with my newfound happiness as a mother, fearing I had not adequately divided my time between school and motherhood. It was not until I had received permission to proceed with my proposal to conduct fieldwork in Dimona, Israel that I felt a degree of peace.

My initial project looked at the African Hebrew Israelite community or Kingdom of Yahweh (KOY), a messianic-nationalist religious community rooted in Black Nationalism and the belief that they are the original descendants of Abraham, and therefore the true Chosen People of Israel. Under the leadership of the charismatic figure Ben Ami, an African-American man from the south side of Chicago who had a vision of liberation and salvation for the Black community, the Kingdom of Yahweh had grown from a band of just over seventy expatriates living first in Liberia in the late 1960s and then Israel by 1970, to a transnational religious movement with followers throughout North America, Africa, the Caribbean, and parts of Europe by 2000. My goal had been to examine the role of women in KOY, a community that practices polygamy, by conducting participant observation in their communities in Dimona, Israel, Atlanta, Chicago, Washington, DC, and Elmina, Ghana. Since I had long been acquainted with the KOY as a frequent customer of their health food store and local restaurant, I was comfortable with the idea of taking my baby into the field with me. Further, it is what ethnographers do—wholly immerse ourselves in the lives of our informants—and if that means strapping our babies on our backs to conduct fieldwork, then so be it. My prospective informants at KOY knew me and had witnessed my development from a young, single graduate student into a new wife and mother. The elder women had given me advice and encouragement throughout my pregnancy, and my contemporary sisters who were mothers had counseled me about what herbs to take to ease my labor and what to eat once I started nursing. In that sense, my pregnancy and the birth of my son gave me greater access to the women I had sought to study in ways I had not anticipated.

SPIRIT TESTED

However in the spring of 2001, the intifada began in Israel and suddenly traveling with a baby through a war zone to conduct research in Dimona did not seem wise at all—scary, in fact. Like many new mothers, fears of something happening to my child on any given day—ranging from SIDS to car accidents to a quirk of fate no one could anticipate or control—plagued me. Seeing the images of carnage in Israel and Palestine on the news fueled my fears about what *could* happen to my child if I took him with me to Israel. I entertained the idea of going ahead with the project and traveling to Dimona alone, but the fear of my death and the thought of my baby growing up without a mother haunted me. I was in a constant, terrible state of fear. Suddenly, going off to conduct fieldwork felt less like an adventure and more like irresponsibility. Most days, I felt like traveling abroad, or anywhere, really for that matter, was not an option.

By the end of June, I had decided to take the rest of the summer to concentrate on my baby and explore my options. In the meantime, the idea for a possible new project had begun to form. I had met an Afro-Brazilian woman who was a *mãe do santos*, or priestess, in the Candomblé religion of Brazil, Doña Rosa the previous year. She has initiated hundreds of believers in Brazil and the United States into this Afro-Brazilian form of the Yoruba religion that has devotees in Brazil and throughout the African diaspora. A trained leader—priest or priestess—initiates devotees into a lifelong community who appease and pay homage to a hierarchical pantheon of *orixas*—spiritual deities—who can and do intercede in the lives of humans. And though I had no particulars for this project yet, I knew my work could provide a valuable contribution to the growing discourse on Pan-African religious identity. For the very first time, I felt truly could negotiate this new life of a scholar-mother.

At least until September 11, 2001. It had begun like every other morning, complete with showering and settling in the rocking chair with my baby nestled against my breast to watch *Good Morning America*. As my husband left for work, I yelled to him to wait. Something had happened in New York City ... something I knew demanded our attention. It had taken a while for us to get a full understanding of what was transpiring, but as we did, I understood thousands of lives had been lost and millions more—including ours—had been changed irrevocably. I thought of my in-laws and my friends in New York City. Had they been hurt? How had this happened? Were we at risk in Chicago? Was my child in danger? Would he have the chance to grow into manhood or was this the beginning of the end for all of us?

In the days and months after September 11th, I became increasingly apprehensive despite having been set to return to work and to my fulltime graduate studies, choosing to stay home with my baby instead of taking advantage of offers to babysit by friends and relatives. I also feared for my husband's safety when he left for work—what if an attack happened while he was there? I had lost my father early in my life; what if the same happened to my son? I had rarely left our apartment; and on those occasions I did, I primarily went to my mother's house across town. While my son needed nurturing, *I needed mothering*; and I yearned for the protection and safety of my mother's presence—even if that presence alone could not truly save me from an impending a terrorist attack.

The emotional turmoil I experienced did not affect my personal life alone. It also influenced my approach to doing fieldwork. Prior to the intifada and 9/11, I had looked at doing fieldwork as my birthright, the manifest destiny of someone who dared to dream about seeing and experiencing the world as the consummate traveler, a keen observer, and a prolific scholar. Had not my parents instilled in me the belief I could do anything I set my mind to do? Had not my mother, who had only been on an airplane twice in her life, told me I could go anywhere I wanted to go?

Nevertheless, because of the dramatic shift of everyone's reality,

I began devising a project that would allow me to do fieldwork closer to home. Surely, I could observe nuances of Pan-African religious identity right in my backyard, but how would such a project rate against the traditional ethnography set forth by pioneering and contemporary ethnographers who traveled to remote places, under dangerous circumstances, as lone, but courageous researchers? I endlessly attempted to reconcile my dreams of becoming an anthropologist and the desire to be a good mother within the realities of the clear and present danger exemplified by the 9/11 terrorist attacks.

While many of my mentors in the academy had raised children while pursuing their graduate degrees, my essentialist anxieties around motherhood and womanhood trumped the need to reveal my fears to my advisor and professors. By acknowledging my fear of traveling to a foreign place for research and the possibility of another terrorist attack, was I not forsaking one of the core elements of anthropological research—that of full immersion in another culture? Was it possible to do ethnography while feeling so unsettled about life itself?

I had also felt unable to speak freely about my reservations to my peers and mentors because I did not want to contribute to the stereotypical image of African-American women as inadequate mothers (Mullings 95) that dominated much of the discourse on American family functioning. I longed for the "willingness to be open about personal stuff" (hooks 2) amongst contemporary mothers who were also trying to navigate motherhood, marriage, and work during those tumultuous times. African-American feminist bell hooks writes on the need to speak and write about our experiences as marginalized women as a radical act—a step toward liberation in that it frees us from our fears and allows us to define ourselves in our own terms (hooks 8-9). I needed a space to discuss my fears about how motherhood complicates career, but I really had no one to turn to, and the shame and guilt about my feelings compelled me to remain silent.

Yet, as I attempted to find my way as a woman and mother and carve out my place as an ethnographer, I began to examine the relationship between my experiences as a mother, and a "mothered" woman, and my ability to teach and conduct fieldwork. I drew strength from the nurturing and encouragement I had received from my mother, mentors, and friends, whose confidence in my work as a scholar and a mother were at times, much greater than my own. Slowly, I began to see my personal foray into motherhood as much like the fieldwork I had always envisioned for myself. Motherhood, then, was the unchartered landscape I would eventually navigate as a participant observer; and as a new mother, I could only rely so much on the stories provided by other mothers, including my own. Ultimately, I would have to trust my own instincts in order to be successful at motherhood, and so too with fieldwork. No amount of research could truly prepare a first-time ethnographer for the various blunders and bouts of naïve realism most of us were bound endure, so too with motherhood.

By and by, I worked through my worries of a subsequent terrorist attack and my vulnerability traveling abroad to develop a fieldwork project that excited both my professors and me. My dissertation entitled "Tell My Feet I've Made It Home: African-American Imaginings of Home and the Journey to Find the Orixas" investigates the experiences of a group of African Americans who travel to Brazil for initiation into the Candomblé religion. Each of my informants was an initiate of Doña Rosa; and ironically, I saw parallels between my experiences as a new mother with those of my informants who sought direction and blessings from Doña Rosa, their newly adopted spiritual mother. We were all seeking answers for questions that held us in limbo—whether to change careers, leave a relationship, buy a particular house, and, in my case, could and should I take my child in the field as conducted my fieldwork.

In Candomblé, the uninitiated are ushered into the world of the *orixas* by a skilled priest or priestess who assumes the role of their spiritual parent. Thus, the themes of "mothering" and "birth" were central to my understanding of the nuances I experienced as a participant observer. While much of my work rests upon my informants' experiences and their interpretation of the rituals they underwent, it also addressed Doña Rosa's role as priestess and spiritual glue to her transnational *terreiro* or temple. During my initial meetings with her, her ability to "mother" every person she met struck me. As a spiritual priestess, Doña Rosa is not only a conduit for the *orixas*, but also a spiritual godmother to each person she initiates. Each initiate then becomes her godchild in the religion, a relationship she takes very seriously. I experienced this relationship first hand as a participant observer during several rituals, but more importantly, as one of Doña Rosa's initiates myself.

Indeed, it was not just the natural progression of time that calmed my nerves about traveling abroad to conduct fieldwork. It was also the prospect of traveling to a place where there was someone with whom I had developed a relationship that, in my mind, had made the project feasible. I had spent many afternoons with Doña Rosa when she visited the United States in 2001 and had established a rapport with her and many of her initiates in Chicago. Additionally, she had fallen in love with my son and had determined she would have a place in his life.

I would eventually conduct dual-site (reflexive) ethnography in Chicago and in Salvador do Bahia, Brazil over the course of 2002–2004. During my first trip to Brazil, I traveled, albeit cautiously, with my one-year-old son. When I returned in 2003, I was five months pregnant with my second child. By that time, I had fully eased into my research and my role as a mother. Yet it was during this second trip my life would change once more.

As an anthropologist and Candomblé initiate, I witnessed and experienced divination and various rituals; thus, I was prepared to have Doña Rosa "read" me prior to my journey back to the United States. I was not, however, prepared for what she had to tell me. According to her divination, my mother was very ill, and asked me a series of questions about my mother's health, to which I had insisted that my mother's health was fine. In fact, she was so healthy she had been helping my husband care for our son while I was away. Nevertheless, Doña Rosa performed several rituals on my behalf, determined I needed fortification in order to face what lay ahead of me.

SPIRIT RESTORED

Not long after my return from the "field," an oncologist diagnosed my mother with Stage Four Non-Small Lung Cancer. In the days after her diagnosis, I replayed our lives together, acknowledging all of my success was the result of the nurturing and encouragement she had bestowed upon me throughout the different stages of my life. She had taught me to read when I was just a toddler; allowed me to grieve my father's death in my own way and pace; worked in factories and then as a certified nurse's assistant to put me through private school and college; and shown me how to nurture my own child. My mother was strong, wise, loving, and compassionate; I dreaded my life without her.

After my mother's diagnosis, I expanded my focus from caring for my toddler and nurturing my unborn child to include saving my mother's life. My mother and I had reversed roles so that *I* had begun mothering *her*. For me, life had suspended and could only resume when and if my mother improved. I had stopped eating and I could not sleep. My friends, family, and doctor had all been concerned about my unborn child, but I could not hear them. The baby in my womb was not here, but my mother, now suddenly childlike, was alive, breathing, and needed me.

During this very stressful period in my life, I held a position as an adjunct faculty member in Women's Studies at Northeastern Illinois University. I taught the introductory summer course—"Women's Perspectives and Values"—to mainly freshmen and sophomores. My reading list included Dorothy Allison's *Bastard Out of Carolina* and Alice Walker's *The Color Purple*, two narratives that explore the complexities of motherhood and female identity. While each novel wrestles with the realities of abuse, oppression, and female desire, I had chosen these texts for their examples of the power and transformative nature of love. Yet, reading these novels during my mother's illness had also transformed me to my core. I especially came to appreciate that mothering is not predicated on a biological link. I drew strength from the characters' redemptive spirits and enduring belief in love in the face of abuse and abandonment. I also learned from the examples of motherhood personified by the central and secondary characters. In both cases, other relatives, fictive kin, and longtime friends often did the "mothering," not the birth mothers, thus signifying the importance and power of motherhood as not simply a biological link. That summer, my students and I poured over the pages of each text, drawing parallels between the fiction we were reading and our real-life experiences. By summer's end, most of my students had a greater understanding of motherhood as an important trope within feminist discourse; but as for me, I had embraced my desire to nurture my mother and hoped that she might live.

I determined to cherish each moment I would have with my mother, my son, and unborn child, showering with each of them as much love and healing touch as I could. Eventually, I learned how important it was for me to mother myself, understanding that my contributions to the world relied upon my ability to be whole. During that period, I recall reading a passage by Robbie Pfeufer Kahn who writes "[A]s a mother, I experienced daily a body in which touch was a faculty of perception that evoked the oceanic feeling, connecting me to forces larger than the self and larger even than the social order in which I lived" (372). My experiences as a nursing mother in the days and subsequent years after 9/11, and role as "nurse" to my mother during her illness, yielded similar insights. Each experience deepened my appreciation for motherhood and my connection to other people. Additionally, each experience reinforced the importance of mothering on women's development as compassionate, loving, and self-actualizing humans—an idea that informs my teaching and my approach to feminist anthropology. As a scholar-teacher, I strive to ensure my students are engaged and inspired in a challenging, yet nurturing environment that encourages thoughtful dialogue. At the same time, I approach my work in the field from the perspective that my informants deserve the right and space to tell their stories in their own words and in their own way. Often, relationships with my students and informants develop organically, making the exchange between us that more meaningful.

The terrorist attacks of September 11, 2001 changed me in profound ways. While I temporarily shirked the thought of fieldwork out of fear for mine and my baby's safety, I also became more acutely aware of my responsibility to protect my child. He needed me and I had to make decisions that would ensure the longevity and quality of his life. I saw the lessons of 9/11 in this manner: hatred and xenophobia were evils that paralyzed and terrorized humanity. I was determined to do my part to love freely, continue to be open to new people and their points of view, and to teach my son to do so as well.

Losing my mother had an entirely different impact of my life. My mother's strength and determination to fight her illness taught me I had an internal fortitude of which I had not even begun to scratch the surface. Her commitment to her family and loved ones and her audacity to laugh, to cry, and to speak her mind—ignited courage I had forgotten I had. When I think about my mother, I do not think about the disease that ravished her body, instead, I remember her spirit and her honesty, and I am reminded I can and must draw from that deep well as often as it is needed. I find myself doing this much more as of late as I navigate the emotions of a burgeoning tween and a feisty eight year old, and in my work in the south, when I find myself always having to point out race and inequity with my colleagues.

These two profoundly different experiences have transformed my thinking about Black feminist discourse from purely philosophical to a real, breathing approach to my work and my life. My experience as an African-American mother and graduate student during those troubling times truly informs my research and approach to teaching. Radical scholar-activist bell hooks reaffirms "it is important that black women in higher education write and talk about our experiences, about survival strategies" (hooks 61). I agree with this premise; and while I did not have the space to freely express myself at that time, I was able to take solace in the fact countless other African-American women—many of them mothers like myself—had labored under similar circumstances and survived. In the end, their wisdom and my own mother's love gave me back my adventurer's spirit.

WORKS CITED

Collins, Patricia Hill. "Learning from the Outsider Within: The Sociological Significance of Black Feminist Thought." *Social Problems* 33.6 (1986): S14–S32. Print.

hooks, bell. *Talking Back*. Boston: South End Press, 1989. Print.

Kahn, Robbie Pfeufer. *Bearing Meaning: The Language of Birth*.

Urbana: University of Illinois Press, 1998. Print.

Mullings, Leith. *On Our Own Terms*. New York: Routledge, 1997. Print.

Turner, Victor. *Ritual Process*. Chicago: Aldine Publishing, 1969. Print.

8.
Walking Tightropes Without Nets

The Adjunct as Single Mother

STACIA L. BROWN

THINGS I WAS NOT TOLD

There is no glamour. Adjuncts are grunts. Pay according to "credit hours" when rationed over twelve to fourteen weeks, is meager at best and well below the poverty line at worst. In order to earn a livable wage, one must work no fewer than 18 credit hours, which means teaching six three-credit classes per term. Typically, a college only lets an adjunct teach three courses per term—which means having to scramble for work within multiple college systems and quickly adapting to the circuitous rules, dates, deadlines, and expectations of each. An MFA, once considered "terminal," is now a mere placeholder degree on the road to the newly minted Ph.D. in Creative Writing.

Gifted, disciplined, industrious creative writers may not need any degree at all to teach on the college level—let alone a master's degree—and successful, published, critically acclaimed novelists need not even attend college to score a visiting professorship. Without significant publications, you will most certainly find yourself seeking a non-academic job within three years' time.

You will work as hard as your full-time colleagues, but the respect conferred upon them via compensation for each of their outside-the-classroom tasks will elude you. Office hours, grading, course preparation, career counseling and impromptu confidante services are all unpaid duties of an adjunct faculty position.

It may have been—and may still be—better for you to teach middle or high school English than College Composition or Basic

Writing. And, because that middle or high school position is full-time with extensive medical, investment, and retirement benefits, people would respect you more for it. You would no longer have to field the question, "Have you ever considered being a real teacher?"

After a year or two of subsisting on saltines, canned soups, and dollar menu meals, while praying seven dollars of gas will get you to and from campus three more times before a week's end, you will ask yourself, "What is so great about pursuing a life of the mind? Why did I ever want this?" And then, as your stomach continues to growl, the follow-up question will come: "Why do I want this still?"

Adjuncts can become invisible at whim—and this is not always a disadvantage, as it means we can avoid bureaucratic red tape and lengthy faculty meetings. Often, however, invisibility is disadvantageous—particularly when we are in need of advocacy, either personal (as it relates to starting or growing a family) or professional (as it relates to being paid in accordance with our labor or receiving the medical benefits critical to ensuring that the stress of this precarious vocation does not doom us to an early grave).

If an adjunct becomes a mother, without having scrimped and saved to afford the countless expenses attendant to pregnancy and parenthood, she and her child will very likely experience prolonged situational poverty.

She will spend more time worrying about how to afford food for herself and her two-year-old daughter each summer than she will spend doing the writing, publishing, and panel-presenting that would better qualify her for a permanent teaching position.

I should have done my research.

MONEY MATTERS

For the college-level English instructor, Baltimore, Maryland is a challenging academic market. In terms of earning, my current institution pays $200 less per credit hour than the colleges where I began my teaching career six years ago in Grand Rapids, Michigan. At $710 per credit, I earn $2,100 over four months. In Michigan, I grossed $2,700 per three-credit course, still significantly less per annum than a full-time associate professor, who may earn between

$45,000 and $65,000—and more if he is white, male, and in the sciences.

Even so, before motherhood, a year's teaching salary could be stretched into anything resembling a livable wage, if I could manage to teach seven or more courses over fall, spring, and summer terms. Budgeting was paramount but I never went hungry. I also never stopped to consider that the output of initiative was not at all equal to my income.

Each semester, that initiative includes but is not limited to creative lesson-planning; curriculum-building extensive enough for a pricey textbook to be "suggested" on a syllabus rather than "required" for classroom success; one-on-one, line-by-line reading and editing of student drafts; half-hours spent listening to students vent about child support arrears, their overtaxing night jobs, the military grant that has yet to pay out much-needed tuition and book money, layoffs, parental disagreements, and the disabled children (or parents) for whom they are financially and emotionally responsible.

In those first years, before I was experienced, none of this mattered. I was too grateful to be breathing the rarefied air of the academe, to have crossed over from impressionable student to hallowed insight-giver.

I would quickly learn, insight-givers are not exempt from bills and empty bellies.

Fortunately, the cost of living in Grand Rapids, where I spent the first four years of my teaching career, is 13.4 percent less than the U.S. city average ("Grand Rapids, Michigan"). Earning more, spending less, and being consistently offered teaching contracts at the three-course-per-term adjunct maximum at two different colleges made the decision to live and work in the Midwest an easy one, despite the ways in which my personal and social life suffered from being away from my East Coast home base. Even as budget cuts reduced the course load for some adjuncts and eliminated employment entirely for others, I still may not have moved back to my hometown of Baltimore, had it not been for motherhood. I remained in Michigan for the duration of my pregnancy and for the first year of my daughter's life.

If money was depleting at an alarming rate during the fall semester, it was practically non-existent at the start of the winter/spring term. I was only offered two classes, on one campus. I had been downsized from the four-year university; enrollment was down. They were thinning their herd of adjuncts. It was not surprising; I had lived in distant fear of it since I started teaching. It figured that when it did finally occur, it would coincide with my moment of greatest need.

I could only hang on for about a month into the new term, before applying for food stamps. I was allotted $150 a month and struggled to stretch it to cover the costs of groceries and formula. My milk dried up when my daughter was five months old, an occurrence I attribute, in part, to financial stress.

My obstacles were not isolated. Results of a 2011 U.S. Census Bureau of Labor Statistics Current Population Survey indicate a marked increase in the number of people with advanced degrees who receive food stamps or other forms of federal aid. This is true even for academics without children. In 2007, the number of master's degree-holders receiving aid was 101,682. In 2010, the number spiked to 293,092. The disparity is much larger for doctoral graduates. In 2007, just 9,776 received aid. In 2010, an alarming 33,655 were social services recipients (Patton). Though the growing numbers do establish a legitimate crisis in academic job scarcity, across disciplines, they do little to assuage the shame and helplessness of finding oneself significantly underemployed and overwhelmed with student loan debt.

By the summer that my daughter turned one year old, I was down to just one course offer for the upcoming fall semester. My best belt-tightening efforts could not have kept us afloat with so little work—not even with the freelance writing and editing assignments I had managed to complete with a newborn lobbying for equal attention. It made more financial sense to give up my apartment, sell my old car, and move back to my home base in Baltimore where I could live rent-free with my grandmother and mother for as long as I needed to, in order to rebuild the home I had cobbled together in Michigan. That plan was more auspicious on paper than it has been in practice. Because Baltimore is a larger market, adjunct positions at multiple colleges are more difficult to procure—and unlike in Grand Rapids, teaching more does not necessarily mean earning more.

According to *The Chronicle of Higher Education*'s web initiative, The Adjunct Project, an adjunct English instructor at The College of Southern Maryland may earn as little as $1,400 per course, just over half of what an adjunct earns for teaching a comparable course in Grand Rapids. Coppin State University offers its English adjuncts $1,700 per course, whereas Frostburg State University and Howard Community College both offer $2,000 ("The Adjunct Project"). It became apparent soon after my arrival in Baltimore that the salary gap was not the only chasm that would lie between me and reestablished financial solvency. The cost of living in Baltimore is also prohibitive. Whereas the Grand Rapids cost of living index is well below the national average, Maryland's cost of living is roughly 25 percent higher than the national average (Basu).

Additionally, as an adjunct, affordable center-based daycare for my two-year-old is currently out of the question. I am fortunate to have the support of my mother and grandmother who are my daughter's primary care providers at next to no cost, during the four to five hours a day I spend en route to and on campus. I had the same assistance in Grand Rapids, as my mother moved in with me during my first post-pregnancy year. However, had I needed to enlist a professional daycare center in Michigan, the average annual cost would have been $10,114. In Baltimore, it is $12,878 and in the nearby District of Columbia, where further adjunct teaching options are available, the average annual cost of daycare for children under four years old is an oppressive $20,178 ("Parents and the..."). Even if I were able to teach nine classes over three terms on three different campuses, and even if I could manage to take on additional writing and editing work, while also remaining present, attentive, affectionate, and instructive for my toddler, affording an apartment, a car note, child care, children's clothing and educational toys, here in Baltimore would be difficult.

As it stands, this semester I am teaching three courses on two different campuses within the same college system. Because two of the three classes suffered from low enrollment, an increasing issue on community college campuses as Pell grant guidelines shift, I was offered half-pay for both. Since the alternative was cancellation of the courses altogether, I agreed to less income.

This term, I earn $555 biweekly for teaching three college courses. This is barely enough to cover my car note and insurance, gas, and groceries.

WHO WILL CRY FOR THE UNWED ADJUNCT MOTHER?

I may not have known what I was getting into as an MFA graduate being offered her first college teaching position two weeks before of the very next school year, but I certainly knew the tightly budgeted lifestyle I managed before motherhood would be unsustainable with an infant in tow. On her second night home, Story screamed practically non-stop for five straight hours. She was inconsolable and too new to the world to extend any real, discernible cues as to what might be wrong. I cried right along with her, big sliding silent tears.

I imagined a long stretch of nights like this—perhaps every night between then and her first day of school. I was deliriously tired and felt an acute helplessness, not just to soothe Story's discomfort, but to handle any of this without a partner.

Before pregnancy, I hadn't anticipated life as a single mother. I had foolishly figured that the eight years I had already spent with my partner would insulate me from abandonment, should we ever find ourselves unexpectedly expecting. Adapting to his emotional absence had been difficult, but manageable. His physical absence, to which I had grown accustomed to over years spent in a long-distance relationship, was positively unbearable in those first weeks at home with our daughter.

Why had I insisted so stubbornly on clinging to my "career?" Was the idea of working my way up to a full-time teaching job, based only on time served and a few anthology publications, so powerful a lure that I would subject my daughter and myself to a life of indefinite poverty? It surprised me that I even wanted to continue gambling on the possibility of a full-time teaching job. I did not like teaching much. I was only then, after six semesters, beginning to feel competent enough at it to find it rewarding.

Writing was still my preferred field—paid writing, that elusive ideal that would have allowed me to work from home and be around enough for my daughter to recognize me more readily than a day care provider. In the absence of that coveted work-from-home income, I was gearing up to leave my delicate newborn with a woman I barely knew for whole days. I could hardly tolerate the thought, which was what had kept me from contracting with a day care provider in the first place. I was hoping against hope for a better plan.

Those first days and months with my newborn were among the darkest. I cursed my stupidity, gingerly moving about the confines of my apartment, still aching and bleeding from a delivery that had left me severely torn and spent, insisting to everyone that I was fine. Every time I cried—and tears were frequent—I quickly issued the statement, "I am not depressed." Even if that much were true, I still felt a great deal of anxiety and guilt. I had not exercised any of the foresight to which I had access, neither in my personal life nor in my professional life.

Why had I been so enticed by the noncommittal process of teaching this way, with the choice at the end of each term to cash in my chips and walk off to start another career? I should have chosen a profession that offered more stability, in the event that I would need time off or a 401k. I should have better anticipated the possibility of an unplanned child. Yet despite all of its problematic components, I cannot entirely abandon teaching, even if it is becoming increasingly impractical, financially. This resolve is not always easy for my peers and loved ones to understand. From an outward vantage—and sometimes from my inward one—it seems like sheer stubbornness or perhaps a romanticizing of struggle is keeping me firmly planted behind college lecterns. This is how many adjuncts are viewed, as willful participants in their own hardship. If we continue to choose to teach in markets that do not pay us enough to live, perhaps we deserve to be grunts. To be sure, adjuncting is not a vocation that lends itself to sympathetic community response.

When *The Chronicle of Higher Education* published "The Ph.D. Now Comes With Food Stamps," a profile on scholars with Ph.Ds. in the humanities whose inability to find full-time work had led them to apply for government assistance, public response was mixed. Early on, the writer makes clear that financial hardship is commonplace for adjuncts:

> "It's difficult to talk about being on aid," says Matthew Williams, cofounder and vice president of the New Faculty Majority, an advocacy group for nontenure-track faculty. "We regularly hear about adjuncts on food stamps," says Mr. Williams, who received food stamps and Medicaid himself when he taught at the University of Akron from 2007 to 2009, earning less than $21,000 a year. "This is not hyperbole and it isn't theoretical."
>
> Some adjuncts make less money than custodians and campus support staff who may not have college degrees. (Patton)

Comments on the article itself ranged from appalled that academicians could come to such a pass to scornful that they had pursued concentrations too broad or too obscure to lend themselves to job competitiveness. To wit, one commenter identified as Yuri Nayazov opined, "Does it make me a bad human being if I feel zero pity for highly educated people who do not understand the basics of supply and demand in their chosen job market?" (Patton).

After six years of barely treading the choppy waters of the university hiring market, I could relate to those who read articles like *The Chronicle of Higher Education's* or reports on adjuncts' battle to unionize—or to simply to survive in the absence of one—with derision. It is difficult to identify with anyone who would continue to subject themselves to unregulated, underpaid work year after year, in many cases with no clear prospects for earning a promotion. But what must be understood about adjuncts is that we all have our reasons for staying the course. Black women—and black mothers in particular—have more reasons than most.

BEYOND BABY MAMA ADJUNCT

Losing my contracts with the four-year colleges where I taught predominantly white Midwestern classes had the interesting benefit of causing me to come into my own as an educator and, unexpectedly, as an activist. That this growing comfort with myself and professional choices coincided with my pregnancy and single motherhood was not happenstance.

Community colleges are just that: communal. Though no class's chemistry is alike, the diversity of culture, class, and background is unparalleled at two-year institutions. Teaching at them can be liberating and instructive in ways that large, impersonal universities and small, private, aggressively homogenous colleges is not. Such has been true for me, particularly since I became a single parent. Nearly each class I have taught over the past three years has included at least one student who is also an unmarried mother.

I acquire this knowledge through many means: a request for an essay extension with a lengthy explanation related to her child; a narrative essay about a single experience that has shaped her outlook on love, hope, or responsibility; an extra, elementary school-aged student auditing my course on a day when his babysitter did not show up or his school was unexpectedly closed.

I find myself investing in these student-mothers' experiences, drawn to the relative ease or the steely determination with which they juggle all their lives' movable parts. Some are far younger than I with much older children than mine. Others are far older, with children around my age. Each upon hearing that I am a mother and upon realizing that I am also single take their own vested interest in updates about my daughter. Most offer gentle advice if I offer up some errant worry about her cognition or social development. "Oh, Ms. Brown," one might warmly reassure, "She will talk when she is good and ready."

I am uncharacteristically open with fellow single parents. I am more like some of them, with their economic obstacles, precarious co-parenting dynamics, and child care expense challenges, than they will ever realize. Their sharing of confidences and frustrations provides me with a kind of education as essential as I hope my lectures provide for them.

It does not matter to the single mother or father of color in my Basic Writing or College Composition course whether my degrees are worth the money I borrowed for them. They do not care if I need public assistance or mock me for wanting to show up and expose them to ideas and history, current events and literature, even though I am not adequately compensated for it. They do not believe I am a bad mother for not taking the salary highway instead of the road paved with four-month teaching contracts. They are just grateful for resources, for a kind word, rolling deadlines, an empathetic ear.

Perhaps this is because they understand quite well what it means to be ridiculed, scorned, prejudged, or belittled because of their choices. Perhaps it is because they perceive community college the way I do, as a haven and a respite, a confessional and a space for meditation. It also is where I generate some of my best ideas.

Beyond Baby Mamas is an online initiative that seeks to amplify the voices of single parents of color in mainstream parenting discourse. I founded it in September of 2012 in order to foster an environment similar to the ones I have found among my parent-students for people who do not have such ready access to other single minority mothers and fathers. Using social media as our primary community-building resource, *Beyond Baby Mamas* offers relevant news and fact-aggregation; video panels and interviews; and a publication space for any single mother or father of color, as well as adults who were raised in minority single-parent households, to write about their experiences.

It is my hope to build a structure that is as adept at strengthening and affirming its members as community colleges aim to be with their students. What I have learned there has served me well in this new, uncharted territory: Be receptive. Assume nothing. Exercise patience until it grows agile, impermeable. Let the narrative come to you. Preserve as much of a person's voice and integrity as possible, but enhance it so that it is strong enough to reach its highest potential. And, perhaps most importantly, there is a lesson I never would have learned without becoming both an adjunct and a single mother: never judge another person's story.

WORKS CITED

Basu, Anirban. "Is the Cost of Living Higher in Washington-Baltimore Area?" *1stMariner Bank*. 18 July 2011. Web. 27 Feb. 2013.

"Grand Rapid, Michigan." *City-Data.com*. Advameg, Inc. 2012. Web. 27 Feb. 2013.

"Parents and the High Cost of Child Care 2012 Report." *Child*

Care Aware of America. Child Care Aware of America. n.d. Web. 27 Feb. 2013.

Patton, Stacy. "The Ph.D. Now Comes With Food Stamps." *The Chronicle of Higher Education* 6 May 2012. Web. 27 Feb 2013.

9.
Mothering Black

A Cross-Cultural Perspective on Mothering in the Nigerian Academy

ROSE A. SACKEYFIO

THE BUSTLING COLLEGE TOWN of Zaria boasts the most diverse community of academics of any of the Universities in Nigeria. Ahmadu Bello University (ABU) is located in Kaduna state and is one of the premier universities in Africa's most populous nation. It is the largest University in Nigeria and the second largest in Sub-Saharan Africa. Established in 1962 it has sustained a reputable prestige and as part of the colonial legacy, the organizational structure and administration is patterned after the British model. ("Our History"). The university has eleven faculties that include nearly 90 departments, five Research Centers, Institutes and Colleges with a student enrollment of over 35,000. The rich and diverse cultural environment shaped the development of ABU as well as the organizational culture that may be described as distinctly African, a feature that holds true for all institutions in the African setting.

The European model adopted by Ahmadu Bello University developed and perpetuated institutional patterns that are inherently favorable to males as a reflection of patriarchy, Islam, and European Victorian values inherited from the British influence that restricted the roles of women, their access to education at all levels and erected barriers to women's professional development. Dzodzi Tsikata has examined gender inequality in the University of Ghana and much of the findings reveal similarities to Ahmadu Bello University. She very aptly observes that:

> Gender inequality was a foundational characteristic of the university, manifesting in various ways and affecting

different elements of the cultures of the university. From gender inequalities in student and faculty numbers, to the male-centered approaches in the residential arrangements and the governance structures, the university has been inequitably gendered space in which women have had to work hard to establish themselves. (7)

The social and cultural environment of predominately Muslim Northern Nigeria unfolds a difficult landscape for women in the professional arena, because the encroachment of "Islam disrupted traditional societies politically and legally, creating new oppressed and subjugated status and roles for women" (Ogundipe-Leslie 30). The Islamic academic environment would create yet another layer of marginality for women who are cultural outsiders and single parents. The vibrant economy of the 1970s oil boom provided lucrative employment opportunities, and material comfort that attracted an influx of expatriates and although the diversity in gender and ethnicity forged significant changes for women, deeply entrenched social patterns prevailed. In the Nigerian cultural milieu, women's role and status is defined by marriage and motherhood, regardless of a woman's educational credentials; to remain unmarried or childless is a social taboo. Within this context of expectations, a professional woman who is single or divorced will experience social stigma, diminished status, and vulnerability to sexual harassment.

Social constraints that inhibit women's advancement and professional development test their capacity to balance academic life with motherhood. Male dominance creates the distorted lens through which women's merit is assessed so that employment, promotion, professional recognition and respect become a negotiable variable in a woman's survival as a single parent professional. This essay will analyze the complex nature of Black women mothering in the Nigerian academy.

While there are real and tangible barriers to mothering and to survival for a single parent, African culture is fertile ground for wholesome and effective parenting. The cohesive nature of Nigerian society, communal values, traditions and codes of behavior can support child rearing in positive ways. My experience in Nigeria spans ten years and what follows in the first part of the paper examines how my status as a cultural outsider formed multiple layers of subjectivity. The second section is an account of my early years in Nigeria that defined me as the daughter of adversity through my struggle to survive and care for my children. The positive and rewarding elements of African culture nurtured my family and illustrate the African proverb, "it takes a village to raise a child." The final section of the paper will discuss the challenges I faced to complete a Ph.D. while raising children alone. Despite the difficult journey into the Nigerian academy, the cultural environment provided a foundation for personal growth, expanded knowledge, and the inculcation of the African personality has enriched my life immeasurably.

CULTURAL OUTSIDER STATUS

Traditional African culture sparked my interest in Africa since I came of age in the 1960s and '70s in America. A major reason I made a commitment to living in Africa was to expose my daughters to the rich cultural heritage of African people and to inculcate them into the African personality. In my effort to re-connect to Africa, I sought to give my children the best of both worlds, and I saw migrating to Nigeria as a way to start a new life in a wholesome environment that would provide a strong foundation for my daughters.

However, when I began teaching in Nigeria in the mid-1980s, I experienced multiple marginalities, and the first and perhaps most far-reaching in its impact on my life was my status as a non-Nigerian single parent. After struggling in Harlem with my two daughters I arrived in Northern Nigeria at the end of the 1970s oil boom that fuelled a thriving economy and nurtured a vibrant community of expatriates from all over Africa and her Diaspora.

When I began teaching, less than five percent of the faculty was female where consistent patterns of female under-representation in the distribution of education have been documented (Assie-Lumumba 48). Teresa Barnes further supports this unfortunate trend when she observes, "gaining an academic position in an African university is challenging for women, and that maintaining it is even more difficult" (4). There is a dearth of research on women in higher education in northern Nigeria. The small community of African-American expatriate faculty was well established and respected though separate from the Nigerian elite. The difference between myself and other African-American and non-Nigerian professionals was my questionable and thoroughly unacceptable condition of single parenthood.

In the African cultural context, single-parenthood is a social taboo and quite literally an abomination. The indigenous cosmological belief system throughout the continent of Africa denotes the principle of duality, or complimentarity of the sexes that imposes balance and harmony of gender, social order and stability (Amadiume 144-151). The institution of marriage and family serves to extend and preserve lineage and kinship ties to promote social cohesion. Unlike the Western world, marriage in Africa is a social contract or bond of kinship between two families or lineage groups and is seldom an affair between two individuals who meet, fall in love and get married without family involvement. In traditional African societies, the incidence of divorce was rare because people married for a lifetime commitment. Divorce was also rare because marriage fostered a sense of security and protection through a binding contract that existed between two families where elders assisted in solving disputes and maintaining healthy relationships between married couples. When there is a divorce, in patrilineal societies, marriage practices and child-rearing customs prevent women from gaining custody of their children. Children beyond the early childhood stage may likely be reared as part of blended families when the father remarries, or may be raised by their father's mother or other female relatives. Social and economic structures do not support independent lifestyles unless a woman is middle or upper class, or educated with a professional career. While in Nigeria with my daughters, there were few single women with children and these were widows.

Although I entered the Nigerian academy with a master's degree, my status as a cultural outsider and single parent did more than raise eyebrows and inevitably, my domestic status colored all social interaction, my professional life, and ultimately my career. The Nigerian perception was that my domestic situation had no legitimacy. According to Molara Ogundipe-Leslie, "A childless woman is considered a monstrosity, *as is an unmarried woman, spinster, or divorcée*. She is often seen by males in the society as an unclaimed and degenerating commodity to be freely exploited in all ways-emotionally, sexually and financially, among other ways" (77).

The stigma of divorce functions as a discrete method of social control to preserve the institution of marriage within indigenous African societies. Women are assumed to be at fault when there is a marital split. Living with children of a former spouse is also a barrier to remarriage, and what is known informally as the 'outcast treatment' or social ostracism is very common. Most African societies are patrilineal and the children *belong to* the husband and his family.

Modernity and urbanization have, to a great extent, influenced traditional attitudes and behaviors so that generalizations concerning how these social mechanisms still operate in contemporary society are unwise in a changing social landscape of western oriented lifestyles and global influence on cultures in transition. In contemporary Africa, more women delay marriage, travel abroad, develop their talents and establish professional careers. African womanhood is defined primarily by and through marriage so that status, recognition and social acceptance is intricately woven into the social fabric of society and is integral to the socialization of girls and women. As a cultural outsider, my perception of myself was constantly challenged by others, and my domestic situation was incomprehensible to many people, especially in the early years.

My commitment to living in Africa and my sense of self worth and esteem were continually tested through experiences related to my "questionable" status.

Jane Bennett underscores the limited cultural expectations for women because "for many women, a personal future in African societies requires permanent, public, culturally legitimated heterosexual liaison: marriage" (10). In Nigerian society the lives of single women are perceived as promiscuous and morally irresponsible. This leads to the widespread assumption of immorality that often results in sexual harassment. Some of these assumptions were because of stereotypes of African-American women's lifestyles as perceived against the background of the image of America as a sexually permissive society. Access to the American film industry and media has perpetuated negative images of women, moral laxity, single parent homes, and many social pathologies. My life was characterized by a struggle to maintain credibility against this barrage of negative assumptions. I experienced repeated sexual harassment and lost my first job because I refused the advances of the director of the research institute where I was employed as an extension editor. Two years later I almost lost my teaching position for the same reason.

As a single parent I came to understand the pervasive nature of women's socialization for subordinate status and lack of control over their lives. In fact, Muslim immigration officers repeatedly asked how I managed to get permission to travel from my former husband while under Islamic patriarchy; a woman needs her husband's permission to travel out of the country.

African women's status and respectability is traditionally conferred by marriage, regardless of educational credentials. Throughout the African continent, marriage is thought to be a sacred duty that all adults must perform. This idea is underscored by pervasive spiritual traditions that celebrate the cyclic flow of life through the individual and society (Mbiti 104). Kwame Gyekye elaborates this point to illustrate that marriage is thus essential to the development and enlargement of kinship ties, which are a characteristic feature of African society. Within this context, my domestic situation was untenable, a subject of controversy and inexplicable to Nigerian people who questioned my coming to Nigeria without the father of my children.

DAUGHTER OF ADVERSITY

Mothering as a cultural outsider in the Nigerian Academy created untold hardship in the early years and forced me to draw upon my inner strength and coping mechanisms to nurture my daughters and survive on meager funds. The nature of my teaching position and the low salary scale made me ineligible for the very comfortable employment amenities that were specially designed to attract and retain international faculty. For example, under ideal conditions the prospective faculty member would be provided airfare, rent free university housing, a car loan, access to the university primary or secondary school for their children, and roundtrip passage to their native country every two years.

I received none of these because I entered the country with a tourist visa, no job and no husband. I was constantly questioned about my marital status by immigration officers when I applied for a renewal of my visa every three months.

The strength of the Nigerian currency on the international market throughout the 1970s and well into the '80s stabilized the economy and made the cost of living very affordable. My family and I survived on the American equivalent of $15.00 to $25.00 per week during the early years. In my spare time I supplemented my income as a seamstress making children's clothing for families in the academic community.

The most serious difficulty I faced was the inadequate housing for which I was eligible, but denied because I am a woman, a single parent, and a non-Nigerian. In the Nigerian educational system, free, on campus housing is provided at secondary and tertiary levels. Ahmadu Bello is a sprawling campus with several residential areas for faculty based upon title and rank. The areas where homes were located indicated varying levels of quality, space and prestige. The northern male Hausa Muslims dominated University administration and the housing department was no exception. Allocation of housing was a political enterprise so that depending upon one's status in the university hierarchy, or informal networks, a male head of the family who is perhaps a senior or tenured professor of long-standing would end up with the best housing available which meant a two-storey home of three to five bedrooms with a garage, huge yard, and garden.

For four years we had no option for housing other than the servant's quarters. As part of the legacy of the colonial administrative structure, all university homes had small buildings on the premises to house the servants. The houses were simple one room unfurnished living quarters. Cooking and bath facilities were shared which meant that essentially my daughters and I led a spartan existence. During these difficult years, my coping strategies were strengthened, and my strong African parenting skills were forged in the midst of terrible stress. I never lost hope of an improved living condition and overall quality of life through a promotion from Temporary Full-time status to a lecturer that would provide economic stability and the opportunity for professional development.

Both Nigerian and expatriate faculty members were amazed that I managed to cope with the stigma of living in the servant's quarters because it carried the mark of poverty and low socio-economic status that was un-becoming to me as a qualified faculty member with foreign status. People who occupied this category of housing were servants, students or needy relatives of university faculty. One may compare this to stereotypical and negative perceptions of low income housing projects in urban areas of the United States.

After four years in this condition, we were allocated a small, one bedroom bungalow with a kitchen and one bath that was fully furnished. The quality of our home environment changed markedly, and the period of adversity never compromised the best elements of our family life. Family rituals and activities that mark a stable, nurturing environment for children were regular and predictable in our family. Meals, homework, chores, birthday parties, playmates, and school events formed a wholesome existence for my daughters that is memorable because of the richness of Nigerian culture and way of life.

On the campus of Ahmadu Bello University there are many preschools, and an elementary and secondary school for the children of faculty and staff. In 1985 my eldest daughter was five and eligible for university primary school; however, my unemployment for, the first fourteen months in Zaria prevented her from attending. I was forced to place her in one of the on-campus nursery schools, which I had to pay for. By the time I was employed at the Center for Adult Education, I was at least in a position to shoulder the expense of school fees.

Another problem I experienced because of the limited nature of my employment contract was ineligibility for a university car loan. Ahmadu Bello University is an enormous campus where transportation is an absolute necessity, and I experienced the inconvenience of always depending on public transportation, assistance from neighbors and friends and mostly walking. I stood out very dramatically in the midst of an affluent academic community that valued status and prestige and the trappings of western life. In the perception of the academic community, the sub-standard housing we lived in, the absence of an automobile, single parenthood and in the early years, having only a master's degree created a stigma and made my life an object of curiosity. For Nigerian women, whether Muslim or Christian, marriage is the key to status, respect and social acceptance for adult participation in African society.

These problems reflect multiple subjectivities that defined my life in the Nigerian academic setting. The barriers that I faced stemmed from my status as an African-American female single parent. In order to survive and provide the best possible care of my daughters under adverse circumstances, I had to be resourceful, resilient, and disciplined as a positive role model for my children.

IT TAKES A VILLAGE

Despite the experience of adversity in the early years, the latter period of my life in Nigeria allowed for personal and professional growth, culminating in the completion of my Ph.D. Parenting my daughters amidst the rich tapestry of African culture became a positive and nurturing experience of support, cultural assimilation, and a sense of belonging. The cultural traditions, customs and way of life aided and enhanced the development of my parenting skills.

One often hears the African proverb "it takes a village to raise a child" without offering an explanation of the depth of this statement in full measure. Raising children in Nigeria allowed me to witness the *living tradition* that is the core, and indeed the foundation of African culture that is the extended family system that included me and my daughters as neighbors of a Nigerian family.

The university environment in Nigeria is very different from a western academic setting for a number of reasons. The vast network of residential areas constitutes a community in a much broader context than in the western university setting, although there is a Christian and Muslim divide. In *The University in Modern Africa,* Marie Sherman notes that "the African university became heir to a dual setting—the traditional African environment in which it was to be rooted, and the modern western sector from which it received its orientation (371). In western settings the university environment is often set apart from the community with the exception of the business sector that might surround and thus service the campus population. Even private American colleges set in small towns where faculty have on-campus housing are no exception.

The reason for this dramatic difference is the nature of African culture. In Zaria, the combination of Islamic and Nigerian culture is infused throughout the social and academic life on campus. For example, there are mosques and churches scattered around the campus so that faculty, staff and students interact not only in the academic workplace environment but in religious and social activities that reflect the elements of a cohesive society. On campus there were cultural displays, ethnic associations, music and dance, naming ceremonies, clubs and recreational activities that bound people together beyond the academic arena. Although the same kinds of activities exist on American campuses and elsewhere, the absence of cultural cohesion as a unifying principle is a marked difference from the African setting. This way of life greatly influenced my family through acculturation, social bonding, parenting, the acquisition of an African language for my daughters and a wealth of cultural knowledge about Nigerian people.

Socio-cultural elements that define the African world-view include humanism, the extended family system, discipline and restraint, strong moral fiber, the hierarchy of respect, generosity, hospitality and the presence of a strong work ethic (Gyekye). These cultural parameters reverberate throughout the socio-cultural fabric and extend from the larger society in rural areas into urban and academic settings. Cultural values and motifs are evident in art, music, dance, language, religion, folklore and myths and rituals of daily life. They are evident in the socialization process, childrearing practices, greetings, and in all institutions within African society transcending national, geographic and language boundaries. African humanism is a salient feature as the African individual is deeply connected to other people in society. For my daughters, growing up in a rich environment shaped their character development, perception of themselves, and this early childhood experience gave them a strong foundation for academic success and personal growth.

Unselfishness and generosity are integral to the African psyche and are ingrained in the African personality beginning with family life and extending outward to the community as an expression of communalism that ensures the survival of *all* people within the community. What was instructive about my own family life in Nigeria is that although I am an African-American, our neighbors and friends extended their hospitality and generosity to us in untold ways. Essentially, my daughters and I became part of our neighbors' families, reminiscent of fictive kin relationships among African Americans. Collective responsibility in society is described by J. A. Sofola in his insightful book, *African Culture and the African Personality,* where he outlines fundamental concepts inherent in the African family such as a feeling of belonging to the family group, the utilization of resources to help needy members, rallying to the support of a family member if he or she is in trouble, and the maintenance of continuity between the parental family and new family units.

It is evident that child-rearing in a communal setting invariably diminishes the alienating context of raising a family in isolation with its attendant stress and strain that is typical of modern life in America. The extended family system provides a social and familial network that assists and re-enforces child-rearing. As a struggling single parent, I was assisted by my immediate neighbors who were Muslim. Their family was very large; my sister/friend had ten children, ranging in age from 2-26. During the early to mid-1980s, this family had a total of 24 extended family members residing in the larger compound to which our house was adjacent. The family patriarch was financially responsible for of the relatives living in his compound. There are several ways in which this family sheltered us during the years of adversity.

For example, in Nigeria childcare in a traditional or rural environment is not a service that requires payment. Throughout a period of several years before we were finally given our own university house, my daughters played, were given meals, and were supervised in the home of my neighbors. It is from my neighbors' children that my daughters learned the language of the dominant ethnic group that is Hausa. Whenever I had long hours on campus or had to travel, I never worried about leaving my daughters because I knew they were safe and well cared for in my absence.

The experience of my daughters and I being treated like members of a Nigerian family in a nurturing environment paved the way for ongoing cultural learning. The order of respect is yet another important cultural value we assimilated because polite, well-mannered and obedient children are a cultural norm, and the expectation for children to behave this way is pervasive throughout Africa. Respect increases with maturity as the elderly are the custodians of society and repositories of wisdom and tradition.

These practices were relevant to my parenting because the values that were important in my home were the same as those espoused in the larger Nigerian society. This meant essentially that there was no conflict of competing values or blurred boundaries of socially acceptable behavior. There were no mixed messages or different standards of behavior displayed outside home life. The Nigerian environment instilled attitudes and behaviors of cooperation and obedience in the school setting that were re-enforced by parents and teachers. Needless to say, respect is one of the strongest African cultural values that govern all social interaction.

The Nigerian environment also helped instill a strong work ethic in my daughters because my values, codes of behavior, discipline and expectations were reinforced by the society at large and the school system. In addition to being a strong and positive role model that my daughters could emulate, the school and social environment supported a work ethic because in Africa all children are expected to complete chores obediently as part of home life and school. This also instills values of cooperation, mutual assistance and shared responsibility that I upheld in my home and through interaction with other families.

DOCTORAL STUDIES

By 1987, with much of the adversity of the early years behind us, my children were happy, healthy, and well-adjusted. They spoke Hausa, achieved academic excellence, had lots of friends, and interestingly, they were popular among their schoolmates. We were still living in the one bedroom bungalow but we were a wonderfully happy family. Actually we were a happy family all along including the years of poverty and uncertainty about the future. One of the interesting features of single parenthood is that mothers become extremely close to their children and display a tendency to share more about life. We had not visited America since arriving in Nigeria because although my university appointment was no longer Temporary Full-Time, I still did not have the higher category of contract that offered my family a paid vacation every two years.

One day another lecturer asked very casually whether I had begun doctoral studies. I was surprised that he thought I was in a financial position to afford further studies. I was even more surprised when he told me that as a lecturer in Ahmadu Bello University, I had the option of pursuing a professional degree without having to pay tuition. I had not known this and the very next day I went to see the dean of the Post-Graduate School to apply for admission for the fall semester. I submitted transcripts, was accepted, and began a course of study in the faculty of education.

This period of my life ushered in another uphill journey to overcome obstacles because of the added responsibility of rigorous study, teaching responsibilities, and lack of transportation that made care of my children a challenge. My expectation was to complete my doctorate. In the Ahmadu Bello university system, some of the graduate course are scheduled during the daytime, unlike graduate programs in America that are offered in the evening to accommodate students who are employed. This meant that throughout the day, I taught as well as attended graduate courses. In Nigeria, school is over at 2:00 p.m. and it was impossible for me to be at home when my daughters arrived and to give them lunch. As a single-parent, I came to rely on my neighbor for child care until I reached home, exhausted from walking long distances on campus in search of transportation. After the afternoon meal, my daughters went to their tutor in English and Math for two hours. Had I been a married Nigerian woman, there would have been other care-givers in my home to take care of my daughters since the nuclear family is an anomaly in Africa.

The conflict between mothering, university teaching and coping with graduate school took a serious toll on my health because I was overworked over a period of years. I was told more than once that if I didn't stop working so hard I would collapse. The chronic exhaustion came from overtaxing my body by walking long distances each day and studying at night. I became sleep deprived because virtually all my academic work was done late at night. I can honestly say that my entire dissertation was written late at night since there was no time during the day because of teaching, and exhaustion.

My dissertation is called *The Organizational Culture of Ahmadu Bello University*, and my research made it necessary to distribute questionnaires and conduct interviews throughout the campus. This became a massive undertaking that challenged my stamina and determination. By 1990, I was so overworked that by 10:00 a.m. each day, I was thoroughly exhausted, almost dragging myself across campus. I had dark circles under my eyes, and the fatigue seemed to have eaten into my bones. In late afternoon I would collapse into bed for at least 3 hours before I could function with my children. My immune system was compromised, and I became ill with malaria although my recovery was speedy.

In addition to the physical exhaustion, near the end of my doctoral program, I experienced another case of sexual harassment. After my dissertation committee had approved my final work, I then learned that curriculum changes were made to my program that would only affect newly enrolled students and would require two additional courses. However, I was approached for sexual favors by a high level administrator in exchange for graduating on time. I refused his advances, took the two extra courses and graduated a full year later than expected.

After completing my doctorate, my family and I remained in Nigeria for one year to enjoy the rewards of nine years of my hard labor at Ahmadu Bello University. The university finally sponsored our visit America. This began a new stage of well-being and prosperity for my family, which I realized after our return to Nigeria. We had unknowingly carved out a special and important status in the competitive university environment, now regarded as full heirs to a highly sought after access to America. Although it took 9 years for me to acquire the proper salary scale, a beautiful 3 bedroom house and other entitlements, when it came, we were suddenly propelled into the spotlight, subject to both envy and admiration from those who witnessed the beginning and the end of my struggle to find my place in the Nigerian academy as a respected colleague and in Nigerian culture as a successful single mother of two teen-aged daughters. My status as cultural outsider was no longer a mark of discrimination but the emergence of a new identity.

CONCLUSION

As a professional Black woman mothering in the Nigerian academy, I have experienced a life-altering journey that began as a bleak, uncertain and risky endeavor into unknown territory. Although there is a growing body of research on gender in African universities in general, there is a dearth of scholarly literature on northern Nigerian universities. This essay is a contribution to the literature in that it explores the multiple subjectivities to which a single woman, whether Nigerian or foreign, may be marginalized in the academic setting since the stigma of divorce and social out-casting is a pre-existing feature of African culture. I have attempted to identify the institutional mechanisms that create personal and professional inequality. Cultural expectations and norms legitimize a woman's role and status in society so that educational credentials and professional career achievements take second place to the marriage mandate. Multi-layered institutional and societal barriers to women's achievement, advancement, independence and autonomy have inhibited the full participation of women in African society at all levels, especially among Muslim women who experience additional religious restrictions.

Parenting under adverse conditions develops inner strength and coping mechanisms, fueled by the old adage that one must learn how to "make a way out of no way" in order to survive. People often ask "why Nigeria?" Perceptive observers remark that my decision to move to Nigeria was the "smartest decision I could have made." In a conversation with a family friend in 1995, I remarked that the early years of adversity were so unnecessary and his response was that "the suffering was the making of the person." This was not an effort to trivialize my hardship but to place it within the context of my path in life and the emergence of inner strength that that was tested every day for many years.

The Nigerian environment nurtured strong and resilient qualities in myself and my daughters that define African identity. In addition to completing a doctorate from Ahmadu Bello University in 1992, the experience of mothering in Northern Nigeria for ten years has added layers of valuable rewards to my grown daughters as well since we returned to America in 1993. My daughters' professional growth and scholarship can certainly be attributed to their Nigerian academic and cultural foundation. They have matured to become Africa-centered scholars, in the fields of African history and political science. Our sojourn in Nigeria was unquestionably the best years of my life as a woman, a mother, and a scholar.

WORKS CITED

Amadiume, Ifi. *Reinventing Africa: Matriarchy, Religion and Culture*. London and New York. Zed Books Ltd., 1997. Print.

Assie-Lumumba, N'Dri Therese. "Gendering and Emerging Challenges in Educational Policy and the Public Sector." *African Women and Globalization: Dawn of the 21st Century."* Ed. Jepkorir Rose *Chepyator*-Thomson. Trenton, NJ: Africa World Press, 2005. 43-66. Print.

Barnes, Teresa. "Politics of the Mind and Body: Gender and Institutional Culture in African Universities." *Feminist Africa* 8 (2007): 8-25. Print.

Bennett, Jane. "Exploration of a Gap: Strategising Gender Equity in African Universities." *Feminist Africa* 1 (2002): 1-16. Print.

Gyekye, Kwame. *African Cultural Values: An Introduction*. Accra: Sankofa Publishing Co., 1996. Print.

Mbiti, John. *Introduction to African Religion*. London: Heinemann Educational Publishers, 1975. Print.

Ogundipe-Leslie. Molara. *Recreating Ourselves: African Women and Critical Transformations*. Trenton, NJ: Africa World Press, 1994. Print.

"Our History." Ahmadu Bello University, Nigeria. n.d. Web. n.p. Retrieved 10 March 2010.

Sherman, Mary A. B. "The University in Modern Africa: Toward the Twenty-First Century." *The Journal of Higher Education* 61.4 (July-August 1990): 363-385. Print.

Sofola, J. A. *African Culture and the African Personality*. Ibadan: African Resources Publishers, 1978. Print.

Tsikata, Dzodzi. "Institutional Cultures and the Career Trajectories of Faculty of the University of Ghana." *Feminist Africa* 8 (2007): 26-41. Print.

10.
Clashing Clocks

Black Women Professors' Perceptions
of Parenting on the Tenure Clock

MARKESHA MCWILLIAMS HENDERSON AND NATALIE T. J. TINDALL

A WOMAN MAY ENCOUNTER two instances in which the prefix to her name changes: when she goes from single to married and when she earns a terminal degree. Whether by choice or a matter of circumstances she is also faced with whether or not to undergo these changes to her identity simultaneously. This chapter specifically explores the phenomena of Black female professors mothering on the tenure track. To understand more about the intersection of the professorate and motherhood, we conducted a study using semi-structured interviews with ten mothers who have either achieved tenure or are in tenure-track faculty positions. The participants were a part of a larger study we conducted on work-life integration of Black female professors. Because of the wealth of data collected, we felt it was appropriate to devote an entire chapter to the experiences of the mothers in our sample as they navigated work-life integration, specifically how they manage their parenting responsibilities while pursing tenure.

Sandra Acker and Carmen Armetti introduced the idea of the clashing clock to describe "a particular source of anxiety ... [at] the conjunction of the 'tenure clock' and the 'biological clock'" (11). Not all women approach their parental responsibilities in conjunction with their professional pursuits with anxiety. However, the purpose of this analysis is to illustrate and explain the consequences when the two clocks collide. For some women pursuing careers as tenure track faculty members, the decision or circumstances surrounding starting a family are carefully weighed. Considering the average age of a Ph.D. recipient is 33 years old

(National Center for Educational Statistics), women in the academy may be faced with an either/or proposition of being on tenure track or "mommy track" (Patterson par 5).

Collaborative relationships, particularly for faculty of color and other underrepresented populations, are important for advancement (Fries-Britt and Kelly 240). For women of color at predominantly White research universities, collaborating can be particularly challenging due to limited opportunities to connect with other scholars of color or difficulty penetrating established networks. Generally, women spend less time than their male colleagues engaging in research activities and more time in service activities (Bain and Cummings 513). Lower levels of scholarly productivity have also been identified as one of the major factors that limit women's advancement in the academy (Bain and Cummings, 508). When family obligations and marginalization further reduce the opportunities for collaboration and engagement, they could have dire consequences for women of color, particularly those on tenure track attempting to meet research and publication requirements for promotion.

Despite existing work-life scholarship that suggests ways in which institutions of higher education can help faculty members and administrators balance family and work responsibilities, institutions are slow to adopt changes to make workplaces more amenable for women faculty. On the other hand, Ann Stockdell-Giesler and Rebecca Ingalls suggest even when colleges and universities adopt better practices for women, the benefits are underutilized or leave is granted on a case-by-case basis and not "formally extended as entitlements" (par. 6). When the juxtaposition of home life and work life occurs, women in the academy are left to construct their own meanings of work-life integration and find ways to manage dual sets of demands.

It is important to divulge that during the conduct of the study we, the researchers, were not mothers ourselves. Advantages and disadvantages of our parental status surfaced during our study. As non-mothers, it was less of a challenge during data collection to identify issues that are inherent to the academy for women in general regardless of their family situation. However, during analysis we identified some differentiating issues for mothers versus non-mothers, and we were careful to avoid oversimplifying circumstances that are extremely complex. To achieve this, we use the direct quotes from the mothers themselves as often as possible. All identifying information has been removed to protect the confidentiality of the participants who were far more candid than expected. Many of the women expressed experiencing a cathartic feeling at the end of the interview and were pleased to not only contribute to knowledge for the purposes of our study, but also give voice to feelings they rarely have the opportunity to express. This study is our attempt to honor their testimony.

INSTITUTIONALIZED SEXISM

Before conveying the findings, it is important to understand the history of educated women and work-life integration. Sexism is ingrained into the fiber of higher education and was never designed to accommodate women nor their reproductive decisions. Academic life was patterned after "the male, monastic, single life" (Stanley 88). Early institutions of higher education in this country were founded in Colonial times. Coincidentally, there is no record of a woman receiving a degree during Colonial times because women were excluded by statute (Thelin 55).

As we recount the history of education for women, most of the early history documents the experiences of White women due to the exclusionary nature of society toward educating women of color. The founding of women's colleges such as Mount Holyoke during Reconstruction provided opportunities for women to be educated. By 1860, there were approximately forty-five institutions that offered college degrees to women (Thelin 83). This also created a notable effect on the family structure and significant shifts in marriage patterns of students. For example, the average age of marriage for graduates of Mount Holyoke from 1837-1850 was twenty-seven compared to age twenty-one for women in the general population (Solomon 31).

Shifts in marriage patterns resulted in women having to choose either education or marriage. In some cases, westward expansion and war created a larger population of young single women, and education was largely considered a placeholder for women in waiting. Similarly, work-life integration and balancing household responsibilities with work responsibilities was a non-issue for many educated women with jobs in this period because work cessation was expected once married. For example, Jane Colden, an accomplished botanist who produced a catalogue of over three hundred plants, ceased her work after she married at age 35 (Solomon 5). This either/or sentiment carried on well into the next century.

Black women undoubtedly faced similar barriers as White women concerning career and family, but with different consequences. Feminist historian Barbara Miller Solomon revealed that the stress of combining career and marriage was relatively the same in the 1930s for both White and Black Women; however, married White women generally had more of a choice to work as opposed to Black women who worked primarily out of economic necessity (180). Fast forward to today to an era where sexism still exists yet women now outnumber men on most college campuses. Despite increased opportunity to pursue education and careers as well as cultural shifts toward women in the workplace, women continue to struggle with the demands of professional pursuits and family obligations.

TESTIMONIES OF BLACK ACADEMIC MOTHERS ON TENURE TRACK

The ten women who participated in our investigation completed semi-structured interviews that lasted on average 1.5 hours. The interviews were conducted by telephone and participants were recruited mainly through referrals and snowball sampling. The results yielded seven dominant themes that will be discussed and illustrated using direct quotes of the participants.

The Trauma of Marriage

> *Who really tells you marriage is a bitch and you're going to have to rethink your entire life? Nobody tells you that. Popular culture tells us marriage is bliss. Popular culture makes it seem like it's wonderful ... jump right in.... Marriage is a completely different transition and nobody tells you that. (Tonya, 45, associate professor/administrator)*

Many of the women interviewed indicated a lack of preparedness for the roles and responsibilities of marriage. Women, who previously led an independent life and had been indoctrinated into the autonomous nature of the academy in graduate school, were challenged with incorporating another person into their routine. Having to schedule start and end times to independent research or writing was an adjustment for them. Even making deliberate decisions, such as when to eat with their spouse, was an adjustment for participants who were accustomed to fitting in meals when it was convenient for them to take a break from their work.

A majority of the participants had more advanced academic credentials than their spouses. Those who were not married to a spouse with a Ph.D. expressed their partner's lack of understanding of what it means to be a faculty member and the frustration and tension that result. Jan, a 38-year-old associate professor who is going through her second divorce, reflects on the tension that it placed on both of her marriages. She stated, "I don't think either one understood what the life of someone in the academy is because it's not a 9:00-5:00 job ... particularly of the life of an administrator trying to do the things you need to do. I think there is a lack of understanding there." Lakisha, who is legally separated from her husband of 15 years, discussed the "emotional distance" she felt when she learned over time her husband began to resent being in the company of her colleagues and friends. She said that although her husband, who is a college graduate but does not hold advanced degrees, did well in social settings with her colleagues and friends, she was not aware of his feelings because he never discussed it. Lakisha has three young boys, and the separation has required her to take more of a primary role in parenting.

However, participants who were married to someone with a doctorate did not express any additional benefit. In fact, the women with spouses of similar educational backgrounds described themselves and their husbands as workaholics, which introduced a conflict of deciding whose career should be prioritized. Although Gail, a 52-year-old assistant professor, started her career around the same time as her husband, he has achieved full professor status. She expressed feeling initially embarrassed for not advancing after achieving tenure, but says she placed her career secondary to parenting while her husband's work was prioritized over family responsibilities.

Tonya, who chose not to marry someone in the academy, recognized the potential for conflict with a spouse with similar aspirations:

> *My prayer was pretty much set on not being with an academic because I didn't want to deal with the competitive edge of being with a partner who is also trying to accomplish the same things I was trying to accomplish and perhaps put us at odds of whose career comes first.*

Not all participants expressed the trauma of marriage. Pam, an assistant professor and mother of three, said she is thankful to have an understanding spouse. She said her doctoral process also trained him to be a spouse of someone in academia. As he learned the culture and demands, her husband was instrumental in helping her set priorities and was very protective of her time. She said he often provides her support when the demands of work and home become overwhelming: "My husband is my cheerleader. He tells me often, 'You are my hero and I want to grow up to be like you.' He recognizes that my role as a mother is very integral and very important to the family cohesiveness…he said, 'If you quit this job, you will be miserable.'"

SINGLE MOTHERS WITH HUSBANDS

Bless my husband, he's a great husband, but I feel like he's a fourth child. (Pam, 41, assistant professor)

Although Pam did not seem to view marriage as traumatic or a barrier to the magnitude of the majority of participants, she, like all of the women we interviewed, felt the primary responsibilities for child rearing and household management were her responsibility. These women also unanimously agreed that delegating tasks to their significant other, rather than expecting them to do things proactively, is source of frustration but necessary in order to get the support they need. Gail speaks of the resentment that creeps in when her husband, who is also a professor, is not pulling his weight. Her advice is to simply get over it:

> *I think years ago there was a certain resentment on my part in feeling that why am I the one who always have to interrupt what I'm doing. But I got over it and I decided these are my kids and so I'm not going to measure how much time who spends with whom. I'm going to do what I feel I need to do for them the way I want to do it. Once I thought about it that way, I no longer measured who did what or how.*

SISTER-WIVES

I wish I had a wife because it seems to be the only way to be successful. (Gail, 52, assistant professor)

All of the women in the study expressed that a majority of the childrearing duties fall to them as opposed to their partner. To manage, many of them have turned to other women to help them, manage their responsibilities. Almost all of the women in the study spoke about the additional help they receive, primarily from another woman in their life or as one participant put it, calling on a "sister-wife." The sister-wife ranged from a paid caretaker, their mother, a good friend, other professional moms, or neighbors with children. These ancillary women helped lighten the load and performed childrearing duties that allowed the women to focus more on their work.

In one instance, the additional help was not specifically for her children, but for her husband. Meal planning for a husband of a different culture proved especially difficult for one participant, so she found other women from his culture to cook more pleasing meals. Some women may find it difficult to allow others to meet the needs of their family and accept help, but the participants unanimously agreed it was necessary in order to manage both home and work responsibilities. Women who had difficulty managing both domains, particularly while pursuing tenure, expressed a greater sense of balance once help was acquired. As Olivia, who was approaching her tenure review at the time of the study, stated, "I found a solution now because we have employed a woman to pick up my child. She keeps her and feeds her and brings her home later. That enables me to feel more comfortable and spend more time at work. She enables me to do that."

SELF-CRITICAL PARENTING

Who knows? My kids may grow up to despise me. "My mom didn't do this or we couldn't do that because she was at work." But I think, you know, I'm managing it all pretty well. I'm managing to do all the things that I think are important, or at least I hope I am. I'm managing to be a good mom, maybe not the best mom out there and I'm managing to be a good teacher, maybe not the best teacher. Those are the things that are really important to me. (Lakisha, 39, assistant professor)

The resiliency demonstrated when dealing with failure on the job is not as evident when the failure pertains to motherhood. The women were extremely critical of themselves when they feel like they failed at parenting. The participants expressed guilt when work demands superseded the demands at home, particularly when it affected their children. Pam, an assistant professor with a dual appointment, had a hard time forgiving herself for a scheduling mishap involving her son and for not keeping a clean house. She said, "I have sat and cried within the last two weeks because I said I'm not a good mom."

The failures the women spoke of hardly qualified as child neglect or abuse, and yet the tendency to be superwoman, the need for perfection, and unrealistic expectations both self-imposed and imposed by others, created a no-win situation. In the end, however, many women expressed that their children come first. Kelly, a 49-year-old assistant professor expressed, "I got the job … and two months later after the fertility doctor told me I would need drugs to get pregnant I got pregnant. I had two babies and did whatever they asked me to. I did whatever was needed for my family."

The mothers all agreed that personal and professional achievements pale in comparison to raising healthy and happy children. Academia is a profession that is very dependent upon recognition from your peers. The tendency to succeed is the initial driving force, but as Gail experienced when her daughter had a major illness, everything was quickly put in perspective:

> *When I got tenured and I didn't get promoted initially it was like oh my gosh, I have to do whatever it takes to get promoted because this is so embarrassing. This was a failure.... And so I came to accept that it is not as though I had done nothing with my life so I really shouldn't be embarrassed because there was no way in the world I could ignore this child's needs just to have a successful career.*

MODELING SUPERWOMAN

> *I think it comes from generations of women like my mom, my grandma, my great-grandma, who managed or seemingly managed to do it all and not take a break.* (Lakisha, 39, assistant professor)

Black women with strong maternal figures are likely emulating the grind they grew up watching from the sideline. Several participants mentioned their mothers as a source of inspiration as well as a source of support. Ironically, many of the women on whose shoulders we stand sacrificed themselves to provide a better life for us. Gail, a 52-year-old assistant professor, echoed that sentiment:

> *I was raised to kind of go for it. You know, my mother is someone who had accomplished things but felt that she could have and should have done more and her mother felt that she could have and should have done more so in a way I was raised that I shouldn't make the same mistake and I should be all that I could be professionally.*

Tamara Beuboeuf-Lafontant says the emotional weight and cultural constructions of the strong Black woman is to our detriment

(25). Although women who are programmed to be a superwoman often complain about the role, they have difficulty relinquishing the burden. Superwomen are cognizant how other people perceive their work habits and feel they have something to prove. Lakisha admits,

> *So maybe secretly inside I get some sort of sick joy from hearing other people say, "I can't believe you do all of this. I can't believe you're able to do the doctorate and you got kids, you got this and you're working full-time." I think sometimes I may let it play out and I can say that I've accomplished a lot.*

What Lakisha describes exemplifies "satisficing," a term Kelly Ward and Lisa Wolf-Wendel borrowed from economics and applied to motherhood (249). The satisficing phenomenon refers to being good enough, but not necessarily optimal. It is especially difficult for women who have been high achievers for most of their lives to adjust to not putting forth their best, but they recognize it is unavoidable given limitations of time, energy, and resources. Internally, women know they are capable of doing better, but ultimately they settle for what they are realistically able to accomplish.

THE DR. MOM LABEL

> *I'm careful how I bring up my children in my life.... I don't want people to say, "She's not pulling her weight," or, "She's debilitated because of her family, she's a 'mommy,'" or characterizes me in some way that undermines my professional status.* (Olivia, 51, assistant professor)

The literature addressing work-life balance often refers to balancing the two lives of mother and scholar. The women in this study frequently referenced this fragmentation. Venitha Pillay suggests there are dangers associated with splitting the academic mother (508). However, as illustrated in the quote above, some of the professors in this study did not embrace the "Dr. Mom" stigma in the workplace.

Their level of comfort with discussing personal schedule conflicts with colleagues varied, and the successful navigation of work and life largely depended on the culture of the work environment. Most participants who expressed working in supportive environments had female department chairs, while the ones with male department chairs expressed less support. However, in those instances where the participants expressed not receiving support from female chairs or other colleagues, the push-back could be attributed to the subjective nature of advice. For example, Tonya, upon learning one of her advisees was planning to get married, advised the student to consider waiting until finishing comprehensive exams. Stopping short of telling the student that she should not get married, her advice, which was ill-received by the student, was to not expect to get married and achieve the things that she hopes to achieve in the program. This advice was rooted in her own negative experience of trying to be a newlywed during her own graduate process.

Lessons learned from personal experience may not necessarily result in a negative perception from those who have had trials with motherhood. Tonya, in her role as department chair, also readily grants extensions and concessions to pregnant students and faculty due to her own experience with multiple miscarriages during her tenure process. She attributes her miscarriages to work-related stress and ultimately had to adopt because of her inability to carry a child to term. This experience allows her to be more sympathetic to expecting mothers in her department.

Experiences related to mothering in the academy can be consistent regardless of race, but having to deal with racism in the workplace along with the Dr. Mom stigma causes even more stress and consternation for Black female professors. As if being misogynistic is somehow better than being racist, Kelly discussed how the schedule conflicts of being a mother were used as an excuse to continue discriminatory practices against faculty of color at her institution. Attacking her abilities based on her race was difficult to substantiate, but the scheduling conflicts could be documented and provided ammunition to be used against her. Kelly expressed how the need to provide for her family kept her in an intolerable environment:

> *That on-the-job stress of not feeling like everything that I professionally accomplished makes any difference, that a White person whether it's a student or an administrator can say something to take this reputation that I worked so hard for away from me—I can't stand it. But at the same time, I can't quit my job. I've got two kids who haven't even started college yet so it feels like you're in prison.*

Several women mentioned how departmental meetings cause conflicts in their parenting schedule. For example, early morning meetings are difficult for one participant who has to get her child to school in the morning. Others expressed how uncomfortable it is to have to miss a meeting or turn down opportunities because of conflicts with their parenting schedule. Another time barrier many of the participants mentioned is the inability to collaborate and socialize with colleagues due to their responsibilities at home. Olivia explained:

> *Most junior faculty/tenure track in their 30s do not have children.... They don't have kids so they have a lot more free time, they are a lot more casual, two of them ride their bikes in, they do a lot of things with graduate students, they're very active on campus. I think that's different than what I'm able to do as a 50-year-old woman. I'm competing with them in a sense. They've got almost 20 years on me and I have these kids to take care of and I can't be hanging around in a coffee shop at six o'clock.*

For Olivia, the demands of the academy required her to delay the start of her family, so at 50 years old, she still has minor children in the household. She perceives not being able to participate in the collegial environment as a professional disadvantage.

Alternatively, several women in the study talked about gaining the respect of their colleagues. One professor said that although she is in a supportive environment and has a department chair who was her mentor; she was sensitive about her colleagues not viewing her as receiving special treatment just because she has children.

CONSEQUENCES OF MANAGED CHAOS

I want to do stuff outside of just being this mama and this wife because that can be all consuming, and that's very irritating to me. (Donna, 37, assistant professor)

Managed chaos can be misleading because it wears the disguise of functionality. As demonstrated by several participants, a person can meet her work deadlines, the kids can be well provided for, and the household can be running efficiently, but all of these things are at the cost of her personal well-being. Tonya, an associate professor describes how other needs superseded her own needs: "Right now I feel like I am operating just by rote. This is what I have to do. And I feel everything I have to do right now is outside of me. And when you say I am at the bottom of the list of my priorities, I feel like I am right there along with my research."

Pam, an assistant professor, encountered the physical manifestation of stress when she could no longer manage the demanding responsibilities of her dual roles. She suffered a breakdown that ultimately forced her to take a break from work and family. What she learned from that experience is that the world did not stop when she was on hiatus. She stated:

I had to pull back, and you understand it may be not as fulfilling because you don't get the accolades and all of that, and I'm not working toward full professor right now, which part of me wishes I was. I see my colleagues publishing and really moving forward. But I'm like, "You know what? I have to be okay with where I am and recognize that where I am is a good place. And I don't have to be everything and perfect in all areas." I say that because I had to hit a wall to recognize that.

Several participants in the study expressed difficulty managing their weight and knowingly ignoring health warning signs. Practicing self-care, finding time to exercise, scheduling doctor appointments or simply taking time for mental and physical relaxation was not prioritized over caring for others. The "others" were not just limited to their children and spouses; care was also extended to parents, other family members, and even students. Not feeling and looking their best had negative consequences to their overall self-esteem. Most of the participants who expressed health challenges were very aware of the physical and mental toil that was occurring but felt their own suffering was a reasonable exchange for the wellness of others.

With self being the lowest priority on many of the mothers' lists, participants also had difficulty articulating what they would do if they had more time to themselves. Some listed hobbies and other interests, but many of the women interviewed had a longing to dive more into their research agenda and publish. Consistent with Kelly Ward and Lisa Wolf-Wendel's findings, our respondents expressed a love for scholarly exploration and the gratification that comes from being recognized for their work (241-242). If given more free time, the participants reported using it to contribute better scholarship. For example, an anthropology professor expressed the difficulty of doing methodologically sound ethnographic research because she does not have the time to truly immerse herself into the cultures she is studying due to her competing demands.

SIGNIFICANCE OF FINDINGS AND IMPLICATIONS

When we initially approached this study, we understood we also had the opportunity for our findings to be instructive for our own lives. As a graduate student and a tenure track professor, both in our thirties, both unmarried and without children, the anxiety of the clashing clocks was ever present. In the larger study, women without families expressed sympathy for mothers with the challenges of raising a family coupled with work obligations. However, the women with families did not want pity from their colleagues as much as they wanted to be recognized as a professional rather than be treated as if motherhood was a liability.

One would only hope that we have evolved as a society to not engage in deliberate oppressive practices that intentionally prohibit women from advancing in their chosen fields. Although women are recognized as essential contributors to the work force in general, many workplaces, including the academy, are still structured as if there is a full-time parent in the household attending to family responsibilities (Schein 164). Many antiquated practices still exist, and in order to meet the realities of today's workforce, policies for achieving tenure require re-examination. Considering the average age for Ph.D. recipients is 33 years old, an assistant professor who achieves a tenure track position in her mid- to late-30s is immediately faced with a window of about six years to demonstrate excellence in teaching, research, and service. The tenure window also coincides with the twilight of childbearing years, leaving women to reconcile which aspect of their life will take priority. Some universities have addressed how family responsibilities can impede tenure achievement and have adopted guidelines to support faculty in their familial roles while pursuing tenure. For example, some institutions add an additional year to the tenure clock when a minor child is added to the household during the professor's probationary period.

Perhaps the greatest lesson to be learned is the manifestation of superwoman tendencies, managing chaos, complicated relationships with significant others, and workplace demands are not all occurring in a bubble. Most importantly, as the participants in the study suggest, the children, particularly daughters, are likely taking their cues on what it means to be a mother from the women who raise them. As we learned, the women in this study cited their own mothers and grandmothers as their first example for work-life integration. We do not believe, however, that the previous generations' intentions were for us to achieve at our own detriment. Successfully navigating work and life has consequences both for our lives and for the children who observe and model our behavior.

Finally, mothers in the academy pay a high tax to achieve professionally and to maintain a healthy home life. Despite the strains to their personal relationships, the missed professional opportunities, and the physical and mental toll on themselves, the women unanimously reported that no sacrifice was too great to ensure the well-being of their children. The findings from this study support Pillay's call to inscribe motherhood into the intellectual work of academic mothers. As the participants suggested, the label of Dr. Mom is not necessarily a badge of honor in certain work environments, and spillover from their lives as moms into the academy is avoided when possible so as not be perceived as inferior and less productive. But Pillay suggests that when a woman is fragmented and attempts to separate her scholarship from herself, fulfillment in either role is compromised (513).

The concept of work/life balance is a misnomer. There will always be a tendency to prioritize one role over another. Instead, women can strive for work/life integration. Weaving personal relationships, childrearing, professional achievements, and workplace camaraderie together and appreciating the intricacies of academic motherhood would allow more women to advance in the profession. More importantly, women maintaining the many obligations in their home and professional lives can come out of the shadows of resentment and regret and embrace a career with deliberate choices for their families and their futures.

WORKS CITED

Acker, S., and C. Armenti. "Sleepless in Academia." *Gender and Education* 16 (2004): 3-24. Web. 12 Oct. 2010.

Bain, Olga, and William Cummings. "Academe's Glass Ceiling: Societal, Professional-Organizational, and Institutional Barriers to the Career Advancement of Academic Women." *Comparative Education Review* 44 (2000): 493-514. Web. 16 Apr. 2011.

Beauboeuf-Lafontant, Tamara. *Behind the Mask of the Strong Black Woman: Voice and the Embodiment of a Costly Performance.* Philadelphia, PA: Temple University Press, 2009. Print.

Fries-Britt, Sharon and Bridget Turner Kelly. "Retaining Each Other: Narrative of Two African American Women in the Academy." *The Urban Review* 37.3 (September 2005): 221-242. Web. 17 Apr. 2011.

National Center for Educational Statistics. "Doctorate Recipients from U.S. Universities 2009." National Science Foundation Survey of Earned Doctorates Web. Dec 2010.

Patterson, G. A. "Managing Motherhood and Tenure." *Diverse: Issues in Higher Education* 25.20 (Nov 2008): 16-18. Web. 16 Apr. 2011.

Pillay, Venitha. "Academic Mothers Finding Rhyme and Reason."

Gender and Education 21.5 (September 2009): 501-515. Web. 16 Apr. 2011.

Schein, Virginia. "Would Women Lead Differently." *The Leader's Companion: Insights on Leadership Through the Ages.* Ed. J. Thomas Wren. New York: The Free Press, 1989. 161-167. Print.

Solomon, Barbara Miller. *In the Company of Educated Women.* New Haven: Yale University Press, 1985. Print.

Stanley, T. "Single Mothering in Academia." *Parenting and Professing: Balancing Family Work with an Academic Career.* Ed. R. H. Bassett. Nashville: Vanderbilt University Press, 2005. 82-88. Print.

Stockdell-Giesler, A. and R. Ingalls. "Faculty mothers." *Academe* 93.4 (July-Aug 2007): n.p. Web. 16 Apr. 2011

Thelin, John R. *A History of American Higher Education.* Baltimore: The Johns Hopkins University Press, 2004. Print.

Ward, Kelly and Lisa Wolf-Wendel. "Academic Motherhood: Managing Complex Roles in Research Universities." *The Review of Higher Education* 27.2 (Winter 2004): 233-257. Web. 17 Apr. 2011.

III.
TRANSCENDENCE

11.
Daughter Dreams and the Teaching Life of Audre Lorde

ALEXIS PAULINE GUMBS

I am
the sun and moon and forever hungry
the sharpened edge where day and night shall meet
and not be
one.
—Audre Lorde, "From the House of Yemanja"

THE RELEVANCE OF THE DREAM ARCHIVE TO BLACK MOTHERS AND DAUGHTERS IN THE ACADEMY

Black feminist dreaming is a publicized critical practice. Farah Jasmine Griffin describes Black Feminist Literary criticism itself as a dream *that the mother's may soar and the daughters may know their names* (336-360). In 1985, literary scholar Carole Boyce Davies pointed out how Black women's fiction participated in the project of dreaming mothering into a healing modality in literature (41-43). Black feminist historian Elsa Barkley Brown uses the precedent of literary figures Alice Walker and Paule Marshall to highlight mothers outside of the academy as sources of intellectual training and to write about how her own mother's complicated disdain for and support of her dream of becoming a scholar shapes her historical practice (74-93). Black lesbian feminist scholar, poet, and publisher Diane Bogus calls her mother the "repository" for her dreams (240). As scholars and writers we inhabit and examine the dreams of our literal and figurative mothers and foremothers, but mothering and dreaming are complicated orientations to the future for oppressed people. In *Mama's Baby, Papa's Maybe*, Hortense Spillers distinguishes between motherhood as a privileged status, usually only granted to middle class white women, and the labor of *mothering* as a form of *work* performed by people who are excluded from a patriarchal gender construct, meaning that it can be a form of forced labor within institutions like slavery or what Audre Lorde calls the "master's house" of the university (Spillers 65-81; Lorde, *Sister Outsider* 110-113). Black feminist critics and queer theorists have built on Spillers's distinction to argue that the labor of mothering, already split from patriarchally privileged gender status, can exceed biological and heteronormative conceptions of motherhood.

This chapter honors the work of dreaming and links it to the work of mothering as an intergenerational Black feminist critical practice. This is an opportunity to move beyond the symbolic invocation of dreams as evidence of the *"huge, rewarding hard work demanded by the huge new ambitions of our mothers"* (Griffin 145) to examine the symbolic work of engaging night-dreams, traces from the subconscious, in this case documented in Audre Lorde's unpublished journals. How might an archive of the subconscious dreams of Black mothers navigating the academy serve as a resource for future or fellow travelers? Practicing a Black feminist theory of dreams, grounded in contemporary Black feminist literary and cultural theoretical practice, this chapter argues that the labor of Black mothering as a knowledge from within capitalism and the university industrial complex is a resource threatened and priceless enough to fill the subconscious and transform the waiting day.

Following the implications of Black feminist literary and cultural theory's focus on mother and daughter subjectivity as key focal points for critical praxis, this essay will focus on Audre Lorde's dreams about teaching and mothering and her journal documentation of her daughter Elizabeth's dreams. It is not hard to imagine why the mother/daughter question that has figured so prominently in Black feminist literary and cultural theory would manifest in the subconscious workings of the minds of Black feminist mothers in the academy. Patricia Hill Collins points out the complication of mother/daughter relationships in general when daughters are taught to identify with mothers, while at the same time the work and status of Black mothers is devalued within patriarchy (7). Collins explains that the further complexity of Black mothers in relationship to patriarchy, charged with teaching daughters how to survive within a racist and sexist system, while also teaching them how to think of themselves beyond the constraints of the system, makes for some complicated silences and resonances under the surface. Further, as Rosalie Troester points out in her analysis of Paule Marshall's work, "Isolation causes the currents between Black mothers and daughters to run deep and the relationship to be fraught with an emotional intensity often missing from the lives of women with more freedom" (13). This emotional intensity in the waking relationships of mothers and daughters makes the psychoanalytic impulse to bring dreams into the conversation a logical step. The subconscious is a key archive for the examination of mothering, daughter subjectivity, institutional navigation, and the complicated labor of teaching. The dream archive of Audre Lorde, a poet, mother, warrior, teacher who assigned her poetry students to keep dream journals as part of their academic work, is an offering toward the waking sustenance of contemporary and future Black Mothers in the academy.

A DIALOGIC APPROACH

As Audre Lorde suggests in one of her rare published analyses of her own pedagogical dreaming, *maybe I am every person in this dream (The Cancer Journals* 14-15). Maybe I inhabit every subject position in this essay, daughter, mother, energetic ancestor, student, critic, poet, and dream-book steward. Maybe my voice is alone echoing off missing Black mother warrior teachers who did not survive the university. But maybe not. Audre Lorde is here. June Jordan is here. Toni Cade Bambara is here. Barbara Christian is here. Nellie McKay is here. Elizabeth Amelia Hadley is here. Presente. Maybe you are here too, waking up, a daughter dreaming whether it is possible to be a mother, a teacher, alive in the context of commodified individuated knowledge. This chapter is not a single author product. It sings in the context of this urgent anthology as a member of a ghostly and anxious chorus. If we are to learn the lessons of our dreams, not as individual intellectual property, but as access to a collective transformation, we need a dialogic approach.

In *Becoming Black: Creating Identity in the African Diaspora*, Michelle Wright offers Audre Lorde's dialogic poetics of maternity (alongside those of Carolyn Rodgers) as a model that anticipates and informs Mae Gwendolyn Henderson's foundational argument that the practice of "speaking in tongues" along with the interpretation of tongues is key in our understanding of the critical, oppositional and spiritual work of Black women's literature (141-144). Wright points to Lorde's "In the House of Yemanja" as a corrective to a masculinist dialectic approach to race (practiced by W. E. B. DuBois, Leopold Senghor and Franz Fanon) as the establishment and re-establishment of Blackness and whiteness as racial opposites. Wright offers Lorde and Rodgers as examples of the dialogic engagement with maternity that she finds necessary for a diasporic understanding of race where whiteness and Blackness are not antithetical, but rather in continual reproduction of each other in a dialogue about what race means. For Wright, the introduction of the figure of the Black mother into this discourse (which DuBois, Senghor and Fanon elide in different ways) is crucial. The mother is the reminder that the future is not produced by one, creating another one, who creates another one. The mother is the reminder that it takes at least two, a dialogue, to produce any discourse, a messy disruption to the would-be purity of race (141-144).

As Wright points out, the figure of the Black mother is burdened with all of the ways we imagine the reproduction of race. However, the reproduction of race is not a biological phenomenon equal to or commutative with the reproduction of phenotypes. The reproduction of race is discursive, enacted through oppressive behaviors and violent definitions of the meaning of life. This specter of the imagined reproduction of race in the bodies of women also adheres to mother/daughter relationships, giving these the conflated weight of oppression in the conscious and subconscious mind.

Audre Lorde's "From the House of Yemanja" performs a modality for addressing the duality of race while facing the complexity of mother-daughter relationships. Describing the critical edge of mothering and creating a language in symbols to describe the internalized racism she experienced with and inherited from her mother, Lorde begins:

> My mother had two faces
> and a broken pot
> where she hid out a perfect daughter
> who was not me. (Lorde, *The Black Unicorn* 6)

But the symbols in the poem exceed the descriptive, and the mother is not only an individual person in the poem. "Mother" is also the name for the production of subjectivity, the catalyst for selfhood and the measure of possible connection. Lorde signals this with her invocation of Yemanja: a goddess who is the mother of the other deities in the Yoruba tradition, and also the ocean, the primordial source of life on earth.

This "mother" who brings the poetic speaker "bread and terror/ in my sleep" has a material, conscious and subconscious role in the subjectivity of this imperfect daughter, and even the maternal reference point whose bed is the primal and complicated scene that prefigures the nightmare-out-of-time sun-and-moon relationship of the poetic speaker.

> All of this has been
> before
> in my mother's bed
> time has no sense. (*The Black Unicorn* 6)

In other words, there is more than one mother in this poem: mother as the force that produces the semiotics of self-knowing, mother as a symbol within that semiotics, and mother as personified portal for transformation. The meaning of mothering is *in production* even in the process of this poem's articulation of itself. Thus Lorde's final address to "Mother" must be multiple.

> Mother I need/ mother I need/ mother I need your blackness now. (*The Black Unicorn* 6)

There is more than one Audre in this poem: Audre as dreamer, Audre as character in her own dreams, Audre as theorist of dreams, Audre as daughter, Audre as mother, Audre as person you think you know already, Audre as imagined reader of *this* text you are reading, Audre whom I am inventing for you now. Like the capitalized and lowercased, goddess, symbol and everyday mothers in "From the House of Yemanja" Audre is *in the making* in this essay, as symbol and more; as multi-present resource for survival.

> Audre we need
> Audre we need
> Audre we need your dreams now.

This chapter will be a dialogue between nightmare mothers and imperfect daughters, between the dreamers and the dreamt of, between Audre Lorde's own dreams and those of her daughter, between Lorde's dreams and her poems about dreaming, between Audre Lorde as theorist and her dreams as text, and between the language of dreams and the birth of a poetic language to describe what we are learning and teaching consciously and underneath. Not least of all because the meanings of our births, rebirths, our mothering and our teaching are dialogic phenomena, a conversation that we still need language to describe.

TOWARD A BLACK FEMINIST THEORY OF DREAMS

> in a room on the 17th floor
> my body is dreaming
> ...while young girls assault my door
> I am afraid
> They will discard my most ancient nightmares...
> *Blackstudies Part 1* (Lorde, *The Black Unicorn* 53)

This is not objective work. Dream reading, like the mothering process of Black feminist teaching, is committed work with bias and forgiveness. As self-chosen daughter disciple to warrior mother Audre Lorde I can find only one place where she misleads us. In her public lecture "Poet as Teacher-Human as Poet-Teacher as

Human" Lorde explains that all life is teaching. Then she offers an exception to prove the rule: "I feel the only state which is not teaching is sleeping…" (2009: 182).

The premise of this essay disagrees with that exception. The sleeping life of Audre Lorde, and the relationship between her dreams and her practices of mothering and teaching, are providing lessons even now to her belated students. I propose that Audre Lorde's use of her dreams as the major source of her own poetic imagery, and her injunction to her poetry students to keep dream journals make the archive of her and her daughter's dreams a shadow body of work that could inform our analysis of Lorde's poetic and pedagogical practices and our own understandings of the relationship between mothering and teaching. If I am one of the young women haunting Lorde's doorway in her post-mortem office hours, looking for answers, I will not fulfill the fear she expresses in "Blackstudies" that her nightmares will be discarded.

It would take a book-length project to analyze the presence of dreams in all of Lorde's poems, and it is a shared task that I hope my generation and future generations of scholars take on. Almost every poem that Lorde published was influenced by the work of dreaming, but in this essay "BlackStudies," Lorde's freeform villanelle about the maternal labor of teaching in the late twentieth century public university, will frame and answer back our inquiry, informing our work to elaborate together as readers, dreamers, daughters, mothers and scholars a Black feminist theory of the teaching work of dreams.

We will take our cue, but not our theoretical lexicon, from Sigmund Freud, much cited "father of modern psychology" and author of a widely referenced, critiqued and drawn on work called *The Interpretation of Dreams*. In this work Freud analyzes his own dreams and uses his experience as a white European, middle-class member of a heteropatriarcal family structure to shape his interpretations. It follows then that to interpret Audre Lorde's dreams from a Black feminist critical and political perspective we would use Audre Lorde's own context: her work as a beneficiary, subject, and practitioner of Black feminist literary theory and as a Black feminist warrior mother within the context of a queer subjectivity and coming from a working class immigrant family.

In "All the Things You Could Be By Now if Sigmund Freud's Wife Was Your Mother: Psychoanalysis and Race," Black feminist literary critic Hortense Spillers signifies on the application of Freud's theories about gender and sexuality to the lives of people far outside his scope of vision (for example ... Black mothers) while centering the complicated subjectivity and intersubjectivity of a Black daughter figure and her conscious and subconscious dreams as a metanarrative for the learning of difference. Spillers references "the child's gift for strange dreams of flying and bizarre, yet correct, notions about the adult bodies around her" (2000: 582) as a way to point out what she calls "the psychoanalytic difference that has yet to be articulated" that of "the stigmatized subject" or "one whose access to discourse must be established as a human right and not assumed" (2000: 596).

A Black feminist theory of dreams reflects the intersubjectivity of the lived experiences of Black feminists as purveyors of an alternative reality in confrontation with the organizing institutions of oppression. To be a Black feminist educator in the context of the contemporary university is a strange trip indeed. The Black feminist mother as a teacher whose right to sleep is never guaranteed and the Black feminist teacher as mother whose consciousness even in her own classrooms is not validated are complicated subject positions, consciousness submerged, dreams coming true. Black feminist dream work is a risk, a recurring articulation. It is happening right now. Are you awake?

THUS SAITH (THE LORDE)

Lorde's most widely circulated published theorization of dreams appears in her essay "Poetry is Not a Luxury." Lorde, always a poet, even in her eloquent essay writing, creates a dream context for the reader, an interplay between light and dark that invokes the circadian rhythm, the organic relationships to light and darkness that make sleep a crucial activity. For Lorde "the quality of light by which we scrutinize our lives" is determined by our relationship to "poetry as illumination" (*Sister Outsider* 36). The illumination of poetry operates in direct relationship to "the dark place within, where hidden and growing our true spirit rises ... against (y)our nightmare of weakness" (*Sister Outsider* 36). This is the dream space, Lorde's challenge to enlightenment and reframing of the subconscious. There is a growing true spirit engaging the nightmares in the subconscious and growing from the same place. Lorde's characterization of this struggle within the subconscious space of rich and complicated darkness also lends power to the position of the oppressed person, cultivating strength within a nightmare reality. She explains, "The places of possibility within us are dark because they are ancient and hidden: they have survived and grown strong through that darkness" (*Sister Outsider* 36). What Freud would call the subconscious, this conflicting and generative dark space, Lorde pointedly calls "non-European consciousness," no longer subsumed to the practice of rationality (*Sister Outsider* 37). Poetry is the practice Lorde offers as a bridge between the strength of dreams and the transformation of lived experience.

For Lorde, poetry was what allowed dreams to be connected with the practice of everyday life. Therefore as an educator she required the documentation of dreams as a crucial practice for her poetry students. In her poetry workshops at Hunter, her syllabus lists the first requirement as keeping a daily private journal for dreams as possible "material" (Audre Lorde Papers, Box 22, Folder 34). As she emphasizes in "Poetry is Not a Luxury": "Right now I can name at least ten ideas I would have found intolerable, incomprehensible and frightening except as they came after dreams and poems" (*Sister Outsider* 37).

PUBLISHING AND THE DREAM DEFERRED

Ironically "Poetry is Not A Luxury," Lorde's most sustained meditation on dreams, was first published in *Chrysalis*, a magazine where ironically or predictably Lorde experienced a dream deferred. Lorde was poetry editor at the literary magazine until the fact that the all-white core editorial collective repeatedly ignored her protests about their disrespect of poetry as a genre, and poetry by women of color within the magazine caused her to resign from her volunteer position. Lorde's publication of this essay in the magazine was an intervention into the luxury economy of what June Jordan would later describe in angry letter in solidarity with

Lorde's resignation as a "profoundly optional profoundly trifling profoundly upper middle-class attic white publication" (June Jordan Papers, Box 85, Folder 1).

Lorde's dream for *Chrysalis* was ambitious and deeply felt. In an early letter upon accepting the invitation to become poetry editor she wrote that the poetry in the magazine:

> must mirror sing warm scream the highest of our journeys, the bloodiest of our failures, the most bizarre and precious of our dreams the most difficult of our future uncharted arrivals and the agonizing elations of reconstructing the route and journeys so that we may come again. (De Veaux 178)

The fact that Lorde's dream (as in intention) for the publication included attention to dreams (as in non-linear sleep narratives) is not a mere coincidence and forms a grounding context for Lorde's theorization of dreams in practice. Lorde believed that the function of poetry, not only as an individual process, but also as a collective resource was the documentation, mirroring, amplification and trans-substantiation of dreams into transformative revolutionary action and a possible world. The work of dreams, intentional and REM sleep-based, to transform lived experience proves its urgency in the context where Lorde invoked it, which is a context that Black feminist mothers and teachers in the academy know all too well: the disjunction between the functions of the publications we often give our labor, and our dreams for their true necessity in the transformation of the discourse and the empowerment of our communities.

Lorde's use of dreams as poetic material in her teaching and publishing life is relevant and evocative for those of us interested in maternity. In conversation with Hortense Spillers' theorizations of the inscription of Black life as flesh in "Mama's Baby Papa's Maybe: A New American Grammar Book," Fred Moten's *In the Break* draws a connection between the predicament of materiality and the denied and silent fact of maternity to talk about the profound denial of maternal subjectivity in the production of capitalist life (18). My work as a scholar and community educator, lives at the intersection of these theories transformed by a dream maternal relationship with Lorde as a poetic mother. Materiality and maternity are linked because of ways that the law of the mother within slave code created a deviant and disempowered form of maternity in order to reproduce subjugation in the form of slavery. The nightmare of slavery and the reproduction of oppression remain present in the dream space of Black feminism. This project, a dream come true, actualized in workshops with Black feminists from across the United States, centers *the most bizarre and precious of our dreams the most difficult of our future uncharted arrivals*, as a crucial resource for our collective transformative impact on the means of production we engage, including the academy, our families, and our possible communities.

II. DAUGHTER DREAMS

I do not know whose legends blew
through my mother's furies
but somehow they fell through my sleeping lips
Blackstudies Part II (Lorde, *The Black Unicorn* 54)

A daughter is a site of dreams imposed, a dream come true, a nightmare about the self that cannot be ignored. Audre Lorde's documentation of her daughter Beth's dreams provide a textual interface for the daughter as a profound catalyst and signifier for Black feminist dreaming, the tricky crossroads where dreams as intention interface with dreams as repressed realities manifesting in sleep. As the editors of *Double Stitch: Black Women Write About Mothers and Daughters* explain, the question of Black mother-daughter relationships beyond biology is the question of "this relationship between Black women over time" (Bell-Scott et al. xv). How indeed do Black women continue to exist over time, how do people continue to construct themselves *as* Black women over time? What is the intersubjective accountability, the story told and silenced that connects the experiences of Black women across generations? In 1981, scholar Gloria Joseph pointed out that the existing feminist psychoanalytic work on mother daughter relationships was insufficient to address the intersecting factors involved in Black mother daughter relationships and conducted a nationwide survey to address this gap (Joseph and Hall 9). However resources on the psychoanalytic elements of mother remain scarce and as Joseph points out in 1981, many people to this day (including my own mother, who is a clinician serving families, in particular Black mothers) turn to fiction or narrative film for depictions of mother daughter relationships (Joseph and Hall80). However, work that looks at the actual documentation of dreams by and about daughters by Black mothers seems to be missing from the discourse. Here we look at the content of Audre Lorde's daughter, Beth's, dreams, as documented by Lorde, and imagine the extent to which Lorde believed that the dreams of her daughter had meaning for her own work as a mother and as an educator. Let this be a start to work that must be taken on within the fields of psychology, psychoanalysis, literature and other fields where Black feminists think through intersubjectivity, intergenerational relationships and the power of waking and sleeping dreams.

Reading through Audre Lorde's journals labeled "1970s" it seems clear that conversations about dreams were normal in Lorde's Staten Island household. Second to her documentation of her own dreams, Lorde repeatedly writes down dreams her daughter tells her about and notable things that her children say during the day. Assuming that Lorde did not write down everything her children Beth and Jonathan said, or every dream Beth mentioned, but rather took time to write the dreams that seemed to have lessons for mother, daughter and maybe posterity, the dreams documented in Lorde's journals must represent issues, topics or frameworks that Lorde thought were important, possibly markers of something to bring into her own work of self-development, or to work on in her relationship with her daughter, her son and herself as a parent.

For example, in July 1976 Lorde documents one of her daughter's dreams: "Dream-Beth-problem shaped buses-you take the one shaped like your problem and you find the solution, then there was the miscellaneous problems bus which was a plain old greyhound" (Audre Lorde Papers, Journal 13). The details of the dream as documented here seem to demonstrate a perception that the dream held a clear message, or reveal some analysis of the dream before the documentation. It is an interpretive rather than descriptive statement to point out that a bus is shaped like a problem. The documentation of the dream does not describe any particular problem or any shape of bus but rather communicates that there is coherence between the problem and the bus, and that the journey on or through the bus will lead a person to the solution. The fact that the bus for miscellaneous problems is a "plain old greyhound" bus seems to suggest a two-part message for the dream. First, there is a bus out there shaped like whatever problem you may be having: i.e., a problem does have a path to resolution and a vehicle to get there. Second, a journey in general (metaphorical? Geographic? Long distance since it is a greyhound and not a local bus?) will have a resolving impact on your problems. What does it mean that a twelve-year-old child is dreaming at night about problems and how they might be solved? This cannot have been surprising for Lorde who points out again and again that children, especially Black children, and especially children being raised by an interracial lesbian couple, face oppression from an early age. Three years earlier, when Beth must have still been in elementary school Lorde documented a nightmare Beth shared with her about being chased by a "child-hater:"

> Beth's dream:
> The child hater was chasing me and there was a deep hole right behind me and I could not go any farther and I turned around and he pushed me over backwards into the hole But it was alright because I got out, and then I ate him up, except yuck! He tasted nasty.
> Why did you eat him?
> Because I was very angry at him!
> (Audre Lorde Papers, Journal 6)

Does Lorde write down this dream because it had a major impact on Beth? Because she is proud of her child's resilience in her dream to eat the nasty child-hater? Because she finds some message for her own healing in the dream? Maybe all of these things are true, but what remains is that Lorde documents the fact that her child, in her dreams, actively experiences being pushed into a deep hole, being physically and emotionally impacted by hate, and developing a way to fight back, even though it is nasty to her. Lorde documents her own questions to Beth about her actions in the dream and Beth rationalizes them. For Beth, anger is an appropriate response to hatred and hatred makes a person taste bad. Responses to hatred form an important core of Lorde's work in the feminist community. In both "Eye to Eye: Black Women Hatred and Anger" and "Uses of Anger: Women Responding to Racism," essays Lorde wrote in the early 1980's, she theorizes the distinction between hatred and anger, arguing that anger is an important form of insight and concluding in "Uses of Anger" that "Anger is an appropriate reaction to racist attitudes," while also pointing out in "Eye to Eye" that Black women live while "metabolizing hatred like daily bread," and that while eating poison might seem to be a way to make oneself immune it is disgusting (*Sister Outsider* 124-133). Clearly the issues in Beth's subconscious and the issues important to Lorde as a scholar and organizer are intertwined, but Beth emerges not only as a teacher and problem-solver in Lorde's journals, but also as a target of disappointment and rage. In her documentation of her own dreams she reveals her own subconscious actions of rage projected towards her daughter because of the violence and degradation of the systems of oppression that impact them both. In a 1976 diary, Lorde writes:

> Beth in a dream slammed down the trunk of the car carelessly and my best gloves dropped out in the gutter behind the car and a police horse came by and shat on them and here they were lying in the gutter, horse turds all mucked over them and I was lurid. I woke up screaming at her "what did you think you were doing?" (Audre Lorde Papers, Journal 13)

Lorde seems to have her own critique of this dream even as she documents it. She wakes up screaming at the Beth of the dream for being careless in relation to a negative experience that involves the police. In 1973, Audre Lorde was teaching composition to armed police officers at the John Jay School of Criminal Justice at CUNY. In the same year, Lorde was also traumatized by the fact that Thomas Shea, a white police officer who was a student at John Jay, murdered an unarmed eight-year old Black boy named

Clifford Glover. In her poems "Power," and "A Woman/Dirge for Wasted Children," she describes her nightmares following the murder of Clifford Glover, and the acquittal by a jury that consisted of eleven white men and one Black woman. The poems, and her journal entries around the time reveal that she felt implicated in this instance of the ongoing extreme police brutality against young men of color in New York, possibly especially strongly because the killer was a student at the university where she taught. I would argue that Lorde wrote down this dream, not only because she woke up screaming, but also because it reveals the misdirection of anger. In "Uses of Anger," Lorde describes several instances where she suppresses her rage at an oppressive force and then goes home to rage at her family over some small detail. She explains to the readers that suppressed anger, eventually harms those closest to us, and we have been trained to suppress anger against our oppressors and to take it out on those who we may have power over. Beth is the person that Lorde's character in the dream can demand accountability from, not the police officer. Her rage at Beth's carelessness may have been intensified because Beth lives in a world where police kill children; even in her dreams child-haters are chasing her down. Like many parents, Lorde's gut instinct, expressed in an extreme way in the dream, may be that as a child from oppressed communities, Beth cannot afford to be careless, or to be a child. Thus her inclusion in her journal of Beth's corrective: "If you want us to grow up and conquer the world, we have to live long enough to grow up," most likely expressed in response to anger, intense discipline or rage expressed by Lorde towards one or both of her children, is part of Lorde's self-critique.

Lorde writes extensively about her own mother's abusive practices and the ways her mother's internalized racism harmed Lorde's sense of self. Beth's nocturnal dreams, Lorde's nocturnal dreams about Beth and Beth's waking critique of Lorde's unconscious actions impact Lorde's theoretical, pedagogical and artistic imperatives. What are the poems she needs to write, methods of learning she needs to create, actions she needs to take and inspire so that her anger is useful for transforming the world that threatens her children, instead of operating as an uncontrolled danger that can harm her children? In this way, Lorde's analysis of her sleeping dreams impact her intentional dreams for what the world can be.

In Lorde's published work about her relationship with her daughter in "Eye to Eye: Black Women Hatred and Anger" she talks about her extreme anxiety at sending her daughter away from home. Three themes, journey, hate and blame, remain relevant in the context of academia, or what Lorde refers to as "the deathlands of the white labyrinth" (*Sister Outsider* 157). Lorde reflects while listening to her daughter cry about the oppression and marginalization she experiences from her professors at the university who "look at her as if she was a benign but unsightly tumor" (157). She recalls that "over the years I have recorded her dreams of death at their hands." And of course Beth's nightmares and lived experiences are not individual. They are traumatic for Lorde because they are the fulfillment and perpetuation of her own sleeping and waking nightmares as a participant in academia. She laments that as a mother she can only hope her daughter finds "less costly pathways" though the deadly labyrinth (157).

Lorde translates her documentation of her daughter's dreams into her published writing in reference to the repeating trauma of academic institutions. Lorde's own dreams and her experiences in academia make her daughter's dreams and their application to an academic context of survival central to her analysis. Therefore reading Lorde's own nightmares about academic space might provide us with some insight into her own "costly paths" and the resources she developed and passed on for survival.

DREAMS OF ACADEME

Chill winds swirl around these high blank places.
It is the time when the bearer of hard new
is destroyed for the message
when it is heard.
Blackstudies Part III (Lorde, *The Black Unicorn* 155)

Lorde's anxiety about her daughter's navigation of oppressive systems they both faced was a manifestation of the traumatic impact of interconnected forms of hatred, systems of police violence, ideological violence within progressive movements and the treacherous world of academia. All of these issues surface in dreams that Lorde documented in her journals and often wrote about in her poetry and speeches. In this section I will focus on two nightmares that take place in the context of academia in order to connect the labor of her teaching and scholarship with the labor of being a dreaming and dream attentive parent.

Audre Lorde's engagement in academia reached towards the fulfillment of conscious dreams of personal and collective advancement. After achieving her undergraduate degree at Hunter College and a graduate degree in library science at Columbia University, Lorde engaged the academy as an educator, theorist and artist. In one short journal entry on July 27, 1977, she explains her decision to engage the academy at the intimidating meta-level of the professional academic association: "I've decided to do the MLA thing, because I owe it to myself to feel able to take what I am fighting for—a voice and amplification enough to be heard to know I am not afraid to live the dreams I dream of" (Audre Lorde Papers, Journal 15, 1977). Lorde did engage the MLA in a way that allowed her to live the dreams she dreamt. She delivered her most famous essay on "be(ing) heard," "The Transformation of Silence into Action and Power" at a Modern Language Association Conference in 1977. She also wrote her groundbreaking biomythography *Zami* in response to hearing Barbara Smith, a fellow MLA member and activist intervening in the committee on the status of women in the profession wonder out loud at an MLA plenary about whether it was possible to be a Black Lesbian Writer and live to tell about it (*The Edge of Each Other's Battles: The Vision of Audre Lorde*).

However, in her everyday work in English Departments in different units of the City University of New York (including City College, Lehman College, John Jay College of Criminal Justice, and Hunter College) she dealt with administrators warning her not to be "too lesbian" (Coss), students with loaded weapons, denied grant proposals, refusal to grant medical leave and the everyday racism that accompanied her role as the first Black person in the English department at John Jay College of Criminal Justice struggling to validate and justify the very first women's studies courses on that campus. One dream reflects the casual disregard for her work of transforming the world through language and lack of autonomy that she experienced as an educator within a huge system with low accountability to Black feminist faculty: "I dreamt that my C(reative) writing class was cancelled and I had instead a class on the History of Peru. Suffer and Savage. I said to ********** But I know nothing of Peru! 'Well' she said 'then it will be a light class'" (Audre Lorde Papers, Journal 13).

Lorde's dream reflects her feelings of expendability within the context of a university system. She likened the university to a plantation structure in her speech at the Second Sex Conference at CUNY. Lorde notes in the speech that she was asked to speak late and in a tokenistic way due to the absence of other working-class women or women of color. She took the speech as an opportunity to chastise white feminists in academia for their racism, homophobia and classism and reminded them that their use of these forms of oppression, the master's tools, would never dismantle the master's house: the patriarchal structure of the university (*Sister Outsider* 110-113). The dream suggests that a woman in a higher position in the department than Lorde completely disregards Lorde's chosen vocation, disrespecting Lorde, the students and the topic of Peruvian history by randomly assigning her to teach a course outside of her expertise.

The proposed title for the course "Suffer and Savage" echoes Lorde's own critiques of structural racism through U.S. systems of discipline in education and law enforcement. In Lorde's syllabi for the John Jay incarnation of her course on "Race and the Urban Situation" (revised from a similar course she designed for teachers in training at Lehman College) she provides a provocative epigraph in all caps: "DEATH OR CIVILIZATION TO ALL AMERICAN SAVAGES," cited as an officer's toast from 1779 (Audre Lorde Papers, Box 17, Folder 60). Lorde's role in a university with a project of discipline and civilization, in a white supremacist genocidal manner, was in conflict with her own vision of a world in which the act of writing enabled people to transform their lives and communities. In her nightmares, Lorde was disturbed by the fact her labor in the university could be changed and mandated to fit the needs of social control at worst and unaccountable liberal multiculturalism at best.

Lorde's anxieties about the consequences of women within the academy destroying each other along lines of oppression with women of color, lesbian women and working class and low-income women bearing the brunt of the destruction were derived from her repeated experiences and transubstantiated in her dreams. In 1979, Lorde had a series of nightmares that took place in an institution where she had the pervasive feeling that she was going to be destroyed. Women gathered in a room to figure out how to sustain themselves, but a bee that was the agent of death landed on one woman and the other women started screaming and beating the woman. Lorde writes that she woke up screaming, but then fell back asleep and was still in the dream. The bee killed the woman for being truthful. She and Adrienne Rich went to a bathroom to grieve, but it was "nasty and filled with people" (Audre Lorde Papers, Journal 17).

This institution, which could represent an academic or community institution, brings to surface Lorde's fears about the power dynamics of institutional spaces in which people are punished for being truthful, and people with a common interest are put in a position to fight against each other by something that is in fact very small. A bee. This is before Lorde moves to St. Croix and becomes a beekeeper with her partner Gloria Joseph. But it is after she writes the poem "The Bees" where she critiques a masculinist violence spree against a hive of bees near a school, while young girls at the school wonder what it would have been like to study honey-making. For Lorde in waking life, a bee is not necessarily a violent threat to the well being of human beings, but in the dream, the women are helpless against the bee and are prevented from solidarity by its presence. It would seem that for Lorde one of the travesties of institutional oppression is that the solidarity and sustainability of the women is not bigger than the impulse for infighting that the institution encourages. The death of their agency comes from the perception of scarcity, fighting for slivers of autonomy in an under-resourced system with overcrowded dirty bathrooms that keeps them completely manipulated by fear. A month and a half before the nightmare Lorde wrote in her journal: "I am an anachronism a sport an oddity. Me and the bee. It was never meant to fly. The bee is dead. It has become Scientific

Instead of magic. I am not supposed to exist. But I do" (Audre Lorde Papers, Journal 17, 1979).

Lorde's nightmares about navigating institutions that use civilization as a force of genocide, where a woman can be killed for being truthful, emerge in her poetry and her essays through her theorization of survival. The alienation of intellectual and activist work within institutions is a nightmare where magic is replaced with science, and where she herself is an anomaly who was never meant to survive. As "Blackstudies" in particular emphasizes, Lorde understood her combined and not always delineated roles as teacher, scholar and mother as intergenerational roles and intending that her truthfulness impact the survival chances and strategies of her students, readers and children.

IV. TEACHING SURVIVAL

> before he could touch the palms of my hands
> to devour my children
> I learned his language
> I ate him
> *Blackstudies Part IV* (Lorde, *The Black Unicorn* 54)

Lorde's nightmares about academic space, her attention to her daughter's nightmares about hate and problems, and her orientation towards using her own dreams as a way to clarify and critique her waking parenting and teaching practices, alchemize into a set of survival dreams that move between the dark space of possibility and insight into the intentional space of visionary teaching, parenting and writing. In her journal, Lorde describes a dream, draws on an insight and then begins charting a poem that will amplify, deepen and share the insight with others. For example, after describing a dream in her journal where her partner and co-parent Frances cried, and another dream in which she could fly, she meditates on survival in what could be the first notes for her poem "A Litany for Survival":

> I have thought much about survival and how it is accomplished and trained for and how the very skills the children

need to survive are the ones giving us so much trouble now. And how we got to let them know how to use and not use them. Like what's necessary and what's not. (Audre Lorde Papers, Journal 15)

As a parent, Lorde realizes that the ways her children resist and challenge their parents' authority will be crucial skills for critiquing the forms of unaccountable power that are imposed on them in an oppressive society. Her challenge is to train her children how and when to use the skills they must develop, and this insight on what is and is not necessary is often gleaned from her dreams. The relationships between problems and solutions, the appropriate response to hate and the consequences thereof, the small deadly dynamics within institutions, what makes us cry, what enables us to fly.

In notes in her journal in 1978 for what would become "Manchild," Lorde's most famous essay on parenting, where she describes the challenges and contours of raising a son as a Black lesbian feminist, she writes: "My responsibility to my children women and men is to teach them how to survive, how to love, and how to let go" (Audre Lorde Papers, Journal 18).

Teaching survival in a context wherein as she repeats in her most cited poem "we were never meant to survive," is an ambitious task requiring intergenerational faith and the willingness to mobilize that which is messiest, most complicated and most revealing in our dream consciousness into material, maternal insight and direction in our waking lives. This process of catalyzing dreams as resources for expression and transformation is a key aspect of Lorde's work and a key lesson for those of us who are the dreamed of daughters inhabiting the academy now, those of us who dream that our modes of inquiry will not only make us better parents, but make a better world for our children and our students to shape.

This intersubjective accountability for a journey of transformation through learning and language is best depicted in one of Lorde's few published extended dream narratives. In *The Cancer Journals* Lorde describes this dream:

I dreamt I had been training to change my life, with a teacher who is very shadowy. I was not attending classes, but I was going to learn how to change my whole life, live differently, do everything in a new and different way. I didn't really understand, but I trusted this shadowy teacher. Another young woman who was there told me she was taking a course in "language crazure," the opposite of discrazure (the cracking and wearing away of rock). I thought it would be very exciting to study the formation and crack and composure of words, so I told my teacher I wanted to take that course. My teacher said okay, but it wasn't going to help me any because I had to learn something else, and I wouldn't get anything new from that class. I replied maybe not, but even though I knew all about rocks, for instance, I still liked studying their composition, and giving a name to the different ingredients of which they were made. It's very exciting to think of me being all the people in this dream. (14-15)

Here, Lorde is cracking rocks and taking classes, advising safety and reaching for something more. Advocating for herself against her own hesitation, suggesting something out of bounds that becomes an opportunity. The study of her own dreams and the transformation of dream truth into poetic inquiry is one of the major ways in which Audre Lorde was her own teacher and modeled the process of learning from the multiple consciousnesses of self. This work of being the teacher, being the classmate, challenging the teacher also reveals why Lorde was such a great teacher to others, inviting her students to draw on their waking and dreaming experiences for transformation.

Rose Partman (a student in a class that Audre Lorde taught as a visiting poet at the historically Black college Tougaloo in the 1960s, where she bravely came out as a lesbian to her students, encouraged their dreams and decided for herself that teaching would always be part of her life's work), reflects in a teaching evaluation that Lorde kept: "I think that something dynamic, something that had to be expressed something very profound and heart-stirring came out of our relationship with Miss Lorde. I will never forget her" (Audre Lorde Papers, Box 23, Folder 47).

There is something to our intentional dreams of unforgettable teaching impact, of resonant and effective parenting that is directly linked to our nightmares of oppression, and our repressed knowledge about what will harm us and what will save us. Following Lorde's example, the charting of our dreams, the attention to the dreams of our children and the encouragement of dream documentation among our students can become a resource for Black feminist transformation inside the institutions that would contain our insight and possibility.

V. TEACHING US QUESTIONS: (NOT A CONCLUSION)

"[O]h speak to us now mother for soon
we will not need you
only your memory
teaching us questions."
Blackstudies Part V (Lorde, *The Black Unicorn* 56)

This is only the beginning, a dream waking into life. This preliminary look at some of the sleeping and waking dreams of Black feminist scholar, mother, warrior-poet Audre Lorde is not nearly comprehensive. This is my attempt to make a dream collective, to ask that our dreams and nightmares, and the dreams of our predecessors and the dreams of our children become a tangible archive for our transformation and growth and a validated part of the mothering work of scholars of all backgrounds in the academic world. These are the questions we are being taught: What do you did you who did you how did you dream? And what do you think (it means)?

WORKS CITED

Bell-Scott, Patricia, Beverly Guy-Sheftall, Jaqueline Jones Royster, Janet Sims-Wood, Miriam DeCosta-Willis and Lucie Fultz, eds. *Double Stitch: Black Women Write About Mothers and Daughters*. Boston: Beacon Press, 1991. Print.
Bogus, Diane. "To My Mother's Vision." *Doublestitch: Black*

Women Write About Mothers and Daughters. Eds. Patricia Bell-Scott, Beverly Guy-Sheftall, Jaqueline Jones Royster, Janet Sims-Wood, Miriam DeCosta-Willis and Lucie Fultz. Boston: Beacon Press, 1991. 239-240. Print.

Brown, Elsa Barkley. "Mothers of Mind: How My Mother Taught Me to Be a Historian in Spite of My Academic Training." *Doublestitch: Black Women Write About Mothers and Daughters*. Eds. Patricia Bell-Scott, Beverly Guy-Sheftall, Jaqueline Jones Royster, Janet Sims-Wood, Miriam DeCosta-Willis, and Lucie Fultz. Boston: Beacon Press, 1991. 74-93. Print.

Collins, Patricia Hill. "The Meaning of Motherhood in Black Culture and Black Mother/Daughter Relationships." SAGE *Journal* 4.2 (1987): 7. Print.

Coss, Clare. "Sister Comrade Event." First Congregational Church, Oakland, CA. November 3, 2007.

Davies, Carole Boyce. "Mothering and Healing in Recent Black Women's Fiction." SAGE *Journal* 2.1 (1985): 41-43. Print.

De Veaux, Alexis. *Warrior Poet: A Biography of Audre Lorde*. New York: W. W. Norton, 2004. 178. Print.

Griffin, Farrah Jasmine. "That the Mothers May Soar and the Daughters May Know Their Names: A Retrospective of Black Feminist Literary Criticism." *Still Brave: The Evolution of Black Women's Studies*. Eds. Stanlie James, Frances Smith Foster, and Beverly Guy-Sheftall. New York: The Feminist Press, 2009. 336-360. Print.

Henderson, Mae Gwendolyn. "Speaking in Tongues: Dialogics, Dialectics, and the Black Woman Writer's Literary Tradition." *African American Literary Theory: A Reader*. Ed. Winston Napier. New York: New York University Press, 2000. 348-368. Print.

Jordan, June. "In Our Hands." *On Call: Political Essays*. Boston: South End Press, 1985. 145. Print.

Jordan, June. June Jordan Papers. N.d. Print.

Joseph, Gloria and Jill Hall. *Common Differences: Conflicts in Black and White Feminist Perspectives*. New York: Anchor Books/Doubleday, 1981. Print.

Lorde, Audre. Audre Lorde Papers. Spelman College, Atlanta, Georgia.

Lorde, Audre. *I Am You Sister: Collected and Unpublished Writings of Audre Lorde.* Eds; Rudolph Byrd, Johnetta Cole and Beverly Guy Sheftall. London: Oxford Press, 2009. Print.

Lorde, Audre. *New York City Head Shop and Museum.* Detroit: Broadside Press, 1968. Print.

Lorde, Audre. *Sister Outsider: Essays and Speeches.* Berkeley: Crossing Press, 1984. Print.

Lorde, Audre. *The Black Unicorn.* New York: W.W. Norton, 1978. Print.

Lorde, Audre. *The Cancer Journals.* San Francisco: Spinsters/Aunt Lute, 1980. Print.

Moten, Fred. *In the Break: The Aesthetics of the Black Radical Tradition.* Minneapolis: University of Minnesota Press, 2003. 18. Print.

Spillers, Hortense. "All the Things You Could Be By Now Sigumund Freud's Wife Was Your Mother: Race and Psychoanalysis." *African American Literary and Cultural Theory.* Ed. Winston Napier. New York: New York University Press, 2000. 582-596. Print.

Spillers, Hortense. "All the Things You Could Be By Now if Sigmund Freud's Wife Was Your Mother." *Black White and in Color: Essays on American Literature and Culture.* Chicago: University of Chicago Press, 2003. 376-427. Print.

Spillers, Hortense. "Mama's Baby, Papa's Maybe: An American Grammar Book." *Diacritics* 17.2 (1987): 65-81. Print.

The Edge of Each Other's Battles: The Vision of Audre Lorde. Dir. Jennifer Abod. New York: Women Make Movies, 2002.

Troester, Rosalie. "Turbulence and Tenderness: Mothers, Daughters, and 'Othermothers' in Paule Marshall's 'Brown Girl, Brownstones'." *SAGE Journal* 1.2 (1984): 13-16. Print.

Wright, Michelle. *Becoming Black: Creating Identity in the African Diaspora.* Durham: Duke University, 2004. Print.

12.
Fighting Phantoms

Mammy, Matriarch and Other Ghosts Haunting
Black Mothers in the Academy

YOLANDA COVINGTON-WARD

I HAVE BEEN A PARENT since my second year of graduate school, when I became the legal guardian of my younger sister. As the oldest of six siblings, and the first in my immediate family to go to college, I spent many nights during my first year of graduate school worrying about my family and what I could do to help from four hundred miles away at a large Research I university in the Midwest. The Bronx, New York, was not the best environment for my siblings, and the two sisters immediately following me in age had both dropped out of high school. My third sister, although just finishing elementary school, was already starting to falter. After doing some research on the public education system in the small city where I lived, and talking to my mother about it, we agreed that it would be in the best interest of the family if I took on the responsibility of raising and educating my third youngest sister. After filing the necessary paperwork, she came to live with me at the age of twelve during the summer of 2002. And there I was, at the tender age of twenty-two, the "othermother"[1] of a pre-teenager. Five years and a marriage later, yet another child entered my life in September of 2007, when I gave birth to my daughter, while simultaneously writing my dissertation.

For the vast majority of my academic career then, I have been a mother. While this has both its benefits and challenges for all mothers, there are some special ramifications for Black women in particular. Using performance theorist Marvin Carlson's concept of "ghosting," this essay examines a number of notorious stereotypes of Black mothers (Mammy, Matriarch, Superwoman, and Welfare Queen) and how they impact Black academic mothers, both inside and outside of collegiate settings.

BLACK MOTHERS IN THE ACADEMY

Black women who are faculty members in the academy have to deal with an interesting conundrum—they are almost invisible in terms of numbers, and yet highly visible as individuals in departments and university settings that are often majority White and male. As the introduction to this volume demonstrates, Black women lag considerably behind White women in attainment of doctoral degrees, and their numbers in the faculty ranks, especially at the Associate and Professor levels, are very small. Overall, there is a discrepancy between the numbers of Black women who earn doctorates and those who go on to earn tenure. There have been a number of studies of the problematic pipeline from graduate school to the tenure track for women in academia more generally (Simeone; Aguirre; Mason and Ekman). One of the major causes for this discrepancy that Mason and Ekman outline is motherhood and parenting, as many of these same female doctorate recipients are in their prime childbearing years. For those women who choose to remain in the academy, their roles as mothers impact their professional advancement in a number of different ways.

Mothering seems to be always out of place in the academy, and many academic mothers worry about their colleagues, administrators, and even students taking them less seriously if they know about or are reminded of their professors also being mothers. Pauline Leonard and Danusia Malina capture this sentiment well when they write:

> Being a woman in academic life is a predominately silent experience. The facts of this motherhood—the personal individual struggles, compromises and solutions to the daily problem of attempting to combine being a good mother and a competent, productive academic—are largely unvoiced at work. (30)

This silence about motherhood often occurs because one is unsure of people's attitudes or ideas about academic mothers. A personal example of this is when I interviewed for my current academic position, I kept the fact that I was a new mother to myself, as I didn't want any potential prejudices leveled against me. My two-month-old daughter was at home with my husband. I was breastfeeding however, and I had pumped some milk in the hotel before leaving for my interview. During the interview process (which lasted an entire day) I was shuttled from one office to another to meet various faculty members. As I conversed with people and moved throughout the department, my breasts slowly became engorged. I became physically uncomfortable and was worried about potential leakage on the front of my suit giving away my hidden motherhood. I was finally able to excuse myself, find an isolated bathroom, and hand-express the excess milk into the toilet. As I have gotten to know my departmental colleagues now, I am sure that being a mother would not have been considered a problem; however, as the primary breadwinner in my family at the time, I was not going to take any chances.

For all female faculty members who are also mothers, many of the same problems abound. Will I be seen as incompetent if I have to ask for maternity leave? How do I deal with a sick child when I have to teach in an hour? However, Black mothers in the academy live at the intersection of both race and sex. This intersectionality[2] can lead to particular interpretations of Black motherhood that are often colored by problematic stereotypes that affect the reception of Black mothers in the academy.

PERFORMANCE, GHOSTING, AND RACIAL STEREOTYPES

My personal story of trying to hide my motherhood during a job interview is one reaction to negative preconceived notions that others may hold about Black mothers. My actions during my job interview were a type of performance in which I responded to a larger imagined, collective memory in our society in which nefarious stereotypes of Black mothers abound. Performance as a concept is useful not only in interpreting my actions, but also as an analytic lens through which to examine ongoing processes of social life for Black mothers in the academy. While the idea of performance is most often associated with events that are framed as special and set-apart from everyday life, I use a broader conception of performance that seeks to capture events both on and off the stage. Erving Goffman, in his classic study and analysis of interactions in everyday life, defines performance as, "all activity of an individual which occurs during a period marked by his continuous presence before a particular set of observers and which has some influence on the observers" (22). Taking this definition of performance as a starting point, performances happen in everyday interactions.

One concept that emerges out of performance studies that is directly applicable to the daily performances of Black academic mothers is that of "ghosting." In his ground-breaking study, *The Haunted Stage: The Theatre as Memory Machine*, Marvin Carlson suggests that theatre acts as a repository of cultural and social memory, such that "the present experience is always ghosted by previous experiences and associations while these ghosts are simultaneously shifted and modified by the processes of recycling and recollection" (2). Carlson examines both the performance of theatre productions and their receptions by audiences in order to formulate the concept of ghosting:

> Unlike the reception operations of genre ... in which audience members encounter a new but distinctly different example of a type of artistic product they have encountered before, ghosting presents the identical thing they have encountered before, although now in a somewhat different context. Thus, a recognition not of similarity, as in genre, but of identity becomes a part of the reception process, with results that can complicate this process considerably. (7)

Here Carlson points to the impact of previous theatrical experiences and even ideas of specific characters on how individual audience members perceive and interpret new theatrical productions. Moreover, "ghosts" can also be seen in the individual bodies of actors themselves. The most obvious example is when the audience recognizes an actor from previously having played another role. "The recycled body of the actor, already a complex bearer of semiotic messages, will almost inevitably in a new role evoke the ghost or ghosts of previous roles ... a phenomenon that often colors and indeed may dominate the reception process" (Carlson 8). Such a process, by which actors are mis-recognized based on past roles that bleed into their present characters, can also apply in settings outside of theatre.

Theatre is clearly a type of performance, and extending Carlson's concept of ghosting leads me to ask, what types of "ghosts" do we encounter in the performances of everyday life? With this essay, I seek to apply Carlson's concept of ghosting to everyday settings, by looking at the impact of racial and gendered stereotypes (ghosts) of Black mothers on their experiences in the academy, especially through how others perceive and interact with them. An actor who previously performed only comedic roles who is seen intoning a solemn monologue from Shakespeare's *Macbeth* will likely not be taken seriously by an audience familiar with his previous characters. Snickers and giggles might be heard in the audience as people struggle to resolve the dissonance between past and present characters. They are thrown off by the physical body of the actor—it is the same face, the same voice, likely the same gait—and yet, they are told to believe that they are seeing a different character. Similar instances of mis-recognition can occur in everyday settings and lead to stereotypes. A Black mother who brings her child to class because of a child care emergency may be seen through a lens that colors her as an unfit parent or matriarch; another mother who struggles to juggle both family and work commitments may be praised as a strong Black woman while her mental and physical health silently deteriorate.

The Mammy, Matriarch, and Superwoman are three debilitating stereotypes that act as ghosts, hovering in the shadows of the halls of the academy as Black women walk by. In this essay I shall first explore these three ghosts and their particular apparition and application to Black mothers both historically and in the present. Then, using personal experiences and some published accounts, I will examine the presence of these ghosts in the academy and their relevance for Black mothers who are professors and graduate students. Then, I will examine another ghost outside of the academy (the Welfare Mother), and close with several suggestions for dealing with these apparitions.

STEREOTYPES OF BLACK MOTHERS: THE GHOST OF THE MAMMY

There are a number of historical stereotypes that have been applied to Black women specifically, dating back to the era of enslavement. The Jezebel, or oversexed, immoral female is one of these, and was often used to justify the sexual exploitation that enslaved women suffered at the hands of their White male owners. Another character that became quite popular post-Civil War in the memories and writings of former owners of enslaved women was the image of the Mammy. "She was a woman completely dedicated to the White family, especially to the children of that family. She was the house servant who was given complete charge of domestic management. She served also as a friend and advisor. She was, in short, surrogate mistress and mother" (White 49). The Mammy was typified by certain characteristics: she was loyal, deferent, obedient, asexual, warm, and nurturing (Collins, *Black Feminist* 71-72). Moreover, for former owners of enslaved women, she symbolized the ideal relationship between Whites and Blacks. "Created to justify the economic exploitation of house slaves and sustained to explain Black women's long-standing restriction to domestic service, the mammy image represents the normative yardstick used to evaluate all Black women's behavior" (Collins, *Black Feminist* 71). The Mammy is an image that emerged at the intersection of reality (Black women as domestic servants), Black women's everyday performances of a "public transcript" (Scott 2) in such positions, and the creative nostalgia of White southerners. Nevertheless, the Mammy is a ghost that haunts Black women in many different contexts, including the academy.

In academic settings, while there are no expectations that Black women dress in an apron with a handkerchief on their heads, there are many ways in which the behavior often associated with the Mammy may be extended to Black female faculty members who may or may not be mothers, through the expectations of both students and colleagues. The expectation that Black women be "warm and nurturing" is one that even extends to Black women executives in leadership positions (Collins, *Black Feminist* 71). In the academy, similar ideas exist. One of the ways in which this is evident is in the interactions between students and Black female professors. Wanda Hendricks recounts some of her personal experiences with students as a Black female historian in the academy:

> Students' general perceptions of Black women academics have further complicated my career. I have simply been overwhelmed by the number who considered me to be more of a psychologist than a scholar. Both Black and White students…have visited me during and after office hours to discuss personal issues rather than academic ones. (155)

This misperception of students can be directly linked to the ghost of the Mammy, as she is understood to be a friend, advisor, and surrogate mother. As a Black female faculty member, I have also had similar experiences. Students have talked to me about domestic and sexual violence, mental health issues, failed relationships, and other problems. In one discussion with Black male colleagues in the department, it became quite apparent that while students talked about a number of personal issues with myself and another female colleague, they rarely discussed such issues with the male faculty members in the department. The ghost of the Mammy can cloud the perception of not just students, but also colleagues, as Brenda Hoke mentions in her experiences at a majority White Women's Christian college (WCC):

> On a daily basis, the lives of African American women faculty members on the WCC campus are affected by the controlling mammy image. For instance, Black women faculty who are supportive of students (both Black and White) are described by their White colleagues as mothering, whereas these White colleagues describe their own supporting behavior as mentoring. (296)

Here, Hoke describes a labeling process that gives different value to the same types of behavior. In this situation, it is clearly "mothering" that is seen as not only less valued, but less appropriate for an academic setting. Another characteristic of the Mammy is that she is always placing herself at the disposal of those around her (Richards 41). This is also a component of the idea of "mothering." As a result, administrators, departments, and even student groups may call upon Black female faculty members for a number of different events/committees, while the same commitment is not expected of White colleagues (Menges and Exum 131). As Debra Harley states, "it is as if African American women faculty members are care providers for groups that are designated as special interest groups" (25), and these students include not only African Americans, but other students of color, women, low-income students of all races, and even sexual minority students as well. White colleagues are most often exempted from such activities (Banks 326-7).

While many Black female faculty members have experienced being associated with Mammy characteristics, there is the potential for the expectation of "mothering" of students to increase if you are very clearly a mother to a child. In order to combat this, especially in regard to students, I minimize the number of photos of my daughter in my office and only mention her on occasion, if at all, in the classroom. In this way, I hope to reduce the number of personal conversations, so that students can see me in a professional manner, and not necessarily as their surrogate mother. Rejecting the "mothering" role can also have consequences, as Black women academics who refuse to nurture can then be classified by their students as "mean," "unapproachable," "unfriendly," or as one of my own student teaching evaluations claimed, "intimidating."

Moreover, the ghost of the Mammy is clearly present in academia with the paradox that Black women professors are expected to nurture and care for our students as the Mammy was expected to offer affectionate care for her White charges (Wallace-Sanders 2), yet we are judged harshly for allowing the care of our own children to interfere with our jobs. Such problematic social expectations are connected to Carlson's concept of ghosting because a figure such as the Mammy is deeply embedded in our nation's social memory. As Carlson states, "all reception is deeply involved with memory, because it is memory that supplies the codes and strategies that shape reception ... the expectations an audience brings to a new reception experience are the residue of memory of previous such experiences" (5). Again, applying these ideas to everyday life contexts, these previous experiences do not have to be first hand—from the figures in popular films to the smiling face on pancake boxes, the ghost of the mammy is omnipresent and continues to affect student and faculty reception of Black women mothers in academia.

STEREOTYPES OF BLACK MOTHERS: THE GHOST OF THE MATRIARCH

The matriarch is yet another image that is often associated with Black mothers. In many of her characteristics, she is seen as the opposite of the Mammy:

> Just as the mammy represents the "good" Black mother, the matriarch symbolizes the "bad" Black mother. The modern Black matriarchy thesis contends that African-American women fail to fulfill their traditional "womanly" duties (Moynihan 1965). Spending too much time away from home, these working mothers ostensibly cannot properly supervise their children…. As overly aggressive, unfeminine women, Black matriarchs allegedly emasculate their lovers and husbands. (Collins, *Black Feminist* 73-74)

The Matriarch has some relation to yet another stereotype—the "Sapphire," a figure created by two White former minstrel actors and popularized by the Amos and Andy radio show from the late twenties to the mid twentieth century (Bennett and Morgan 489; Thomas, Witherspoon, and Speight 429). Sapphire was an aggressive, sharp-tongued and emasculating Black woman, having many of the same characteristics that Hill Collins associates with the matriarch figure. When considered as a mother, the Matriarch is not seen as nurturing. She is responsible for the failures of her children and for passing on negative values (Collins, *Black Feminist* 74).

A relevant attribute of Carlson's notion of ghosting is that people encounter the same actors in multiple theater productions, performing in new and different contexts. "…Even when an actor strives to vary his roles, he is...entrapped by the memories of his public, so that each new appearance requires a renegotiation with those memories" (9). The everyday performances of Black academic mothers are often tied to the ghost of the matriarch.

One particular instance comes to mind in my own experience as a graduate student at a large Research I university in the Midwest. I was teaching a summer course, and my eight-month-old daughter was attending a campus day-care facility. One morning, her center had to suddenly close due to some unexpected emergency. Because of the short notice, I was forced to bring her to my class (my husband and sister were in school and we had no family in the area). I taught the class as normally as possible, as she sat in her stroller. Occasionally, I held her to stop her from whimpering, as I didn't want her to distract the students, but for the most part she played quietly as I gave my lecture. At the end of the term, I was shocked when one student evaluation claimed that I "brought my baby to class all the time, and if I couldn't get a babysitter that was my problem, but the students shouldn't have to be subjected to it," among other things. While this was just one student, what surprised me (besides the obvious untruths) was the vitriol of the comments. While White mothers who bring a child into the classroom may also be criticized, the decision to bring a child to class by a Black mother may be further associated with irresponsibility and bad choices in ways that evoke the ghost of the matriarch. By claiming that I brought my child into the classroom frequently, the student seemed to imply that I was trying to shift the responsibility for taking care of my daughter to the students themselves. This parallels the characteristics of the Black matriarch as a bad mother—a "good mother" would, in fact, stay at home with her child or have made prior arrangements, regardless of the unexpected nature of the closing of the day-care center.

Shanti Parikh, who in 2010 became the first Black female to complete the tenure track at Washington University in St. Louis, has experienced similar situations when motherhood and academia clash. In an interview with the student newspaper, she had this to say: "'I probably don't spend enough time with my kids,' she confessed. Rushing into her office last Wednesday morning, Parikh described the chaos of having a sick baby at home. 'The doctor can't see him until tomorrow, but that's my long teaching day so I have to be here'" (Marcal 2010). While Parikh's situation is not unique, as it can happen for all academic mothers, her choice to teach rather than stay at home with her child can once again be interpreted by others as a sign that she is a bad mother and does not care for her child's well-being. If she were a White academic mother, her choice to teach with a sick baby at home would more likely be interpreted as an exceptional occurrence, whereas for Black academic mothers, it would more likely be seen as the rule, as their normative behavior. The ghost of the matriarch can once again appear as observers try to make sense of how Black academic mothers deal with their competing obligations.

STEREOTYPES OF BLACK MOTHERS: THE GHOST OF THE SUPERWOMAN

Yet another ghost that continues to haunt Black women in the academy is the apparition of the Superwoman, also known as the Strong Black Woman (SBW). Having its origins in the mythic physical strength of enslaved Black women working in the fields, this concept has evolved into an image of a woman who is both physically and emotionally strong, capable of surviving the most horrendous of circumstances. In the words of Michelle Wallace, she is "a woman of inordinate strength, with an ability for tolerating an unusual amount of misery and heavy, distasteful work. This woman does not have the same fears, weaknesses, and insecurities as other women, but believes herself to be and is, in fact, stronger emotionally than most men…. In other words, she is a superwoman" (107). The Superwoman/Strong Black Woman is able to juggle multiple feats simultaneously, and is heralded by some as the backbone of the Black community, a source of pride among all of the other negative stereotypes. However, at the same time, because the Superwoman often puts others first, her own needs suffer.

One author discusses her intentional act of "retiring" from being a Strong Black Woman, by rejecting the idea that: "…by the sole virtues of my race and gender I was supposed to be the consummate professional, handle any life crisis, be the dependable rock for every soul who needed me ... retirement was ultimately an act of salvation. Being an SBW was killing me slowly. Cutting off my air supply" (Morgan 87). In this excerpt, Joan Morgan points out one of the disturbing realities of the superwoman stereotype, which is that many Black women internalize it as an image that they must uphold or try to live up to. While on its face heralding the strength of Black women can be seen as positive, Black women who internalize this image can do so to the point that they do not seek help from others or take care of their own needs when it is most necessary. Tamara Beauboeuf-Lafontant's study, for example, shows that the Superwoman/Strong Black Woman image is a limiting construction that can lead to compulsive overeating, obesity, depression, and other debilitating issues for Black women who are overwhelmed with the many loads and responsibilities that they carry (Beauboeuf-Lafontant, "Keeping up Appearances").

There were quite a few moments in my own life when performing the role of the Superwoman began to threaten my own health and wellbeing. Upon taking my current academic position, my family relocated to Pittsburgh, and my sister returned to the Bronx after graduating from high school. However, because of the serious economic downturn, my husband had trouble finding a job in his field, although he sent out countless applications. I became the primary breadwinner (a role which I also held while we were both attending universities in the Midwest). To further complicate matters, my sister-in-law (who lives in another state) was gravely ill at the time, which led to many anxious phone calls and nights of fervent prayer. My family was also dealing with child-care issues. Because of the competition for spots in quality day-care programs in Pittsburgh, my daughter was on the waiting list at several centers, and a spot had finally opened up. As a result, my husband and I did not want to take a chance of taking her out of the daycare and losing her spot, especially when we did not know how soon he would find a job.[3] Times were very difficult for us, and my daily schedule was tedious as I commuted in highway traffic with my daughter to her day-care each morning, went to work, taught my classes, tried to write and research, commuted back home, and then had a number of other domestic obligations after work. My daughter, who has both serious food allergies and asthma, also became ill a number of times during our first semester in our new city. Each day as I worked in my office, I would hope the phone wouldn't ring with another emergency call from the daycare. Moreover, because of constant worry and other issues, I was only getting about five hours of sleep per night. I became worn down, and my relationship with my husband suffered. Physically, I lost over ten pounds. Yet, each day as I interacted with students and co-workers, I tried to pretend that everything was fine. One day, on yet another early morning commute, I noticed that my hands were shaking as I was driving. I decided right then that something had to be done and talked with my husband that evening. He began to step in and share some of the daily tasks that I had executed selflessly for months. It was not long after that that he was offered a job. The search had taken nine months.

While this is just my own personal experience, one of the lessons that it taught me was to be willing and able to ask for help. At the time, I thought that I should be able to handle all of the responsibilities that I was juggling—financial matters, child care, commuting, food shopping and preparation, doctor's appointments, helping with my husband's job search—not to mention all that was expected of me as a tenure-track faculty member. In addition, because I am the first person in my immediate family to go to college, I have a number of other obligations with my own family in the Bronx—financial and emotional support, advocating for my family against unscrupulous landlords, interpreting and explaining paperwork, creating resumes and helping with job searches, even helping with yearly taxes. The Strong Black Woman is a different kind of ghost, however, because there are expectations from your own family and community that you will do all of these other tasks that they need you to do. The burden became too much for me however, and my own body had to "tell" me that I could not accomplish everything all alone. In this case, the ghost of the superwoman is one that I willingly invited into my life, with no regard to the detrimental effects of trying to embody the woman who can "do it all."

In her book *Behind the Mask of the Strong Black Woman*, Tamara Beauboeuf-Lafontant points out that the Strong Black Woman is a "racialized construction of gender" based on normalizing struggle and responding with performances of strength, so that Black women keep up the appearance that they have everything under control (70-72). Relating this to Carlson, the ghost of the Strong Black Woman operates like theater productions in which actors have to live up to a memorable original performance where "...for a generation or more all productions are haunted by the memory of that interpretation, and all actors performing the role must contend with the cultural ghosts of the great originator" (66). In this case, the "originators" of the Strong Black Woman may be mothers or grandmothers, community leaders or civil rights activists, women whose own performances of strength became the model upon which we based our own actions in everyday life. Sadly, as my narrative clearly demonstrates, I had fully embraced and believed in my everyday performance of strength until my body rebelled against the lack of self-care and total neglect of my own well-being.

My experience is by no means unique. A single mother of three children who was also a student in a doctoral program, Lesa Covington Clarkson explains the numerous roles she has to play: "I am the sole bread winner, hand holder, nose wiper, tear dryer, homework helper, cookie baker, microwave-button-pushing-dinner maker. Succinctly, I am sufficiently challenged" (Covington Clarkson 161). Her challenges became even more overwhelming after she had physical complications after a very intensive first year as a doctoral student.

> ...by the time I finished the first year, I was exhausted. I felt like I had been running a race for months. In fact, my health had suffered from the experience. At the end of my first year of study, I had to have surgery on both feet.... My children took turns pushing me around in the wheelchair. They brought books to me, handed my crutches to me, and brought water to me. I was used to being the provider, protector, and transporter. Now I had to depend on everyone else. (165-166)

The numerous roles that she played in her family as a single mother, as well as being a doctoral student and teaching several classes each week, contributed to the decline of her physical health. Her story is also a warning to other Black women who mask themselves with the ghost of the superwoman, and then suffer the consequences when they take on too much.

OMNIPRESENT GHOSTS, FROM SUBWAYS TO SUPERMARKETS: THE WELFARE MOTHER

One of my primary motivations for writing this essay is to try and deal with the presence of these ghosts—the Mammy, the Matriarch, and the Superwoman in my own life, both inside and outside of the academy. One of the hardest lessons that I have come to learn is that, regardless of my hard-fought Ph.D. and other academic degrees, income, accomplishments, and intelligence, in the eyes of many in my everyday life encounters, I am just another Black woman with a child whose real image and identity is hidden behind the many ghosts of stereotypes past and present. The first example of this occurred when I was visiting my family in New York City. I was about eight months pregnant with my daughter and was in the subway station at Times Square, purchasing a bus ticket. Out of breath, hot, and weary as I walked slowly to my train, a random White man stopped in front of me and said "Congratulations" gesturing toward my belly. Before I could get out a response, he continued, "I hope the father is in the picture." Then, he quickly stalked off. Catching my breath, I said, "I'm married," but he was gone and there was no one there to hear me. I looked down at the obvious wedding ring on my finger, and stood there, reeling from the unexpected verbal attack, the few words that placed me into the category of the Matriarch, and more specifically, the Unwed Mother, likely on welfare, bringing yet another child into the world. The Welfare Mother is another negative stereotype, emerging post-World War II and explicitly connecting ideas about Black women's fertility to state assistance programs. "Typically portrayed as an unwed mother, she violates one cardinal tenet of Eurocentric masculinist thought: she is a woman alone" (Collins, *Black Feminist Thought* 77). By implying that I was alone, unmarried, and having children, this random man tried to connect my pregnant body with the ghost of the Welfare Mother. I will never know what his intentions were with his comment, but for that moment, that few seconds of "misrecognition," I was masked by this ghost, with all of the negativity and shame that comes with it.

Yet another incident demonstrates the constant presence of these ghosts in Black women's everyday lives. I was at the supermarket with my daughter, who was three years old at the time. I was in the check-out line, and my daughter saw a balloon of her favorite Disney character, Princess Tiana. She asked me to buy it for her, and began to whine when I refused. This is a common scenario for many parents, and I clenched my teeth in frustration as I tried to watch the screen to make sure that my order was tallied properly while simultaneously giving her the "eye" to make her quiet down. After handing the cashier my few coupons, I waited for the final tally and began to reach for my wallet. "That's $53.62 ... or $51.62 with food stamps." Stunned, I looked at him, and said, "I don't have food stamps" and he pressed the debit key. By this point, my daughter is openly crying and people are starting to look at us. I was upset, thinking about what I should have said as I walked away with my cart. I know he hadn't mentioned anything about food stamps to the White woman in front of me, who had a stack of coupons. I have been shopping at this supermarket for two years, and this is the first time someone had said something like that to me. However, I rarely take my daughter with me shopping. Was it her presence that evoked the ghost of the "welfare queen/unwed mother on food stamps?" Or was it just the ignorance of this cashier, a young White man who looked to be under twenty, who might have said the same thing whether I was with a child or not? What is clear is that these everyday indignities, these slights of hand that may seem trivial to casual observers, serve to reinforce the sense of marginalization that people of African descent continue to feel nearly one hundred and fifty years after the end of slavery.

CONCLUSION

In this essay, I sought to delineate the pernicious ghosts of Black mothers in the academy in the forms of: the Mammy, the Matriarch, the Superwoman, and the Welfare Mother by grounding these images in the lived experiences of Black women. However, there are also many wonderful things about being a mother in the academy; having the responsibility of providing for children will often make you more motivated to succeed. In the words of the great educator Mary McLeod Bethune who established her own historically Black college, "having a child made me more than ever determined to build better lives for my people..." (Bethune 137). Similarly, KaaVonia Hinton-Johnson writes the following, "My son serves as a powerful motivational force for me...his mere presence reminds me daily that I must be persistent in my effort to obtain a terminal degree" (Hinton-Johnson 164). Likewise, both my sister and my daughter were great motivators for me as well. Nevertheless, my everyday experiences as a Black mother have been impacted by negative stereotypes of Black mothers more generally.

In order to deal with this recurring problem, I have three suggestions for other Black academic mothers: 1) Self-definition: Allow who you are as an individual to center and ground you, rather than letting other people's misperceptions define you. Defining who you are on your own terms is a critical part of reaching your full potential in a society in which you are often marginalized, maligned, and looked down upon. 2) Battle wisely: Take proactive steps to combat these ghosts when necessary, but do not allow the battle against these ghosts to consume your life. You have to make informed choices about which battles to fight and which are not worth your time or effort. 3) Know the history: Recognize the historical trajectories and pathologies of these apparitions, and do not internalize them as real. By remaining informed about the histories of these ghosts, you can immediately recognize their appearance, assess the larger socio-political moments when they tend to reappear, and thus educate others on their use in the larger oppression of Black women. These ghosts of Black mothers have been around for decades, and you cannot ignore their existence. However, you cannot allow them to define your identity or your destiny.

While these are three general suggestions that are relevant to everyday life in multiple contexts, I also have some ideas for alleviating problems in terms of the reception of Black mothers in the academy in particular. Effective mentorship by senior colleagues can help Black academic mothers judiciously avoid or deal with additional pressures and competing commitments for their time. Producing and sharing scholarship about these stereotypes—in workshops, academic courses, and general discussions—can help to increase awareness about their negative impacts. Moreover, Black academic mothers must learn to ask for help—from their loved ones and colleagues alike.[4] In closing, these ghosts of Black mothers may never be completely exorcised. But much can be done so that Black mothers are seen in a different way: as individuals with hopes and dreams, fears and anxieties, like everyone else.

NOTES

[1]An othermother is defined as "those who assist blood mothers in the responsibilities of child care for short-to long term periods, in informal or formal arrangements. They can be, but are not confined to, such blood relatives as grandmothers, sisters, aunts, cousins, or supportive fictive kin" (James 45).

[2]I follow Deborah King's idea of multiple jeopardy in recognizing that race and sex can be multiplied by other positions in society, such as class and sexual orientation, in affecting the life chances and outcomes of Black women in comparison to other groups (King 1988).

[3]Currently, our daughter is now enrolled in our university's day care center—it was three and a half years before a spot opened up for her.

[4]In writing this chapter, I have benefitted from the help of several people. I would like to thank Grace Okrah for her encouragement and feedback. I would also like to thank the Department of Africana Studies and my student research assistant, Shannon Finley, for her excellent research efforts.

WORKS CITED

Aguirre, Adalberto Jr. *Women and Minority Faculty in the Academic Workplace: Recruitment, Retention and Academic Culture.* San Francisco: Jossey-Bass, 2000. Print.

Banks, William. "Afro-American Scholars in the University: Roles and Conflicts." *American Behavioral Scientist* 27.3 (1984):325-338. Print.

Beauboeuf-Lafontant, Tamara. *Behind the Mask of the Strong Black Woman*. Philadelphia: Temple University Press, 2009. Print.

Beauboeuf-Lafontant, Tamara. "Keeping Up Appearances, Getting Fed Up: The Embodiment of Strength among African American Women." *Meridians: Feminism, Race, Transnationalism* 5.2 (2005): 104-123. Print.

Bennett, Dionne and Marcyliena Morgan. "Getting Off of Black Women's Backs." *Du Bois Review* 3.2 (2006): 485-502. Print.

Bethune, Mary McLeod. "A College on a Garbage Dump." *Black Women in White America: A Documentary History*. Ed. Gerda Lerner. New York: Random House, 1972. 134-142. Print.

Carlson, Marvin. *The Haunted Stage: The Theatre as Memory Machine*. Ann Arbor: University of Michigan Press, 2001. Print.

Collins, Patricia Hill. *Black Feminist Thought*. London: Harper Collins Academic, 1990. Print.

Collins, Patricia Hill. "The Meaning of Motherhood in Black Culture and Black Mother-Daughter Relationships." *Double Stitch*. Eds. Patricia Bell-Scott, Beverly Guy-Sheftall, Jacqueline Jones Royster, Janet Sims-Wood, Miriam DeCosta-Willis and Lucille P. Fultz. New York: Harper Perennial, 1991. 42-57. Print.

Covington Clarkson, Lesa Marie. "Sufficiently Challenged: A Family's Pursuit of a Ph.D." *Sisters of the Academy: Emergent Black Women Scholars in Higher Education*. Eds. Reitumetse Obakeng, and Anna L. Green Mabokela. Sterling, VA: Stylus Publishing, 2001. 160-173. Print.

Gillespie, Marcia A. "The Myth of the Strong Black Woman." *Feminist Frameworks: Alternative Theoretical Accounts of the Relations between Men and Women*. Eds. Allison M. and Paula S. Rothenberg Jaggar. New York: McGraw-Hill Book Company, 1984. 32-36. Print.

Goffman, Erving. *The Presentation of Self in Everyday Life*. New York: Anchor Books, 1959. Print.

Harley, Debra. "Maids of Academe: African American Women Faculty at Predominately White Institutions." *Journal of African American Studies* 12.1 (2008):19-36. Print.

Hendricks, Wanda A. "On the Margins: Creating a Space and

Place in the Academy." *Telling Histories*. Ed. Deborah Gray White. Chapel Hill: University of North Carolina Press, 2008. 146-157. Print.

Hinton-Johnson, KaaVonia. "Choosing my Best things: Black Motherhood and Academia." *From Oppression to Grace: Women of Color and Their Dilemmas in the Academy*. Eds. Theodora R. and Nathalie Mizelle Berry. Sterling, VA: Stylus, 2006. 155-167. Print.

Hoke, Brenda. "Women's Colleges: The Intersection of Race, Class, and Gender." *Black Women in the Academy: Promises and Perils*. Ed. Lois Benjamin. Gainesville: University Press of Florida, 1997. 291-301. Print.

James, Stanlie M. "Mothering: A possible Black feminist link to social transformation." *Theorizing Black Feminisms: The Visionary Pragmatism of Black Women*. Eds. Stanlie M. James and Abena P.A. Busia. London: Routledge, 1993. 44-52. Print.

King, Deborah. "Multiple Jeopardy, Multiple Consciousness: The Context of a Black Feminist Ideology." *Signs* 14.1 (1988):42-72. Print.

Leonard, Pauline and Danusia Malina. "Caught Between Two Worlds: Mothers as Academics." *Changing the Subject*. Eds. Cathy Lubelska, Jocey Quinn and Sue Davies. Bristol: Taylor & Francis Publishers, 1994. 29-41. Print.

Marcal, Kate. "Tenured professor overcomes obstacles of race and gender." *Student Life* 22 September 2010. Web. 20 July 2011.

Mason, Mary Ann and Eve Mason Ekman. *Mothers on the Fast Track: How a New Generation can Balance Family and Careers*. Oxford: Oxford University Press, 2007. Print.

Menges, Robert and William Exum. "Barriers to the Progress of Women and Minority Faculty." *The Journal of Higher Education* 54.2 (1983):123-144. Print.

Morgan, Joan. *When Chicken-Heads Come Home to Roost*. New York: Touchstone, 1999. Print.

National Center for Education Statistics. *Digest of Education Statistics*. Web. 9 September 2011.

Richards, Hilda. "Reflections of a 'Mother Confessor': African American Women's Roles and Power Relationships in Historically White Institutions." *Coloring the Halls of Ivy*. Ed. Josephine D.

Davis. Bolton: Anker Publishing Company, Inc., 1994. 38-44. Print.

Scott, James. *Domination and the Arts of Resistance*. New Haven: Yale University Press, 1990. Print.

Simeone, Angela. *Academic Women: Working Towards Equality*. South Hadley: Bergin & Garvey Publishers, Inc, 1987. Print.

Thomas, Anita, Karen Witherspoon, and Suzette Speight. "Toward the Development of the Stereotypic Roles for Black Women Scale." *The Journal of Black Psychology* 30.3 (2004): 426-442. Print.

Wallace, Michelle. *Black Macho and the Myth of the Superwoman*. New York: Verso, 1990. Print.

Wallace-Sanders, Kimberly. *Mammy: A Century of Race, Gender, and Southern Memory*. Ann Arbor: University of Michigan Press, 2008. Print.

White, Deborah Gray. *Ar'n't I a Woman?* New York: W. W. Norton & Company, 1985. Print.

13.
Mothering and Mentoring

Relational Dynamics Among Black Women in the Academy

KAREN T. CRADDOCK

SOCIALLY CONSTRUCTED DISCOURSES, beliefs and practices about race, gender, class and power negatively impact Black women and has been documented by many scholars (Cole and Stewart 136; Collins, *Black Feminist Thought* 555; Lawson 22). The marginalization of Black women within society reflects their membership in groups that are perceived as having less worth and being lower in status; this has an impact on their identity formation and opportunities for professional and personal advancement. Research documents the power of Black mother-daughter relationship as central to the way that Black women mediate and form identity in the midst of hegemonic forces that attempt to define them as subordinate. Awareness of this phenomenon, of course, does not dismiss or disregard the powerful importance of role of fathers or male influences, nor does it lock women into rigid assumptions of motherwork as an element assigned gender role. As many scholars note, mother figures play central roles in daughters' lives and especially in their understanding of intersecting identities of race and gender in a society where the identities of non-Whites and non-males are socially constructed as inferior (Bynum and Kotchick 530; Collins "Meaning of Motherhood"; Ceballo and Olsen 108; Wade-Gayles 9). In addition, writers have discussed models of relationship-based mentoring and interventions and have associated them with useful strategies of support and parenting within marginalized communities (Pinderhughes, Craddock, and Fermin 191).

Based on this salient framework of mothering and Black women, an analogy to the mentoring relationship between and among Black women is worthy of exploration. Especially within the academic context, the mothering/mentoring framework is an appropriate area to investigate relational dynamics, as Black female scholars often face marginalizing circumstances attached to their race and gender. Excavating patterns of relational dynamics among Black women in the academy offer opportunities to examine links to other relational theories that point to dynamics of race, gender and power such as Relational Cultural Theory (RCT) (Walker "How Relationships" 4). Key tenets of the RCT theoretical construct include engaging in authentic, growth-fostering relationships that are mutually empowering and take into consideration the socio-cultural context of the relationship (Comstock, Hammer, Strentzsch, Cannon, Parsons and Salazar 280). Such considerations of the role of relational dynamics in context further emphasize a relevant link between frames of mentorship and motherhood for Black women in higher education.

BLACK WOMEN IN THE ACADEMY AND MENTORSHIP

Catherine Hansman suggests that there is a powerful role that mentoring plays for women as they develop their careers (63). Researchers have specifically noted the importance and challenges of mentoring for women in academia, with particular attention to women of color. Christy Chandler reports the strikingly low rates at which women of color are recruited into, and advance in, higher education; these are glaringly evident in the fields of math, science and engineering. She points to the cyclical loop by which increasing the numbers of women of color faculty leads to higher rates of women of color completing doctoral programs (84-85). Often in isolating or hostile climates, female graduate students of color seek role models, mentors and a network of faculty and administrators of color in order to survive (Morgan 22; Reid and Wilson 100; Wheeler 96). Additionally, experimental researchers have delved into more nuanced challenges for women and minorities in academia by exploring faculty responses to doctoral students' request to meet. They found that Caucasian males received more and faster responses compared to women and doctoral students of color (Milkman, Akinola and Chugh 711).

In the aforementioned study, results showed that decisions about investing time to meet with students in the distant future activated more discrimination against women and minorities triggered by an increased reliance on stereotypes that privilege males and Whites (Milkman et al. 713, 716). Thus, the continuous process of attracting, fostering, and supporting the careers and needs of women of color in the academy, especially through mentorship, is necessary as a central vehicle for their recruitment, retention, and renewal.

For Black women faculty, the stress associated with multiple layers of life as an academic, added to the isolation, vague tenure and promotion requirements, and high service commitments, also creates a great need for mentorship (Holmes et al. 109). As stated in the volume's "Introduction," key data affirms the challenges described here: according to a 2009 data set, 7 percent of U.S. college faculty were Black women compared to 75.5 percent white women ("Racial Breakdown").[1] Disproportionately high numbers of Black women hold joint or part-time appointments; meanwhile, they reach lower academic ranks, and are less likely to be tenured. Black women in the academy are often required to engage in specific service to represent and support diversity, but such tasks also bring costs. Tokenism can be a precursor of work overload, leaving less time for vital research (Evans and Cokley 54). The lower representation of Black women in higher education institutions has also been attributed to a "pipeline" problem. For example, Gina Evans and Kevin Cokely found that there was a direct connection between successful Black female mentors and development of a "pipeline" for future Black female academics (50).

Specifically then, Black women in academia play a critical role through the mentoring of other Black women which has an individual impact on the professional development and career trajectory of Black female scholars, as well as an overall institutional impact on the numbers of Black women in higher education as indicated in the literature. The aforementioned research highlights specific areas of mentorship, but also focuses on the level of involvement and relational dynamics as critical components of success in academia.

BLACK WOMEN AND THE MOTHERING RELATIONSHIP

Parallel to the ideas above, two areas of the mother-daughter relationship provide particular insights into the mentoring relationship between Black women in junior and senior positions. The *levels of involvement* from the senior colleague (mother) to the junior colleague (daughter) and the *relational dynamics* between them are platforms that offer insights into such relationships in both the mothering and mentoring contexts.

Nancy Apfel and Victoria Seitz offered a conceptual model for mother-daughter relationships among Black adolescent mothers and their mothers. The researchers assessed the mothers' degree and mode of involvement in their caregiving of their grandchildren and to elaborate on the roles these women play in "their adolescent daughters' transition into parenthood" (Apfel and Seitz 422). Their research provides a broader understanding of the mother-daughter dyad in this context of exploring the mothers' level of involvement in their daughters' parenting practices. They found specific "adaptational approaches" among the pairs that were anchored in the mothers' level of involvement emerging from her own mothering practices and beliefs.

A later study (Craddock, *Mother to Mother*) built on this model of adaptive approaches using three lenses to examine qualitative case data to uncover the involvement of Black mothers in the lives of their parenting daughters. The lenses used were: (a) the caregiving practices of both the mother and the daughter; (b) approach belief statements, orientations, or actions of both daughter and mother; and (c) relational dynamics of the dyad that describe levels of intimacy (warmth, comfort, tension), autonomy (independence, dependence) and proximity (close, distant) captured in the interviews with daughters. Collectively these features formed the Model of Mother Involvement (MMI) by exploring caregiving practices, beliefs about how to approach parenting, and relational dynamics in the lives of the young Black mothers and their mothers (Craddock, *Mother to Mother* 38-39).

Following the qualitative methods of ethnographic data collection and analytic techniques (Miles and Huberman), a sample of ten African-American mothers was interviewed over a period of two-and-a-half years. Six to ten meetings occurred in the home or community of the mother who had elected to participate in an ethnographic sub-study of a larger home-visiting program evaluation. Interviews ranged from one to four hours in length. Each visit included in-depth observations, field notes and assessments to document mother-child/family interactions, home environment and activities. Informal conversation, naturalistic observation and semi-structured interviews to capture dimensions of parenting, help-seeking, family and program perspectives were also implemented, along with other protocols pertinent to the larger study regarding program perceptions and race/gender socialization (Craddock, *Mother to Mother* 41-49).

To define the models of mother involvement, the relationships between the three elements of *practice*, *belief*, and *role relationship* were considered. From the data analysis four models were developed:

(1) *Instrumental*. In this model, what prevails is practical activity and a provisional outlook on involvement with the parenting teen; this represents the stewardship role that the mother takes on in her daughter's life. The mother provides general support and some guidance; the core belief is that the daughter is the primary caregiver and does most of the caregiving.

(2) *Complementary*. In this model, what are most evident are a daily functional practice and a shared approach to parenting; the mother takes on a partnership role with her daughter in raising the child. The core belief is that the mother and daughter are equal in a co-parenting role, sharing in the caregiving practices.

(3) *Surrogate*. In this model the mother is totally involved in the practices of caring for the child; the mother believes that she is the primary caregiver. The mother is seen as taking more of an ownership role as head of household and ultimately parent to both the daughter and her child. The caregiving practices vary somewhat, but the mother is still the lead.

(4) *Instructive*. In this model a teaching practice represents a developmental belief about becoming a parent: the mother is engaged in a mentorship role with her now parenting daughter. The core belief is that the daughter is learning to become a mother under the instruction of her own mother. Caregiving practices vary, with

the daughter conducting most of them under some supervision.

EXPLORING MENTORING THROUGH THE MOTHERING LENS

Using the framework above to further examine these ideas of models of involvement and relational dynamics, a pilot qualitative case study (Craddock, *Mother-Mentor*) explored Black women's mentoring relationships in academia. An initial sample of ten Black women academics representing a range of higher education experience across the United States of America (i.e. research universities, teaching colleges, single sex institutions) were interviewed about their relationships with other Black women in senior positions while they were graduate students or junior faculty. Using interview protocols adapted from the Craddock (*Mother to Mother*) study, these women were interviewed for 2-4 hour blocks and asked to (a) reflect on the mentoring practices they experienced; (b) share specific messages they received from their senior colleague about issues related to race and gender marginalization as a Black female academic; and (c) to rate their relationship, in accordance with the aforementioned mother-daughter relational dynamic framework on *proximity* (distant, median, close), *intimacy* (tense, neutral, warm) and *autonomy* (independent, consultant, dependent). Qualitative case study methodologies (Miles and Huberman; Mishler; Riessman) were used to collect and analyze interview data. Narrative data was clustered into themes and used the MMI as an analytical tool and guiding construct.

Five models of mentorship emerged analogous to the MMI

(1) Instrumental mentoring. Practical activity and a provisional outlook on involvement prevail in this model. The junior member takes on the primary lead role in their academic program or career activity while the senior member takes on varying levels of very basic instrumental support.

(2) Instructive mentoring. Teaching practice represents the developmental approach used in this model. The senior member is engaged in a mentorship role with the junior member, offering purposeful guidance. Based on some level of consonance between junior and senior, the junior actively looks to and receives mento-

ring instruction and advice from the senior as the major lead for teaching and the junior is expected to carry it out.

(3) *Complementary mentoring.* Regular functional practice and a shared approach to the relationship and associated job related tasks are most evident in this model. The senior takes on a partnership role with the junior. The core belief is that the junior and senior are viewed as peers/colleagues. The senior does not take on a hierarchal role and she views her relationship with her junior colleague as complementary.

(4) *Surrogate mentoring.* In this model the senior colleague is involved in every area of the junior colleagues' tasks and professional development. The senior colleague fully identifies with the junior's struggles and virtually takes on, or fully vests herself in, the primary role in carrying out tasks or providing a lead role in the junior's academic career path.

(5) *No-involvement mentoring.* In this model the relationship is not substantive. The senior is not truly involved and she may be distant from or dismissive of the junior.

CASE BRIEFS: EMERGENT MENTOR/MOTHER DYADIC THEMES AMONG BLACK WOMEN IN THE ACADEMY

A sub-sample of five of the pilot interviews were captured as case briefs for further interrogation and to more fully understand the overall model of mentor/mother involvement in the scenarios that the participants described. The following participant information offers a few key points about the junior colleagues academic placement and personal background at the time of their narrative reflections. This information provides additional grounding data useful for future research questions (participant numbering coincides with cases):

Participant 1 reported on her experience as a new faculty member in a rural college setting. She was part of a recruitment effort to attract more faculty of color to the school.

Participant 2 reported on her experience as an advanced doctoral student in an urban university. She was one of a few African-American women who advanced from the Masters program into the Ph.D. program and had not withdrawn.

Participant 3 reported on her experience as a new faculty member in an urban southern U.S. university. She had been a member of a national fellows program for doctoral students of color.

Participant 4 reported on her experience as a new science faculty member at a small women's college. She was concerned about how she would be perceived and treated as a Black female scientist.

Participant 5 reported on her experience as new faculty member in a large university setting. She was particularly enthused about joining a faculty where there was highly celebrated and recognized senior faculty.

Case Summaries

Brief case overviews capture key elements of the senior and junior colleagues' relationship and the emerging mother/mentor model:

Participant Case 1. In this case, only two women of color were teaching in the department. The senior colleague took no overt interest in the junior colleague and she neither articulated nor demonstrated any support. (*No involvement*)

Participant Case 2. This case reflected a very involved faculty member (senior colleague) with a doctoral student (junior colleague). The faculty member actively engaged in a "maternal" stance, gave clear direct messages regarding marginalization in the university, and encouraged the student to combat them directly. The faculty member often stepped in to fight those battles for the student. (*Surrogate*)

Participant Case 3. This case revealed an engaging mentorship where the senior faculty member exhibited a clear understanding of her role as mentor. The senior colleague guided and advised the junior faculty member who was expected to—and did—behave as an agent for herself while receiving detailed support from senior. (*Instructive*)

Participant Case 4. In this case, the senior faculty member took on a basic mentorship role, based in pleasant personal exchanges and being available for basic information on department protocols. The junior raised questions about marginalization but the senior colleague did not focus on these issues as they arose; instead she suggested that it would be best for the junior colleague to focus energy on her own professional development and research. (*Instrumental*)

Participant Case 5. In this case, the senior colleague was involved

Table 1: Mother Mentor Case Overview

Case	Model of Mother/Mentor Involvement	Relational Dynamics: Proximity, Intimacy, Autonomy	Messages of Marginalization
1	No Involvement	Distant Tense Independent	No mention of marginalization as a career issue.
2	Surrogate	Close Warm Dependent	It is prevalent and you must be assertive in combating it.
3	Instructive	Median Warm Consultant	It can be covert and complex and you must be informed and strategic in dealing with it.
4	Instrumental	Median Warm Independent	It may happen but do not focus on it. Focus your energy on your own development.
5	Complementary	Close Warm Independent	It all depends. Just see what happens and I am here to listen if you want.

The above table provides an overview of the Model of Involvement, Relational Dynamics and Messages of Marginalization conveyed by the junior colleagues regarding their relationships with their senior colleagues.

with and responsive to the junior colleague, providing collegial support concerning her provisional needs as the junior colleague encountered and identified them. The aim of the senior colleague was to be supportive and encourage as needed, but not in an overly involved manner. (*Complementary*)

As seen in Table 1, these selected cases from a sub-sample reveal the range and multiple layers of level of involvement, along with the underlying relational dynamics and messages about marginalization that emerge in senior/junior relationships among Black women in the academy. Case 1 exemplifies an isolating and competitive climate in which the Black senior faculty member showed self-protective and competitive behavior toward the junior, so the case was categorized as *No Involvement*. This is in stark contrast to the mother/mentor model in Case 2 where the senior faculty member actively positions herself to protect and to develop the junior as a *Surrogate*. Surely the junior colleague's status as doctoral student lends itself to this more overtly maternalized approach, but other faculty-student relationships in the larger study (not reported here) reveal other mother/mentor models including *No-Involvement* and *Instrumental*. Case 5 provides yet another model in which the senior minimizes her hierarchical status and seeks a shared partnership with the junior in the *Complementary* mother/mentor model.

When the junior members interviewed for this study reflected on their relationships and their future outcomes, those in Case 3 (*Instructive*) and Case 5 (*Complementary*) found them to be the most adaptive professionally and the most satisfying personally. In Case 3, the junior colleague described appreciating the clarity with which her mentor understood the dynamics of their institution, engaged in strategic brainstorming with her, and then allowed her to implement a plan herself while also being available for ongoing guidance. She described acquiring skills that have been helpful in her career and also provided a "road map" about the kind of mentor she hopes to become herself. In Case 5, the junior faculty member appreciated the deep friendship that emerged from this partnership approach: the senior did not assume leadership or impose her thoughts or ideas onto the junior colleague. She explained that she was eventually able to define her own path in the institution and to cultivate a deep and trusted friendship with someone who may have otherwise felt too intimidating.

Although these two models of mentorship appear to offer the most adaptive and sustainable approaches among those in this study, it is important to remember that each approach is embedded in sociopolitical context. Thus one approach may be more appropriate or the only one possible given the institutional context and climate. This is most evident in Case 2: the senior faculty member took a firm and involved approach with the doctoral student, an approach driven by a particularly hostile environment. In this case, the doctoral student said she might not have made it through the program had it not been for this mentoring approach. She also reports that it left her somewhat cynical and perhaps ill equipped to deal with the hostility of academy in the future. Despite the retrospective nature of the data, the reported mentoring approaches and models that took into account the institutional context and the knowledge base of both senior colleague and junior colleague, and that value and incorporate *partnering* rather than hierarchy and *guidance frameworks* rather than didactic frameworks, seemed to have the greatest impact on the junior faculty members' professional development.

INTERSECTIONS: MOTHER/MENTOR INVOLVEMENT, RELATIONAL DYNAMICS, AND MESSAGES ABOUT MARGINALIZATION

Three salient domains provide a useful frame for exploring the relevance of and intersections across levels of involvement, relational dynamics, and messages about marginalization among Black women in the academy: context, content and concept.

Context. Models of mother/mentor involvement provide a dyadic frame for exploring parallels between motherhood and mentorship among Black women in the academy. This contextual grounding presents a good opportunity to set the stage for better understanding relationships, race, and gender in academia.

Content. The relational dynamics that amplify intimacy, autonomy, and proximity allow us to excavate rich content that can aid in learning more about the nature of and connections between mentoring and mothering and the overarching role that marginalization may play in either fostering or hindering relationships among Black women in academia.

Concept. Investigating the perceptions, experiences, and messages related to marginalization that Black women experience in the academy can broaden and deepen a conceptual understanding of how racism and sexism emerge in the academy; in turn, this may lead to more fine-tuned strategies to combat and eliminate its prevalence in higher education.

IMPLICATIONS: THE MOTHER/MENTOR PARADIGM

As the current study is only a pilot, there are limitations to this case analysis given the small sub-sample of five and the numerous remaining aspects of the data to interrogate, such as across the intersecting salient domains noted above in context, content and concept. Future analysis will more deeply explore possible variations of the mother/mentor relationship among Black women in the academy, such as in single sex schools, Historically Black colleges and universities and across specific disciplines or departments.

The Mother/Mentor paradigm has great potential to provide insights into Black women's experiences in academia. For senior faculty, the mother/mentor role may provide a vehicle through which they can understand and affirm the marginalizing experiences they themselves have faced in the academy. In relationships with junior faculty or doctoral students, this mothering/mentoring positioning can potentially reveal elements of the unseen or unacknowledged hegemony of the political climate of the institution. That is, in the context of these mother/mentor relationships and constructs women can find ample opportunities to interrogating areas of potentially discriminatory treatment of Black women in academia that may otherwise be dismissed as personal issues. Also, the process of engagement between Black women may provide more opportunities for self-reflection, transparency, and acknowledgement of marginalizing experiences; this can bring to light areas of institutional inequity and pathways toward institutionalized improvement.

Moreover, the frame of the mother/mentor role may offer strategies and opportunities for cultivating leadership within a network of Black female academics and promote professional development across the institution. For example, seeking research funding that furthers the senior faculty member's work and provides a platform for junior faculty growth, or they may develop mission-aligned structures in the academy and meanwhile create sustainable vehicles that support existing and upcoming black female academics. The mentors' messages regarding marginalization may also reveal knowledge of havens and hollow spots in the academy that could provide opportunities to both showcase strengths and highlight opportunities for growth for the senior faculty, junior faculty and perhaps even the institution itself.

Upon reviewing some areas of intersection between messages of marginalization and relational dynamics within Black female dyads in the context of the academy, once again the salience of the Relational-Cultural Theory is reinforced. The RCT theoretical construct is consistent with feminist, multicultural, and social justice theories and emphasizes that the context of relational development is invariably linked to individuals' cultural, racial, and social identities (Walker "How Relationships" 2). In the RCT framework, the essentiality of relationship-building translates into core mechanisms for empowerment that are particularly linked to those areas of one's identity that may have been historically linked to socially constructed ideologies of deficiency (Comstock et al. 283; Walker "Critical Thinking" 52). For Black women in the academy, locating and strengthening channels where they can cultivate their mutual relationships could promote both personal and professional development in a sector that has often left Black women isolated and devalued.

The concept of Black mothering in the academy, for which there is a growing body of literature and inquiry in its own right, coupled with the idea of mother/mentor models provides room for inquiry and expansion across many fields. Opportunities emerge for innovative research and practice to address Black motherhood, research that further delves into these mentoring relationships and pushes against the power paradigms as they become manifest among and between Black women. By pursuing these concepts, we may even be able to push back against some of the more frequently circulated public media portrayals of the Black mother/daughter relationship that too often reflect dysfunction marked by biting harshness or drastic neglect. By examining the emergent mothering/mentoring connections among Black women in the academy as outlined in the aforementioned pilot study, we can highlight the range and variety of mother/daughter or mentor/mentee relationships for Black women in ways that signal intellectual strength and leadership, domains where our general social discourse does not always include Black women.

Some key questions arise for future study. For example, how might we discuss and discern shared power, instructional power, and "power-over" in our relationships as Black women? How might we identify, embrace, and retain growth-fostering relational dynamics among Black female academics in settings that can perpetuate race and gender marginalization? How does a maternal identity as Black female scholars, practitioners and colleagues inform our professional and personal decisions? Considering these questions, and the many possible answers, reminds us of the role that mentors, like mothers, can play for Black women by potentially offering both "roots" and "wings": a grounding in critical tools of information and instruction that can guide paths, while also aiding in developing the skills and opportunities necessary to fly and succeed as scholars and practitioners in academia.

NOTES

[1] Reference is based on research and statistics from the United States of America; however, patterns of marginalizing realities for Black women scholars in other academic institutions around the world also prevail.

WORKS CITED

Apfel, Nancy H., and Victoria Seitz. "Four Models of Adolescent Mother-Grandmother Relationships in Black Inner-City Families." *Family Relations* (1991): 421-429. Print.

Bynum, Mia Smith, and Beth A. Kotchick. "Mother-Adolescent Relationship Quality and Autonomy as Predictors of Psychosocial Adjustment Among African American Adolescents." *Journal of Child and Family Studies* 15.5 (2006): 528-541. Print.

Ceballo, Rosario, and Sheryl Olsen. "Emotional Well-Being and Parenting Behavior Among Low-Income Single Mothers: Social Support and Ethnicity as Contexts of Adjustment." *Women's Ethnicities: Journeys Through Psychology* (1996): 105-123. Print.

Cole, Elizabeth R., and Abigail J. Stewart. "Meanings of Political Participation Among Black and White Women: Political Identity and Social Responsibility." *Journal of Personality and Social Psychology* 71.1 (1996): 130. Print.

Collins, Patricia Hill. *Black Feminist Thought: Knowledge, Con-*

sciousness and the Politics of Empowerment. Boston: Routledge, 2009. Print.

Collins, Patricia H. "The Meaning of Motherhood in Black Culture and Black Mother-Daughter Relationships." *Double Stitch: Black Women Write About Mothers and Daughters.* Ed. Patricia Bell-Scott et al. Boston, MA: Beacon, 1991. 42-60. Print.

Comstock, Dana L. et al. "Relational-Cultural Theory: A Framework for Bridging Relational, Multicultural, and Social Justice Competencies." *Journal of counseling and Development* 86.3 (2008): 279-287. Print.

Chandler, Christy. "Mentoring and Women in Academia: Reevaluating the Traditional Model." *NWSA Journal* (1996): 79-100. Print.

Craddock, Karen T. *Mother-Mentor Relationships among Black Women: Pilot Study 1.* Waltham, MA: Brandeis University Women's Studies Research Center, 2009. Print.

Craddock, Karen T. *Mother to Mother: Profiles of Psychological Resistance in Young Black Mothers and Models of Mother Involvement in the Relationship with their Mothers.* Diss. Tufts University, 2007. Ann Arbor: UMI, 2007. Print.

Evans, Gina L., and Kevin O. Cokley. "African American Women and the Academy: Using Career Mentoring to Increase Research Productivity." *Training and Education in Professional Psychology,* 2.1 (2008): 50-57. Print.

Hansman, Catherine A. "Mentoring and Women's Career Development." *New Directions for Adult and Continuing Education* 1998.80 (1998): 63-71. Print.

Holmes, Sharon L., Lynette Danley Land, and Veronica D. Hinton-Hudson. "Race Still Matters: Considerations for Mentoring Black Women in Academe." *Negro Educational Review* 58.1,2 (2007): 105-129. Print.

Jordan, Judith V. "A Relational-Cultural Model: Healing Through Mutual Empathy." *Bulletin of the Menninger Clinic* 65.1 (2001): 92-103. Print.

Lawson, Erica. "Black Women's Mothering in a Historical and Contemporary Perspective: Understanding the Past, Forging the Future." *Journal of the Motherhood Initiative for Research and Community Involvement* 2.2 (2000): 21-30. Print.

Miles, Matthew B., and A. Michael Huberman. *Qualitative Data*

Analysis: A Sourcebook of New Methods. Thousand Oaks, CA: Sate Publications, 1984. Print.

Milkman, Katherine, Modupe Akinola, and Dolly Chugh. "Temporal Distance and Discrimination: An Audit Study in Academia." *Psychological Science* 23.7 (2012): 710-717. Print.

Mishler, Elliot George. *Research Interviewing: Context and Narrative*. Cambridge, MA: Harvard University Press, 1991. Print.

Morgan, J. "Women Leaders of Color Call for Coalition and Unity to Advance Concerns." *Black Issues in Higher Education* 10.4. (1993): 22-23. Print.

Pinderhughes, Ellen, Karen Craddock, and Latasha Fermin. "Adolescent Parents and the Juvenile Justice System." *Juvenile Justice: Advancing Research, Policy, and Practice*. Eds F. T. Sherman and F. H. Jacobs. Hoboken, NJ: John Wiley and Sons, 2011. 174-196. Print.

"Racial Breakdown of Full-Time Women Faculty in the U.S." *Women in Academia Report WIA Report* July 7, 2011. Web.

Reid, Pamela Trotman and L. Wilson. "How Do You Spell Graduate Success? N-E-T-W-O-R-K-S." *Black Issues in Higher Education* 10.10 (1993): 100. Print.

Riessman, Catherine K. "Narrative Analysis." *Qualitative Data Analysis: A Sourcebook of New Methods*. Eds. Matthew B. Miles and A. Michael Huberman. Thousand Oaks, CA: Sate Publications, 1984. Print.

Walker, Maureen. "Critical Thinking: Challenging Developmental Myths, Stigmas and Stereotypes." *Diversity and Development: Critical Contexts That Shape Our Lives and Relationships* (2005): 47-66.

Walker, Maureen "How Relationships Heal." *How Connections Heal: Stories from Relational-Cultural Therapy*. Eds. Maureen Walker and Wendy B. Rosen. New York: Guilford Press, 2004. Print.

Wade-Gayles, Gloria "The Truths of Our Mothers' Lives: Mother-Daughter Relationships in Black Women's Fiction." *SAGE: A Scholarly Journal on Black Women* 1.2 (1984): 8-12. Print.

Wheeler, P. H. "Fallacies about Recruiting and Retaining People of Color into Doctoral Programs of Study." *Black Issues in Higher Education* 9.10 (1992): 96. Print.

14.
Black Women Occupying the Academy

Merging Critical Mothering and Mentoring
to Survive and Thrive

JULIA S. JORDAN-ZACHERY

Those of us who stand outside the circle of this society's definition of acceptable women, those of us who are poor, who are lesbian, who are Black, who are older—know that survival is not an academic skill. It is learning how to stand alone, unpopular and sometimes reviled, and how to make common cause with those others to define and seek a world in which we can all flourish. It is learning how to take our differences and make them strengths. (Lorde 112)

AUDRE LORDE POIGNANTLY CAPTURES the challenges faced by those construed as the "Other" in academe. Her words also capture the challenges faced by those of us whose mothering co-exist with systemic and multiple forms of oppression. We often stand on the outside and we often stand-alone. I walked into both roles, academic and mother, knowing but never fully grasping the work that was required to resist the negative implications of living on the outside. While the impact of my marginalization ebbs and flows I must be constantly vigilant in my fight against it. As the mother of a Black girl, I am also in a perpetual battle with a society that espouses "post-racialism" but continues to read my daughter's body in a racialized manner. My attempts to embolden her and teach her to understand and resist the raced-gendered-classed construction of her body are sometimes unpopular and even resisted in our current community. I operate in and resist the trouble spaces, as both a mother and mentor, Audre Lorde describes.

Below, I explore my experience as a mentor by offering an autoethnographic narrative case study that explores the often-symbiotic relationship between my mothering and mentoring selves. I focus primarily on how my parenting relationship influences my mentoring relationships. Relying on my memory and journal entries, I tell my past and current story in a relational manner, in the sense that it is told in relation to hegemonic discourses of race, gender and class. The story considers, directly and indirectly, the political contexts in which I perform my mothering and mentoring work. Employing a self-narrative approach allows me to explore how I make meaning in my life and attempt to share, explore and (re)think that meaning in concert with others. From my perspective as research subject/author, I strive to challenge the crisis of representation of Black women in academia. This "story" is intended to offer the reader tools for challenging and navigating the trouble spaces within which so many of us (Black) women operate.

A key question many Black women face as we negotiate and navigate trouble spaces is how do we create and nurture self, both inside and outside the institutions in which we serve. In other words, how can we generate critical agency? The dominant approach to mentoring in academia does not offer the context that affords us the resources to thrive. This approach, as it is heavily structured on hierarchy, can be damaging to all of us regardless of race, class, sexuality and gender. However, the consequences for those of us who occupy the "othered" spaces, as a result of this model, can be even more severe. In my experience, Black women tend to draw on more connected and interwoven experiences of self. Consequently, mentoring for Black women must include these realities. Critical mentoring targeting Black women specifically should not compartmentalize and treat in a hierarchal manner the multiple practice of self-mothering, partnering, community advocacy, self-care, teaching, and publishing.

As I explore how I mentor and mother in these troubled spaces, I first explore the notion of belonging in academe through a lens of "nation state building" and its relation to the family. After which I offer the theoretical lens, Black feminist ontology and epistemology, that I employ to engage in a form of critical mentoring and mothering designed to challenge others' attempts to marginalize and mute me. The essay then transitions into the narrative thematic area where I interrogate my relationship between mothering and mentoring. I present three narratives: finding space; waiting to see, and the only one. In the presentation of my narratives, I move between various modes: descriptive, discursive, and reflexive. In the conclusion, I interrogate how my position as an immigrant, Black feminist serves not only to resist a particular understanding of my role and relationship in academia, but how I use my position to encourage others to not only survive but thrive within these spaces.

ACADEME'S PROJECT OF NATION STATE BUILDING AND RESULTING MARGINALIZATION

I, like others, posit that Black womanhood is socially produced, via discursive practices; thereby, producing a particular form of Black female subjectivity (Collins, *Black Feminist Thought*; Guy-Sheftall; Higginbotham; Wallace). The discursive practices, which rely on scripts, myths, images and stereotypes, have significant political implications for how Black women are treated—politically, socially, and economically. Additionally, these discursive practices influence how Black women see themselves and how they organize their responses. As suggested above, my mothering and mentoring are not free from social and political constraints. They are both anchored within raced-gendered-classed institutions and practices. These institutions and practices ascribe particular meanings to my body and as a result to my mothering and mentoring.

The notion of reproduction—biological and intellectual—binds both roles. Reproduction is intimately tied to the longings and desires of the nation-state. Reproduction, as it has implications for family structure, is a key principle for social organization and ultimately the development and imagination of a nation-state. Nation-states, as suggested by Benedict Anderson, are "imagined political communities" which are systems of representation that permit individuals to imagine a shared experience of identification with an extended community (Anderson 6). Anderson argues that as part of the imagination of nations there tends to be a de-emphasizing of difference (particularly socio-economic, but I also include race and gender in the case of the U.S.) in favor of the idea of a "deep, horizontal comradeship" which binds members that share a set of cultural prescribed features together as a community. These cultural norms/features provide narratives around notions of the family—in terms of what it should look like, the duties to be performed by each member, and how it will be treated by society.

> In the United States, understandings of social institutions and social policies are often constructed through family rhetoric. Families constitute primary sites of belonging to various groups: to the family as an assumed biological entity; to geographically identifiable, racially segregated neighborhoods conceptualized as imagined families; to so-called racial families codified in science and law; and to the U.S. nation-state conceptualized as a national family. (Collins, "It's All in the Family" 63)

Those "families," biological and racial, that are perceived as not prescribing to the norms are often punished (Alexander-Floyd; Roberts). Within the U.S's nation-state building project the "other" is treated with suspicion and as such is never fully invited in. As a result there are parallel realities structured along race, class, gender, and sexuality and their intersections.

My embodiment of race, class, gender and sexuality scripts often renders me as the "other." My self-presentation has cultural meanings and is read differently depending on the receiving public. For example, when I present myself on some college campuses, which can be thought of as a form of "family," I am often asked if I belong. It is as though Black women cannot be present in and represent academia unless we are there to clean up the messes or offer support to those perceived as entitled to be there (Harley).

Citizenship within the academic building project is never fully extended to Black women. In essence Black women are not perceived as being a part of the academic family. My challenge of such dynamics often further pushes me to the margins as I am then perceived as being the "angry Black woman." According to this stereotype, the angry Black woman is not only unjustifiably upset, but tends to also be disproportionately upset. She is emotionally expressive and easily provoked to hostility—in words and deeds.

The stereotype of the angry Black woman is in direct contrast to the notion of rationality that permeates much of academia. Such stereotypes render Black women invisible in academia in terms of them being seen as intellectuals. My understanding of Black feminist praxis helps me to resist this projected understanding of Black women and myself that I do not belong in academia.

BLACK FEMINIST PRAXIS AND ETHOS

Black feminist practice and ethos is born out of Black women's experiences with and challenges against multiple forms of oppression. There are three central elements that inform Black feminist practices (Collins, *Black Feminist Thought*; Combahee River Collective). The first key element is the recognition that there are multiple and interlocking systems of oppression which systematically influence the everyday experiences of Black women. While there is recognition that Black women are oppressed differently because of race in comparison to White women and also differently, because of gender, in comparison to Black men, Black feminists realize that oppression is experienced differently among Black women. Furthermore, there is recognition that privilege and penalty can simultaneously exist. The second principle is the belief that self-empowerment/awareness, coupled with broader collective action (often involving coalition building with various groups), is central to the transformation of oppressive structures and processes. The final element of Black feminist practice is the commitment to humanism.

Black feminists are not solely concerned with theorizing the multiple and interlocking systems of oppression faced by Black women. They are also concerned with doing—engaging in political works that challenge these systems. One of the core areas in which these women engage in political work centers on mothering, both biological and community—though I am not suggesting that all Black women engage in this project and in the same way.

The work of mothers (biological and non-biological) has the potential for radical social change. Mothers can teach their children resistance strategies; they can subvert gender and race norms. According to bell hooks, Black homes serve as a respite that offers refuge from the external brutalities resulting from the intersection of multiple oppressive structures. The "Homeplace" provides residents a safe space within which their humanity is recognized and honored. Homeplace serves as a site of resistance as it offers to the inhabitants tools and tactics designed not only to encourage them to survive, but to flourish. While hooks recognizes that multiple individuals contribute to creating safe spaces, she emphasizes the "mother work" of Black women and the role they play in resisting oppressive structures in their children's lives (41-49).

Our public work often carries over into the so-called private realm and vice-versa; thereby, blurring the false dichotomy of the public and private realms. Our realties force us to often look inward and outward as we navigate trouble spaces. My mentoring and mothering embodies this in-ward and out-ward view of living as a Black woman. Both roles symbolize hooks's understanding of homeplace as my actions seek to create a safe space for those who are systematically "othered."

APPROACH

I offer my testimony as a mother/mentor using an ethnographic approach. Doing such allows me to unveil the cultural and political work I do in my attempts to create a homeplace and subvert the dominant narratives I receive from the U.S. and academe nation-state building project. As the Combahee River Collective assert, "Even our Black women's style of talking/testifying in Black language about what we have experienced has a resonance that is both cultural and political." The narratives I present are my truths based on my worldview and experiences. I make no claim that they are universal.

Autoethnography involves "turning of the ethnographic gaze inward of the self(auto), while maintaining the outward gaze of ethnography, looking at the larger context wherein self experiences occur" (Denzin 227). An autoethonographer's critical self-reflection on their social location should encourage others to also engage in self-reflection within the socio-historical context in which he/she lives (Ellis and Bochner; Goodall). The narratives reflect on: my notion of identity and self-definition, my experiences with marginalization and oppression, and my social and professional integration.

I am an immigrant who migrated to the U.S. from Barbados. I have been a professor in various institutional settings: small liberal arts colleges, large research institutions, historically White and historically Black institutions. Currently I am an Associate Professor at a historically White institution. Concurrently, I mother an adolescent daughter. The story of my experiences in academe is told from my memory of multiple experiences in concert with a series of journal entries recorded through the years. The three narratives I present below, which are presented by way of composite first person stories, highlight the simultaneity of tension and resistance that I experience in academia.

FINDING/CRAFTING MY OWN SPACE

Early in my mothering experience, someone told me that my needs will always be in conflict with the needs of my daughter. The key, he/she said, is how I choose to respond. Mothering showed me how much I value quiet time—time to nourish my soul and quiet my mind. Raising a child sans a community means that there is no immediately established support network to share these duties. My already existing feelings of isolation increased as my ability to find quiet time decreased. This represented a moment when our needs were in conflict. In response to this "conflict," I realized that I needed to be honest with myself and my family about my need to replenish in order to participate in their care.

Simultaneously, I faced a similar situation at work. As one of a few Black women at a small liberal arts, historically White institution, the needs of my students were often in conflict with my needs. It was there that my students (primarily Black students and other students of color) christened me with the title "Dr. J-Z." As there was often a line outside of my office door, one student said, it's just like being at the doctor's—thus the title (in part). More importantly, the moniker was used by students of color to "claim" me as theirs. Like motherhood, my service to and with these students was exhausting. Students came to me with varied needs: academic counseling; questions about sexual health; needing help dealing with rape and sexual assault, deaths, and unplanned pregnancies. They wanted someone "like" them if only in theory.

At some level, the increased demands on my time reflected the failure of the institution to adequately meet the needs of its multicultural students. The students I encountered at historically White institutions face a dearth of individuals with whom they can establish and foster interpersonal relationships. Debra Schroeder and Clifford Mynatt's analysis of female graduate students suggests that female majors with access to female professors indicated that their interactions were more positive in comparison to interactions with male professors (563). The problem we continually face is the shortage of Black women who can serve as role models for those who aspire to successfully complete their degrees and possibly join the ranks of academia. While academia espouses to inclusiveness, often the policies and climate portends otherwise. Although I felt and feel valuable filling a gap for students, I was and, at times, am still overwhelmed. Consequently, I quickly learned that I needed to establish boundaries if I wanted to thrive and survive.

Establishing boundaries was not always easy because I lacked a "homeplace," where I could turn to for help in responding to the growing demands on my time and knowledge. I was one of four Black women on the entire campus at the time of my initial appointment. Additionally, I did not attend graduate school with a cadre of Black students and as such my cohort was rather limited. This forced me to be creative in finding and defining for myself an adaptive "homeplace."

For one, my varied strategies included speaking with some of my more demanding students and informing them that although I was present on campus, there were times when I was not available. When I could not be present, I used a dry erase board where students could leave me a note. If they opted against leaving a public note, they were encouraged to leave a note in my mailbox or slip a note under my door. In order to gain their trust and assure them that I valued them, particularly because some did not feel valued in this environment, I responded within the time frame specified. Like my daughter, my students came to learn and accept that once I said I would be available within a specified time frame that indeed I was.

Additionally, I learned to encourage students to seek solutions on their own. This means that I also resist the urge to "fix" all the issues that I am presented with—something that I also practice in my private life. We taught our daughter, at a young age, that accidents are a part of life and whenever possible she should clean them up. In the event that she found that she could not manage on her own, then it was more than appropriate to ask for help. This requires that I resist the need to fix these "messes" and to accept the approach she chooses. These have also been invaluable lessons for me to learn as a mentor. I have to resist the urge to "fix" the problem. Instead, I ask "What do you want to do?" Sometimes by simply posing this question, mentees are able to think through a strategy on their own and I have to be willing to accept their response. This is a practice of self empowerment encouraged by Black feminists. In order to help others and ourselves we have to recognize our strengths and our limits.

"EVERYBODY IS NOT NICE AND YOU JUST HAVE TO ACCEPT IT"

There was a young boy in my daughter's class who at that time was experiencing some adjustment challenges. At times he was rather disruptive and did not always respect others' private space. During one of our conversations, I encouraged my daughter to extend to her classmate some time to better adjust and learn different modes of interacting with others. With eyebrows raised she said that she "would give it a try." A couple weeks went by and she eventually came to me and said, "some people are not nice and you just have to accept that!" She was seven years old at that time.

Two years later we moved into a predominately White community. She was one of two Black girls in her class. Wanting her to form a relationship with girls that looked like her, I encouraged her to build a relationship with the other Black girl. I believed this was needed to help protect her from racism, in its explicit and implicit forms, and help her in developing a positive racial identity. A few weeks went by and I asked her about the other young girl. She replied, "I'm waiting to see." I asked, "Why? What are you waiting to see?" "I'm waiting to see how she behaves, because everybody is not for me."

Indeed every mentor is not for me and neither is every mentee. I once encountered an individual whom seemed full of rage. At that time I wrote, "[name] scares me. s/he seems angry and volatile. I really am uncomfortable with him/her being in my office. I realize that very few want to be in his/her presence. Dear God, show me what to do." I was not necessarily afraid physically; it was more of a psychological/emotional fear. This person was not for me. As such I made a conscious decision not to encourage a mentor/mentee relationship.

In a much more recent experience, I was reminded of my daughter's prior cautionary approach regarding relationships. By happenstance, I met an individual who was an assistant professor at a historically White institution. At the time of our meeting this individual was approximately eighteen months away from having to submit their tenure packet. During that time I worked with the individual on his/her research projects, often reading drafts. We met almost weekly and in between meetings we would often converse via phone or email. The individual was tenured but never called to let me know. As a result of a chance meeting and months after learning of their tenured status, she/he did indeed share with me that she/he had been tenured. Initially I was hurt and I felt used and taken advantage of. This experience caused me to be rather cautious in terms of how I extend myself to others.

How do we reconcile that not all Black women are for us as we seek out mentoring experiences? How do we wait and see who is indeed for us? How do we reconcile our desires to be mentored by someone who looks like us but for reasons often unknown to us are not available to mentor? How do we acknowledge and push beyond the pain of mentoring experiences that end on less than a positive note? These were questions that I pondered as I reflected on my varied mentoring experiences. Mentoring relationships, like all relationships, means that both the mentee and mentor are vulnerable. Mentoring involves taking risks and being resilient.

As suggested above, the racial-gender order of academia limits how many of us are allowed to walk the halls of academia. As a result, there can be sense of competition that is more harmful than helpful. Some of us become bruised along the way and as such might not be psychologically available to mentor. At other times, the individual might not feel equipped to mentor. Or maybe the person simply has no interest in mentoring. Regardless of why that individual cannot be available to mentor we have to remember that everybody is not for us and vice-versa, we are not for everyone.

Academia can place an enormous burden on Black women by failing to offer students and faculty of color with the necessary resources needed to thrive and often by failing to openly confront the impact of race, gender, class and sexuality hierarchies that impact how we are able to flourish. As a result, academia creates and perpetuates trouble spaces. Often, the expectation is that Black women will fill in the gaps and provide to multiple and diverse individuals the resources they need. This is often an unfair burden placed upon Black women. Coupled with this burden is the feeling of alienation often experienced by Black women. Some Black women opt to extend themselves in the face of these challenges, others choose not to. As we explore our mentoring relationships we must be mindful of imposing our institutional expectations onto the bodies of a few.

BEING THE ONLY ONE

As a parent, I have to address the cultural dissonance encountered by my daughter and I. One episode stands out. When my daughter was in fourth grade, the students (she attends an all girls school) and their parents would read the same book and then gather for discussion led by the students—this was often held during the school day. I walked out almost in tears after my first meeting. As I walked into the room, it seemed like every girl and her mother had some shade of blond hair. In a room filled with 16 girls, two teachers and about ten mothers, approximately six of us did not have blonde hair. This experience brought to reality the lack of diversity we were experiencing. My fear for my daughter's psychological safety was particularly intensified at that moment. It was not that I feared overt racism. Instead I feared more subtle forms of exclusion and marginalization. I feared that I was exposing my daughter to the same experiences I have had while occupying space in historically White institutions. I know what it feels like to exist but not be seen. For example, in the hallway I get the complimentary "Oh, hi Julia," after I offer my greeting. I am not seen until I "force" them to see me. My experience has taught me how such encounters leave invisible scars and the emotional and psychological work required to heal.

While the literature on mentoring discusses how Black women in academia face these struggles, it does not adequately inform us on how mentors who occupy these spaces "make it through" and as such make themselves available to mentor. This has indeed been one of the most difficult challenges I face as a mentor. How do I survive and thrive while simultaneously supporting others in their quest to do the same?

After my experience with the fourth grade book club, I sat in my car for about 30 minutes as my mother talked me through the experience. She reminded me that this was not the only space my daughter occupied, that I had available resources, including my experiences, to teach her how to handle such circumstances. She also encouraged me to use my resources to reach out to other mothers of color for support. I relied on the advances of computer-mediated communication to ensconce myself in a supportive community. I also encouraged my daughter to create supportive communities of her own.

I have applied something similar in my attempt to mentor. As I matured as a teacher and mentor, I have accepted that mentoring does not have to be my singular responsibility. My experience of being one of three self-identified Black women on campus has resulted in me having to be creative in how I mentor. I came into the institution without an on-site mentor and indeed encountered the only other Black female professor on two occasions within a period of three years. During my second year, another Black female was hired, eventually a rather small cadre of women of color was also hired. Given my experience at this institution and the basic failure of academic institutions to think about and respond to what it means to be "one" in a majority setting, I reached out to the my new colleagues.

Although I found myself in the position of being the only "one" openly, accessible, and available colleague, I made a conscious decision not to approach mentoring alone. My initiative involved organizing a group of women of color, from diverse disciplines, to engage in peer-mentoring. We meet monthly with the sole purpose of putting our mask down. Robin Hughes and Mary Howard-Hamilton assert that as a consequence of the physical isolation that is the result of the low numbers and dispersion of Black women in academia, many women experience sporadic and haphazard interactions with other Black women. Given this, we have to be creative in how we form community both within and outside of our institutions.

As a so-called mid-career faculty member, I find myself even more isolated in the sense that there is an increasing expectation for me to help others coming behind me, while I have limited access to women who are ahead of me. This is another manifestation of tension that I experience in my role as mentor—the desire to extend oneself, while seeking help for oneself. This is the result of the small numbers of Black women at the associate and full professor ranks in Political Science (Alexander-Floyd, "'Written, Published...'" 821). Given the limited number of Black women in my discipline, while I attempt to address the sporadic and haphazard interactions experienced by many of my colleagues, I am left with sporadic and haphazard experiences of my own. To address this deficit, I have reached out to others via social media in an attempt to have my needs met. Over time, I have transcended the boundaries of fields and geography to create a patchwork of support. Some of these experiences have been short-lived, but have filled the void. These relationships are tenuous and evolving and often require nurturing in a manner that is different from relationships forged face-to-face.

FOSTERING AND NURTURING CRITICAL MENTORING

Research on mentoring, from a Black woman's perspective, tends to privilege the voices and experiences of the protégée. The voices and experiences of Black women who mentor tend to receive less focus. This leaves a void for some of us who mentor—in terms of theorizing on how we mentor and also how to avoid the challenges of mentoring in spaces within which we are in constant negotiation for our own survival. Based on my experiences, I present an understanding of critical mentoring. There is no singular model for mentoring as we are talking about a dynamic interactive process. As such, I am not proposing that my suggestions will meet the needs of every Black woman nor are they relevant to Black women exclusively. I start by defining what I mean by the term critical mentoring.

Tracey Patton (190) posits that "rather than the university being a place to explore diversity and to embrace diversity, universities often become complicitous in domination and oppression." My understanding of critical mentoring is designed to challenge the domination and oppression usually faced particularly by Black women in academe. Drawing on Black feminist thought and praxis, my understanding of critical mentoring recognizes the impact of the intersection of multiple oppressive structures on the lives of Black women. Critical mentoring challenges the nation-building project of academia which is based on a rather limited understanding of who belongs and how members should behave. Beyond empowering Black women, my understanding of critical mentoring engages a project of social justice within academia. My praxis of critical mentoring engages individual and institutional level strategies. The basic elements of critical mentoring are: empowerment, advocacy, and reciprocity.

According to Lori Patton and Shaun Harper (71) Black women's mentoring needs are better served when they are in relationship with each other. This is the case because Black women are better positioned to "understand the complex intersection of race and gender in the academy and society" in comparison to those of other racial/ethnic and gender backgrounds. What do we do when we are the only one? What do we do when there are so many demands placed on our time; thereby limiting our time to mentor? What do we do when organizations fail to adequately offer programs designed to encourage and foster our success? What do we do when our mentoring activities are not valued as service to the college nor are weighted positively in our tenure and promotion reviews?

For one, we work to create community where none exist. Mentoring networks are key to surviving and thriving in academia. We will benefit by developing a cadre of individuals who meet our diverse and evolving mentoring needs. Recognizing this has led me to foster several mentoring networks (Kram and Isabella; McCormack and West). Within these networks, I have brought together women of color and women at various ranks. This helps to create a reciprocal relationship where we recognize and honor that some of us hold different sets of knowledge based on experience, but none of us are particularly "superior" to the other. Organizing mentoring networks across various boundaries challenges the notion that mentoring has to be constructed in a hierarchical manner. Such mentoring networks also work to foster cross-generational solidarity. Furthermore, they work to alleviate some of the pressure of one individual having to serve as the mentor.

Given that Black women are often "the only one" or one of a few, we face the challenge of finding and crafting relationships across geographical boundaries. Technology affords us with tools to cross these geographical boundaries. A growing trend is to offer services where academicians pay others to create such communities. This is but one mean for creating community, but it is not the only one. We can create these communities without having them being commodified. It involves risk and it will take time to build relationships; however, we can use technology to dialogue with one another.

Additionally, we have to work to create counter-narratives. One counternarrative should recognize that not all Black women will possess the emphatic motivation and ability to mentor. There are times when we enter into spaces with the expectation that Black women are to lift as they climb. This can be a misplaced expectation. Simply put, this mindset can cause unnecessary pain. Sometimes, in the words of my daughter we "have to wait and see" because not everyone is for us and neither are we suited for everyone.

Another narrative that we must work to counter is the narrative of individualism that permeates much of academia. Such a counter-narrative to individualism should involve social organizing that pools resources. Black women should cultivate allies and form coalitions with multiple sectors both within and outside of the academy. When I entered academia there was one dominant narrative presented to me. This narrative suggested that success resulted from individual hard work. No one told me that behind the individual hard work were often individuals who read drafts of papers, who called editors, etc., to inquire about publishing options for others; no one took me to lunch to offer me insight into the unspoken rules of academia. This was the case until I met three men, one older White man and two Black men, who took the time to share their experiences with me and to mentor me. My first publishing opportunity was a result of one of these men using his capital to secure me access to the journal. My experience speaks to a different method for surviving and thriving.

Beyond the narrative of individualism, we also have a counternarrative institutions often offer when confronted about the dearth of Black women and other women of color. We often hear "We are trying to hire more faculty of color, but we don't seem to know how to attract them." As a collective, we must continue to pressure universities to address their hiring and retention practices. Also, we can ask our institutions to offer additional resources that would allow us to access professional development and advocate for mentoring to be valued at the institutional level.

The above strategies have helped me to negotiate the often trouble spaces I occupy as both a mother and a mentor. For those of us who for various reasons stand outside the "circle of society" we must develop strategies and skills to address our marginalization. We have to look both in-ward and out-ward in our attempts to develop a community within which we are valued and nurtured. That is, we have to create our "homeplace" or homeplaces. We have to maintain a resistance to the often-negative constructions of Black womanhood and the invisibility of the Black woman intellectual.

Institutions must also be held accountable for offering support to Black women and women of color that allows them to thrive. To encourage such accountability, we cannot be silent about our experiences. We cannot allow the dominate group to mute us and as such render us invisible. Institutions committed to substantive integration should engage in practices including, but not limited to providing resources that would support Black women's professional development. Institutions have to also move beyond statistical representation and promote a culture that encourages substantive representation where Black women share in the decision-making powers of the institution.

WORKS CITED

Alexander-Floyd, Nikol G. *Gender, Race and Nationalism in Contemporary Black Politics*. Basingstoke: Palgrave Mcmillian, 2007.

Alexander-Floyd, Nikol G. "'Written, Published ... Cross-Indexed, and Footnoted': Producing Black Female Ph.Ds and Black Women's and Gender Studies Scholarship in Political Science." *PS: Political Science and Politics* 41.4 (2008): 819-829. Print.

Anderson, Benedict. *Imagined Communities*. 1983. London: Verso, 1991. Print.

Collins, Patricia Hill. "It's All in the Family: Intersections of Gender, Race, and Nation." *Hypatia* 1998: 62-82. Print.

Collins, Patricia Hill. *Black Feminist Thought: Knowledge, Consciousness, and the Politics of Empowerment*. New York: Routledge, 1991. Print.

Collins, Patricia Hill. "Shifting the Center: Race, Class, and Feminist Theorizing About Motherhood." Ed. Donna Basin, Margaret Honey and Meryle Mahrer. *Representations of Motherhood*. New Haven: Yale University Press, 1994. 56-74. Print.

Combahee River Collective. *The Combahee River Collective Statement*. n.d. 1 August 2012. Web.

Danley, Lynette L. and D Green. "I Know I've Been Changed: The Impact of Mentoring on Scholarship." *National Association of Student Affairs Professionals Journal* 7 (2004): 31-45. Print.

Denzin, Norman K. *Interpretive Ethnography: Ethnographic Practices for the 21st Century*. Thousand Oaks, CA: Sage Publications, 1997. Print.

Ellis, Carolyn and Arthur P Bochner, eds. *Composing Ethnography: Alternative Forms of Qualitative Writing*. Walnut Creek, CA: Alta Mira Press, 1996. Print.

Goodall, H. L. Jr. "Notes for the Autoethnography and Autobiography PNCA." A paper presented at the National Communication Association Convention in New York City, November 1998. Print.

Guy-Sheftall, Beverly. "The Body Politics: Black Female Sexuality and the Nineteenth-Century Euro-American Imagination." *Skin Deep, Spirit Strong: The Black Female Body in American Culture*. Ed. Kimberly Wallace-Sanders. Ann Arbor: University of Michigan Press, 2002. 13-63. Print.

Harley, Debra A. "Maids of Academe: African-American Women Faculty at Predominately White Institutions." *Journal of African American Studies* 12 (2008): 19-36. Print.

Higginbotham, Evelyn B. "African-American Women's History and the Metalanguage of Race." *Signs* 17.2 (1992): 251-274. Print.

Holmes, Sharon L. "Black Female Administrators Speak Out: Narratives on Race and Gender in Higher Education." *National Association of Student Affairs Professionals* 6 (2003): 45-63. Print.

hooks, bell. *"Homeplace: A Site of Resistance." Yearning: Race, Gender, and Cultural Politics*. Boston: South End Press, 1990. Print.

Hughes, Robin L. and Mary F Howard-Hamilton. "Insights: Emphasizing Issues That Affect African American Women." *New Directions for Student Services. Meeting the Needs of African American Women*. Vol. 104. Ed. B. F. Howard-Hamilton. San Francisco, CA: Jossey-Bass, 2003. 95-104. Print.

Kram, Kathy E. and Lynn A Isabella. "Mentoring Alternatives: The Role of Peer Relationships in Career Development." *Academy of Management Journal* 28 (1985): 110-132. Print.

Lorde, Audre. *Sister Outsider*. Freedom, CA: The Crossing Press, 1984.

McCormack, Carolie and Damian West. "Facilitated Group Mentoring Develops Key Career Competencies for University Women: A Case Study." *Mentoring and Tutoring* 14.4 (2006): 409-431. Print.

Patton, Lori D. and Shaun R. Harper. "Mentoring Relationships Among African American Women in Graduate and Professional Schools." *New Directions for Student Services: Meeting the Needs of African American Women*. Vol. 104. Ed. B. F. Howard-Hamilton. San Francisco: Jossey-Bass, 2003. 67-78. Print.

Patton, Tracey O. "Reflections of a Black Woman Professor: Racism and Sexism in Academia." *The Howard Journal of Communications* 15 (2004): 185-200. Print.

Roberts, Dorothy. *Killing the Black Body: Race, Reproduction, and the Meaning of Liberty*. New York: Random House, 1997. Print.

Schroeder, Debra S. and Clifford R. Mynatt. "Female Graduate Students' Perceptions of Their Interactions with Male and Female Major Professors." *The Journal of Higher Education* 64 (1993): 555-573. Print.

Turner, Caroline S. V. and Samuel L. Meyers. *Faculty of Color in Academe: Bittersweet Success*. Needham Heights, MA: Allyn & Bacon, 2000. Print.

Wallace, Michele. *Black Macho and the Myth of the Superwoman*. 1978. New York: Verso, 1990. Print.

Contributor Notes

Candice Bledsoe is currently pursuing a doctoral degree in Education and a certificate of advanced study in Human Rights at University of Southern California. She works at Tarrant County College as an instructor of developmental English. Candice has previously worked as an Instructor at Yonok College in Lampang, Thailand. She is the Founder of Poetic Diamonds and the Cutting Edge Youth Summit. She also supports women in ministry through conferences and local organizations.

Stacia L. Brown has a Master of Fine Arts from Sarah Lawrence College. She has taught at various colleges in Michigan, including Grand Valley State University and Grand Rapids Community College. Her writing has been featured in several publications, including *Reverie: Midwest African American Literature, It's All Love: Black Writers on Soul Mates, Family and Friends, Mosaic* magazine, and *The Huffington Post*. She currently resides in Baltimore, Maryland with her daughter, Story.

Yolanda Covington-Ward has a BA from Brown University and a MA/Ph.D. from University of Michigan. She is a Cultural Anthropologist and an Assistant Professor in the Department of Africana Studies at the University of Pittsburgh. Her research examines how the body is used to transform social relationships and identities through performances in everyday life. She has previously published in *Women and Performance, Transforming Anthropology, The Journal of Religion in Africa,* and *The Journal of Black Studies,* among others. Funded by a Ford Postdoctoral Fellowship, Yolanda is currently revising her book manuscript, *Gesture and Power: Religion, Nationalism, and Everyday Performance in Congo*, for publication. She and her husband Lincoln have a young daughter, Leyeti.

Karen T. Craddock is a Developmental Psychologist concentrating on the socio-cultural context of child and family development within the fields of Education and Health. Her core interests and publications include psychosocial functioning and social-emotional development within frameworks of relationship, identity and representations of mothering/hood, especially among ethno-culturally diverse and marginalized communities. Building strengths-based capacity and collaborative partnership within. Craddock's senior academic and administrative roles in the public and private sectors include Harvard University, Brandeis University and Education Development Center, Inc. She is the proud mother of two young adult sons.

Giovanni N. Dortch is a scholar activist with a history and agenda of social justice activism and research. Currently a doctoral candidate of Sociology at the University of North Texas, her dissertation examines the processes of identity formation in African Immigrant communities. Her larger research interests include the creation and inclusion of Womanist pedagogies and methodologies in formal and community education, social inequality, and the representation of race, class and gender in society and the media. Her activist work is centered in community based education for youth and creating media examining the experiences of under-represented groups. She is a mother of two elementary and middle school aged sons.

Tokeya C. Graham is an Aassistant Pprofessor of English at Monroe Community College. She has an MA in English from the University of Rochester. Mrs. Graham is an accomplished writer and an inspirational public speaker. She lives in Rochester, New York with her husband and their children.

Alexis Pauline Gumbs has a Ph.D. in English from Duke University with certificates in African and African American Studies and Women's Studies. Her work emphasizes the poetic and narrative dynamics of gender and resistance in the African Diaspora with an emphasis on Black feminist publishing. Alexis is the instigator of the Eternal Summer of the Black Feminist Mind Community School in Durham and the co-creator of the Mobile Homecoming Project, an experiential archive amplifying generations of Black LGBTQ brilliance! She was named one of UTNE *Reader's* 50 Visionaries Transforming the World in 2009, a Reproductive Justice Reality Check Shero in 2010, and received a Too Sexy for 501-C3 trophy in 2011.

Marcelle M. Haddix is an Assistant Professor of English Education at Syracuse University who specializes in Literacy, Language, and Learning. Dr. Haddix's scholarly interests center on addressing the literacy achievement gap that persists for children of color and on increasing the racial and linguistic diversity in literacy teacher education. Her work is featured in *Research in the Teaching of English, Urban Education, and Journal of Adolescent and Adult Literacy*. Dr. Haddix also directs the "Writing Our Lives" project, a program geared toward supporting the writing practices of urban youth within and beyond school contexts.

Julia S. Jordan-Zachery is an associate professor of Political Science and the Director of the Black Studies Program at Providence College (RI). Her interdisciplinary research focuses on African American women and public policy. She has authored a number of articles including: "Blogging at the intersections: Black women, identity, and lesbianism *(Politics & Gender)*, "The Female Bogeyman: Political Implications of Criminalizing Black Women *(Souls: A Critical Journal of Black Politics, Culture, and Society)* and "Let Men be Men: A Gendered Analysis of Black Ideological Response to Familial Policies" *(National Political Science Review,)*. She is also the author of the award winning book *Black Women, Cultural Images and Social Policy*.

Patricia Williams Lessane is the Director of Avery Research Center for African American History and Culture at the College of

Charleston in Charleston, South Carolina—a post she has held since 2010. She holds a BA in English from Fisk University, a MALS from Dartmouth College and a doctorate in Cultural Anthropology from University of Illinois at Chicago. She currently serves on the Executive Board of the Collegium of African American Research (CAAR) and was the 2011 Diversity Fellow for the Seminar for Historical Administration.

Markesha McWilliams Henderson is an Assistant Professor in the Department of Leadership and Instruction at the University of West Georgia. Her research interests include role conflict, college student development, and the intersection of student affairs and intercollegiate athletics. She and her husband Derrick reside in Atlanta and are the co-founders of Operation P.L.A.Y., a non-profit organization dedicated to childhood obesity prevention and awareness in Georgia.

Vanessa L. Marr is a proud native of Saginaw, Michigan. Vanessa has dedicated much of her graduate studies to critical service-learning as a form of grassroots activism. Her research interests include instructional communication, womanist/queer pedagogy, socio-spatial construction of urban classroom identity, and performance ethnography. In addition to being a communication doctoral candidate at Wayne State University in Detroit, Vanessa holds a Bachelor of Arts in English and a Master of Liberal Studies in American Culture. She currently hustles part-time for the Department of Women's and Gender Studies at Eastern Michigan University.

Sekile Nzinga-Johnson is an Assistant Professor of Gender and Women's Studies at University of Illinois at Chicago. Insert: She holds an MSW from Ohio State University and a Ph.D. in Human Development from the University of Maryland. Her research focuses on the intersection of race, class, gender, family and work. Her current projects center on the working lives of work women of color in academics. Her activist work focuses on youth development, family-school-community partnerships and reproductive justice. She currently resides in Oak Park, Illinois with her partner and three children.

Rose Sackeyfio is an Assistant Professor of English at Winston Salem State University. Her research interests and publications explore various aspects of the lives of African women in the global arena. She completed her Ph. D. (1992) at Ahmadu Bello University, Zaria, Nigeria where she taught English for ten years. She is the proud mother of two academic daughters, Dr. Naaborko Sackeyfio and Dr. Naaborle Sackeyfio.

LaToya L. Sawyer is a doctoral student in Composition and Cultural Rhetoric at Syracuse University. Her research interests are Composition and Rhetorical Studies, Women of Color and Hip-hop feminisms, Pan African languages, and Black and Brown literacies. Her research explores Black women and girls' discourse practices, online identity, Black feminism, and rhetorical agency. She has taught in numerous community-based and educational settings in the United States and China.

Rosalyn Terborg-Penn is currently University Professor Emerita at Morgan State University, where she served as Professor of History and the Coordinator of the Graduate Programs in History for many years. Her research and writing include over 40 articles and seven books, including *African American Women in the Struggle for the Vote, 1850 to 1920*. The recipient of numerous awards for scholarship and service to the Historical profession, in 2010 the Southern Historical Association awarded her the John Blassingame Prize for Distinguished Scholarship and Mentorship in African American History and was honored by the Association of Black Women Historians as the winner of the 2011 Letitia Woods Brown Best Article on Black Women Prize.

Natalie T. J. Tindall is an Associate Professor of Communications at Georgia State University. Her research interests include diversity in media, identity and power of public relations professionals, intersectionality, and the situational theory of publics, fundraising and philanthropy for higher education, and health communication. Her research has been published in nonprofit management, higher education, and public relations journals. She holds a B.S. in graphic arts technology from Florida Agricultural and Mechanical

University, a masters in mass communication from the University of South Florida, and a doctorate in communication from the University of Maryland-College Park. She lives in Atlanta, Georgia.

Index

A
abandonment, 61, 160, 169-170
abolition, 77, 83-84
abortion, 94
abuse, 117, 160, 199, 225
academic community, 181, 183, 276
academic motherhood, 30, 99, 110, 207-208
academic mothering, 1-2, 4, 11, 16, 21, 27, 93
academic mothers, 13, 92, 94-95, 97, 100, 104, 106, 127, 137, 145, 195, 206-207, 237-239, 245-246, 252-253
academy as site of resistance, 103, 106, 127, 279
accommodations, 45, 60, 70, 187, 194
accountability, 225, 227, 288
acculturation, 184
activism, 9, 13, 20, 49-50, 54, 71, 75-77, 80, 83, 86-88, 97, 129, 150
activist, 6, 10, 14, 18, 20, 23-24, 50, 54-55, 57, 70, 80-82, 86, 88, 140, 162, 171, 227, 230, 249
activist scholars, 20, 77
actor, 1-2, 87, 239-240, 244, 249 18, 160, 164-168, 170-171
adaptational approaches, 260
adjunct faculty, 7,
administration, 18, 38, 63, 119-120, 131, 139, 141, 175, 181, 188, 193, 195-196, 203, 227, 237, 243, 258, 290
advantage, 51, 69, 85, 120-121, 144-145, 156, 193
adversity, 177, 180, 182-183, 185-186, 189

advisees, 202
advisor, 38, 103, 129, 152, 157, 241-242
advocacy, 12, 20, 43, 50, 53, 76, 81, 107, 112, 120, 165, 171, 232, 248, 274, 286, 288
affirmative action, 114
Africa, 23, 146, 154, 175, 177-179, 183, 186-187, 190-191
Africana, 52, 54-56, 253
Africans, 67
ageism, 152
aggressive, 38, 172, 244
aging parents, 141
aid, 69, 113, 167, 171, 183, 267, 270
alienation, 12-13, 23, 68, 96, 102-104, 185, 230, 283
Allen, Jeanie, 11, 30, 109
alliances, 3, 30, 42, 70, 107, 287
Allied Media Conference (AMC), 70
alternate border zones, 8
alternative reality, 218
ambivalence, 27
American Association of Community Colleges (AACC), 113
American Association of University Women (AAUW), 96, 99, 107
ancestors, 85-86, 213
ancient, 216, 219
anger, 223-225
angry Black woman, 276
antebellum, 38, 56
anthropology, 22, 130, 148, 150, 152, 157, 159, 161, 205
anti-family, 11, 127, 131, 145
anxiety, 64, 157, 170, 192, 205, 213, 226, 228, 247, 253

298

INDEX

Anzaldua, Gloria, 63, 71
apathy, 62, 97
Apfel, Nancy, 260
apolitical, 4
Armenti, Carmen, 93
artist, 10, 148, 225, 227, 239
asexual, 241 aspirations, 5, 197
assault, 7, 9, 216, 279
assertive, 8, 15, 27, 66, 93, 103, 265, 278, 285
assessment, 15, 58, 62, 152, 176, 252, 260-261
assets, 43, 52, 144
assigned gender role, 257
assimilate, 183, 186
assistant professor, 81, 102, 104, 133, 196-201, 204, 206, 282
associate professor, 130, 165, 195-196, 204, 279
Association of American University Women (AAUW), 93, 99
attitudes, 94, 186, 238
autobiography, 24, 289
autoethnography, 3, 20, 22, 74, 77, 89
autonomy, 18, 94, 189, 196, 229, 260, 262, 265, 267, 270

B

babysitting, 134, 156, 172, 245
backlash, 6, 25b
bad Black mother, 101
bad choices, 245
bad mother, 10, 102, 172, 245-24
balancing, 11, 26, 29-30, 42, 65, 70, 84, 92, 102, 107, 109, 117, 128, 137, 195, 201, 208
Balderrama, Maria, 105
Bambara, Toni Cade, 213
bargaining, 63
Barkley Brown, Elsa, 211
Barnes, Teresa, 177, 190
barriers, 17, 23, 31, 65, 94-95, 98, 100, 109, 114, 127-128, 175-176, 179, 183, 189, 195, 197, 203, 207, 256
Basset, Rachel Hile, 92
being broke, 19, 58, 60-61, 73
bell hooks, 9, 15, 63, 69, 104, 157, 162
belonging, 7, 25, 36, 68, 94, 179, 183, 185, 274, 276-277

Bennet, Michael, 105, 108
Beuboeuf-Lafontant, Tamara, 200
bias, 98, 108, 110, 117, 216
bias avoidance, 96, 107
bias resisters, 107
binaries, 4, 99, 102
biography, 134, 234
biological, 1, 4, 18, 44, 46, 76, 95-96, 160, 212, 214, 275-277
biological clock, 192
biology, 9, 11, 95, 221
biomythography, 227
biosocial, 109 birthright, 156
bitch, 195
Black boys, 20, 78-79, 89
Black communities, 27, 51, 78, 87-88, 113-114, 136, 154, 246
Black women faculty, 91, 116-119, 121, 192, 202, 241-243
Black feminist, 3, 9, 11, 18, 20, 24, 29, 56-57, 68, 74-76, 87, 89, 109, 145, 150-152, 162, 211-212, 216-218, 220-221, 227, 233-234, 241-242, 244, 250, 254-255, 257, 270, 274-275, 277, 286, 289
Black feminist critics, 212
Black feminist discourse, 152, 162
Black feminist dreaming, 211, 221
Black feminist literary criticism, 211, 234
Black feminist mother, 218
Black feminist teaching, 216
Black feminist theory, 11, 18, 152-, 212, 216-218
Black feminist theory of dreams, 212
Black feminist transformation, 233
Black lesbian, 10, 211, 227, 231
Black men, 5, 7, 26, 75, 277, 288
Black mother-daughter: dynamism, 26; relationships, 10, 18, 221, 257, 269
Black motherhood, 8, 20, 49, 53-54, 75-77, 87-88, 149, 238, 255, 269
Black nationalism, 154
Black parental dissatisfaction with public schools, 80
Black students, 112-119, 140, 279-280
Black tax, 139
Black women's designated status in academia, 15

Black women's fiction, 211, 234, 272
Black women's literature, 214
Black women's resistance, 102
Black women's work, 11, 13, 16-17, 27, 53, 99, 119
blackness, 68, 113, 214-215
blame, 53, 226
blogs, 70
bloodmothers, 76
blurred boundaries, 21, 186, 278
Bogus, Diane, 211
bondage, 9
bonding, 10, 115, 144, 184
borders, 14, 16, 18, 27, 61, 107
Bordo, Susan, 93
boundaries, 1, 11, 17-18, 21, 24-25, 35, 56, 75, 80, 87, 110, 117, 120-122, 184, 280, 285, 287
Bousquet, Marc, 7, 28
boycott, 36
breakdown, 204, 259, 272
Breastfeeding, 238
Brenda Hoke, 242
Bridging, 46, 59, 71, 73-74, 89, 219, 271
Brutalities, 277
Budget, 166, 169
Burden, 4, 7, 65, 141-143, 201, 214, 248, 283
Burnout, 116, 118
Bush, Esther, 136
Butler, Judith, 15

C
camaraderie, 104, 207
capitalism, 6, 8, 16, 76, 98, 212, 220
care providers, 168, 243
career disruption, 1, 97
career dissatisfaction, 7 c
career penalty, 105, 107, 277
career-life balance, 97
caregiving, 1-2, 7-8, 12, 15, 17, 20, 23, 36, 45, 49, 68, 77, 87, 89, 97, 99, 108, 114, 121, 141, 146, 160, 198, 204, 260-261
caregiving practices, 260-261
Carlson, Marvin, 25, 236, 239
census, 96, 146, 167
ceremonies, 184

challenges, 1, 12, 17, 21-22, 24-25, 29-31, 36, 56, 70, 84, 86, 88, 99, 103, 112-113, 121-122, 144, 172, 177, 190, 205, 231, 236, 249, 258-259, 273, 277, 281, 283-287
chaos, 245
child care, 39-40, 51-52, 69-70, 131-132, 168, 172-174, 185, 187, 240, 248, 253
child rearing, 27, 177, 184, 197-198, 207
child support, 135, 166
childbearing, 4, 206, 237
childless, 27, 131, 176, 179
choice, 6, 101, 103, 156, 255
Christian, Barbara, 63, 21
Civil Rights, 5, 76-77, 109, 129, 153, 249
Civil Rights Activism, 129
classism, 35, 115, 151-152, 228, 273, 275
cloaking, 96-97
closing the gap, 136
co-parenting, 261
coalition, 272, 287
coalition building, 277
Colbeck, Carol, 96, 107-108
collaboration, 6, 19, 72, 81, 100, 193, 203
collective, 4, 17, 27, 72, 76, 80, 94, 106-107, 150, 185, 213, 219-221, 227, 277-278, 288-289
collective action, 70, 277
collective gain, 8
collective memory, 238
collectively, 3, 9, 11, 18, 21, 24, 38, 76, 84, 100, 107, 260
collectives, 70
collegiality, 59
Collins, Patricia Hill, 1, 3, 10, 24, 28, 49, 52-54, 56, 74-77, 88-89, 95, 99, 107, 150-151, 162, 212-213, 234, 241-242, 244, 250, 254, 257, 270-271, 275-277, 289
colonial, 175, 181, 194
colored, 178, 238
Combahee River Collective, 277-278, 289
combat, 69, 86, 243, 252, 264-265, 267

comfort, 26, 63, 65, 69, 112, 122, 154, 171, 176, 180, 199, 202, 260
commercial, 1-2, 14, 84
commitment, 15, 68, 81, 104, 112, 118, 152, 162, 177-179, 243, 27
commitments, 14-15, 88, 137, 240, 253
commodification, 2, 179, 213
communal, 18-19, 23, 35-39, 46-47, 49-55, 172, 176, 185
community cognizant research, 36
community college, 21, 111-113, 118, 121-123, 131, 168, 173
community mothering, 13, 49, 95
community property, 19, 35-37, 39, 41, 43, 45, 47-49, 51, 53, 55, 57
community service, 53
competency, 100, 103-105, 169, 237, 271, 290
competing demands, 205
competing obligations, 246
Complementary Mentoring, 263
compulsive overeating, 247
Conaway, Carol, 49-50, 52, 54, 56
conflict, 13, 17, 24, 68, 89, 99, 186-187, 196-197, 202-203, 219, 228, 234, 254, 279
conformist, 91
confront, 3, 8-9, 11, 13, 17, 20-21, 23-25, 92, 98, 103, 106, 218, 283, 288
conglomerate, 1
consent, 37
conspiracy, 79, 89
constraints, 9, 13, 20, 23, 48, 93, 96, 98, 104, 176, 213, 275
consume, 204, 252
contested, 18
Contingency, 6-7, 17, 19, 42, 63
continuous presence, 239
Cooper, Anna Julia, 9
cooperation, 137, 186
coping, 180-182, 187, 189
corporate, 6, 40, 73, 142
corporeal control, 92, 95
counseling, 51, 109, 116, 118, 136, 138-139, 164, 271, 279
counter narratives, 3, 20, 77, 87, 106, 287
courage, 147, 149, 157, 162
creative, 3-4, 7-8, 22, 24, 29, 37, 46, 50-51, 55, 66, 69-70, 75, 152, 164, 166, 176, 180, 183, 194, 199, 214, 220, 235, 241, 244, 248, 255, 278, 280, 284-285, 287
credentials, 43, 139, 176, 180, 189, 196
credibility, 151, 180
criminal, 67, 224, 227
crisis, 22, 30-31, 144, 167, 246, 274
critical agency, 274
critical mentoring, 274, 285-286
criticism, 6, 9, 15, 30, 211-212, 234, 245
Crosby, Faye, 97
cross-generational, 45, 51, 287
cultivate, 76, 82, 116-118, 121, 143, 219, 266, 268-269, 287
cultural and social memory, 25, 239
cultural dissonance, 283
cultural outsider, 23, 177-180, 189

D

desire, 9-11, 15, 21, 28, 45, 88, 95-97, 101, 103-104, 107, 112, 121, 149, 157, 160-161, 275, 282, 285
devalued, 16, 24, 213, 269
deviant, 220
diaspora, 26, 55, 83, 140, 146, 155, 177, 214, 235
dichotomies, 16, 51, 59, 99, 150
Dickerson, Vanessa, 105
didactic frameworks, 267
digital, 87, 90
dignity, 64, 121
dimensions, 6, 14, 98, 261
diminishment, 13, 104
disability, 45, 95, 99, 166
disadvantage, 13, 92, 118, 121, 139, 165, 193, 203
discipline, 61, 122, 129, 133, 164, 183-184, 186, 225, 228, 285
discrimination, 12, 96, 99, 107, 109, 115, 120, 133, 146, 189, 202, 259, 272
discursive practices, 214, 275
disembodiment, 21, 96, 98, 100, 102
disembodied individualism, 6, 8
disempowered, 105, 220
disenfranchised, 12, 106
disobedient, 96

disparity, 5-6, 13, 144, 167
disrespect, 104-105, 121, 219, 227-228, 257
dissertation, 39, 46, 91, 132-134, 139-140, 143, 153, 158, 188, 236
dissonance, 4, 240
Davies, Carole Boyce, 211
Davis, Angela, 9, 150
daycare, 168, 247-248
deadbeat, 62
deadlines, 164, 173, 204
debt, 67, 144, 167
defiance, 3, 19, 94, 104
deities, 155, 215
denial of education, 220
depression, 149, 247
descendants, 115, 154
diversity, 15, 18, 21, 63, 79, 81, 86-87, 89, 104, 106, 118, 123, 129, 143, 172, 175-176, 207, 259, 272, 283-284, 286
divorce, 135-136, 176, 178-179, 189, 196
doctoral student, 37-38, 44, 83, 103-104, 249, 263-264, 266-267
doctorate, 5, 35, 38, 41, 44-47, 101, 132, 145, 187-188, 190, 196, 201, 207, 237
documentary, 134, 142, 254
documentation of dreams, 219, 222
domestic, 15, 179-180, 241-242, 247
domestic service, 241
domestic sphere, 97
domestic status, 178
domestic labor, 143
domesticated, 14
dominant discourse, 1, 66, 81, 278
domination, 75, 157, 181, 240, 256, 286, 288
double duty, 119
double jeopardy, 98, 110
Drago, Robert, 96, 107
dream Collective, 233
duality, 12-13, 20, 100-101, 147, 150, 159, 178, 183, 193, 199, 204, 214
dyke, 59

E

echoes, 119, 228

economics, 7, 10, 18-19, 22, 47, 95, 98, 106, 118, 201, 241, 275
educational Motherwork, 13, 18-19
educator, 81-82, 86, 112, 151, 171, 218-220, 222, 227, 252
Edwards, Arlene E., 15-16
elder, 37, 44, 141-142, 153, 155, 178, 186
elitism, 12, 127, 140, 145
Ellis Crone, Martha, 97
email, 47, 100, 282
emancipation, 31, 77, 95, 143
embodied, 3-4, 15, 18-21, 52, 91, 94, 98-99, 105-108, 127, 150, 152, 207, 248, 254, 276, 278
emotional, 36, 39-42, 46, 48-51, 65, 68-69, 98, 118-119, 142-143, 153, 156, 162, 166, 169, 179, 196, 200, 213, 223, 246, 248, 270, 276, 282, 284
empathy, 59, 132, 173, 271
employment, 5, 7, 18, 30, 38-39, 45, 51, 61, 64, 66, 98, 109, 111, 116-117, 122, 144-145, 166, 176, 180, 182, 187, 199, 274
empowerment, 8, 26, 56, 69, 74, 88-89, 119, 220, 269, 271, 277, 286, 289
encouragement, 22, 38-39, 42-44, 47, 51-52, 67, 85, 101, 115, 130, 133, 147-148, 151, 155, 158, 160, 232, 253, 264, 280-281, 284
equality, 4-5, 256
equity, 30, 89, 92, 97, 109, 114, 123, 190
ethic, 15, 19, 36
ethic of care, 15
ethnicity, 98-99, 104, 176, 184-185, 270, 286
ethnography, 74, 88, 148, 152, 154, 157-159, 205, 260-261, 278, 289
ethos, 277
evaluation, 15, 59, 96, 232, 243, 245, 261
Evans, Elrena, 12, 92
everyday indignities, 251
exclusion, 4, 6, 12, 95, 101, 107, 194, 212, 283
exploitation, 7, 14-15, 17, 19, 21, 118, 179
extended community, 39, 275

extended family, 23, 37, 52, 183-185
extensive mothering, 16, 28

F
Facebook, 39, 46, 83-84, 87
faculty, 1-2, 5-8, 11-12, 14-15, 18-19, 21, 26, 29-30, 59, 63, 70, 91-92, 96, 101, 104, 107-110, 112, 115-119, 122-123, 131-134, 139, 161, 165, 171, 176-178, 181-182, 184, 187, 191-193, 196, 202-203, 206, 208, 227, 237-238, 242-244, 248, 253, 255-256, 258-259, 262-264, 266-269, 272, 285, 290
faculty of color, 2, 21, 31, 193, 202, 263, 283, 288, 291
failed relationships, 242
false dichotomy, 278
familial, 8, 22, 24, 35, 37, 53, 85, 135, 138, 185, 206
family friendly, 12
family leave, 97-98
family responsibilities, 139, 197, 206
fatigue, 132, 188
female graduate students of color, 258
female identity, 152, 160
feminism, 3-11, 14, 16, 19-20, 26-30, 56, 74, 76-78, 87-89, 93, 95, 97, 101, 106-109, 140, 145-146, 149-152, 157, 161, 190-191, 195, 211, 218, 221-222, 224, 228, 231, 234, 254-255, 269, 277, 281, 289
feminist Anthropology, 161
feminist praxis, 10, 20, 24, 277
feminist Psychoanalysis, 221
fertility, 199, 250
fiction, 62, 161, 222
fictive kin, 160, 185, 253
fieldwork, 22, 147-149, 152, 154-159, 161
figurative mothers, 14, 211
first generation, 2, 42, 44, 51
folklore, 184
food stamps, 64, 68, 71, 73, 167, 170-171, 174, 251
forced labor, 212
foremothers, 3, 11, 211
freedmen, 55, 133
freedom, 19, 54, 56, 70, 74, 80, 83, 89, 107, 112, 145, 213, 290
Freud, Sigmund, 217-219, 235
Friendship, 40, 266
frustration, 59, 62, 65, 78-79, 119, 172, 196-197, 251
fulfillment, 21, 39, 44, 51, 55, 83, 104, 107, 204, 207, 217, 226-227, 244
Full Professor, 5-6, 140, 196, 204, 285
full-time, 5, 27, 38, 81, 83, 85, 113, 116, 130-131, 137, 143, 156, 164-165, 169-170, 182, 187, 201, 206, 272

G
gender, 1, 3-5, 7-8, 11-13, 15-17, 21, 24, 28-31, 42, 51, 54, 56-57, 66, 74, 85, 89, 91-93, 95-100, 103, 105, 107, 109-110, 112, 115-116, 120, 122, 132, 139, 143, 145, 150, 153, 176, 178, 189-190, 207-208, 212, 218, 240, 246, 255-258, 261-262, 267, 270, 273-277, 282-283, 286, 289-290
gender inequality, 175-176
gender role, 24, 257
generational, 22, 24, 37-38, 41, 49-50, 53-55, 76-77, 81, 88, 96, 141, 151, 200, 206, 217, 221, 249, 256
genocide, 79, 94, 229
George Washington University, 129-130
ghost of the matriarch, 244-246
Giffen, Allison, 104
glass ceiling, 207
Glover, Clifford, 224
goddess, 215-216
good mother, 10, 59, 99, 102, 157, 237, 245
Goulden, Marc, 30, 96-97, 109-110
government, 18, 48, 129, 170
grace, 28, 107, 253, 255
graduate student, 36, 44, 62, 127, 133, 149-151, 155, 162, 205, 245
graduating, 35, 37, 40-41, 43, 47-48, 51, 112, 128, 141, 167, 188, 194, 247
graduation rate, 78
grandmothers, 36, 41, 44, 51-52, 55, 60, 102, 138, 142, 167-168, 200, 206, 249, 253, 270

Grant, Caroline, 12, 29, 92, 108
grassroots, 77, 87
Gregory, Shelia, 97
Griffin, Jasmine Farah, 211
groceries, 59-61, 71, 167, 169
Grounded Theory, 100, 110
guidance, 3, 28, 49, 52, 116, 120, 261, 266
guidance frameworks, 267
Gutierrez y Muhs, Gabriella, 93, 109
Guy-Sheftall, Beverly, 77, 275
Gyekye, Kwame, 180

H
Hadley, Erma Johnson, 37, 47-49
Halpert, Jane, 96
Hammonds, Evelyn, 93, 109
Harkins, Chandra, 37, 42, 51
Harlem, 152, 177
Harley, Debra, 15, 243
Harris, Angela, 93
having it all, 51
Hays, Sharon, 27, 29
head of household, 261
health challenges, 50, 205
hegemony, 8, 95, 257, 268, 274
help-seeking, 261
Henderson, Gwendolyn Mae, 214
Henderson, Tammy, 15
heterogeneous, 37
heteronormative, 11, 93, 95, 106, 212, 217
heterosexism, 8, 152
heterosexual, 19, 52, 104, 116, 179
hierarchy, 1, 5, 66, 155, 184, 263, 266-267, 274, 283, 287
high service commitments, 259
Hildreth, Gladys J., 15
Hinton-Johnson, Kaavonia, 252
hip-hop, 3, 20, 55, 76-78, 87-89
Hispanic, 122, 144
Historically Black Colleges and Universities (HBCU), 41, 129, 140, 232, 252
homeplace, 9, 29, 69-70, 277-278, 280, 288, 290
homeschool with freedom, 83-84
homeschooling, 20, 75, 77-78, 80-89
homophobia, 152, 228
hostile environment, 267

house servant, 241
house slaves, 241
housing, 130, 135, 181-182, 184
human rights, 37, 40, 145, 218
humanism, 105, 184, 277
humanities, 18, 140, 170
humility, 19, 148
hunger, 60, 149, 166, 211
Hunter, Andrea, 15, 29
hustle, 19, 58, 68-70, 76
hypersexual, 95
hypervisibility, 102

I
ideal, 68, 98-99, 102, 169, 181
ideal mother, 99
ideal relationship, 241
ideal workers, 98
identity, 2, 10, 15, 17, 66, 78, 82, 85-87, 90, 108, 111-112, 116, 120, 156-157, 189-190, 192, 214, 235, 239, 250, 252, 257, 269-270, 278
ideological violence, 226
ideology, 11, 17, 27-28, 83, 94-95, 105-107, 121, 255, 269
illness, 160-162, 200
imagined political communities, 275
immigration, 66-67, 98, 180-181, 217, 275, 279
immoral female, 241
indigenous, 178-179
individualism, 11, 15, 19, 97, 107, 213, 287-288
inequality, 4-5, 16-17, 20, 22, 69, 114, 162, 176, 189, 268
inferior, 5, 207, 257
injustice, 6, 13, 15, 17, 104
innovative research, 269
institution of motherhood, 150
institutional, 1, 8, 12, 17, 22, 68, 91, 106-107, 117, 120, 143, 175, 189-191, 207, 213, 229, 259, 266-268, 279, 283, 286, 288
institutional change, 120
institutional oppression, 229
institutionalized discrimination, 115
institutions of oppression, 218
instructive mentoring, 262
instructor, 7, 38, 40, 66-69, 130, 133,

153, 165, 168
instrumental mentoring, 262
integrity, 117, 173
intellectual, 2-4, 6-7, 10-12, 14, 17-22, 24, 36, 94, 98, 101-103, 107, 112, 116, 122, 128, 141, 206, 211, 230, 269, 275, 277, 288
intellectual labor, 6, 14, 17
intellectual mothering, 13, 18
intellectual property, 213
intensive mothering, 10, 13, 16, 27-28
intentional dreams, 225, 232
Interconnected, 18, 226
intercultural, 56
interdependent, 86
interdisciplinary, 18, 100, 140
intergenerational, 11, 14, 16, 19, 22, 24, 50, 212, 222, 230-231
intergenerational mothering, 13, 18
internalized racism, 214, 225
internet, 23, 56, 83, 90
interracial lesbian couple, 223
intersecting identities, 68, 257
intersectional feminist, 3
intersectionality, 4, 238
intersubjective accountability, 221, 231
intersubjectivity, 218, 222
intifada, 155-156
intimacy, 2, 7, 9, 262, 265, 267, 275
invisibility, 16-17, 19, 63, 93, 102, 104, 120, 165, 237, 277, 284, 288
involvement, 20, 25, 42, 70, 77-79, 81, 83, 86-87, 119, 178, 199, 221, 243, 259-267, 271, 277, 284
Islam, 175-176, 180, 184
isolated, 7, 36, 39, 51, 54, 68, 84, 116, 119, 121, 167, 185, 213, 238, 258-259, 266, 269, 279, 285
Israel, 154-155
ivory tower, 63, 110, 146

J
James, Stanlie M., 27, 139
Jordan, June, 213, 219
journals, 212-213, 217, 222, 224, 226, 231, 235
Joy, 4, 9, 12, 19, 27, 29, 56-57, 201
juggle, 72, 116, 127, 138, 143, 172, 240, 246, 248

junior colleague, 260, 263-267
junior faculty member, 264, 266
justice, 8, 67, 224, 227, 272

K
Kaiser Family Foundation Poll of Black Women in America, 7
kinship, 71, 115, 153, 178, 180
Kunjufu, Jawanza, 79

L
labor of teaching, 213, 217
laboring, 1, 3-4, 11-14, 16-18, 26, 108, 110, 162
laboring of mothering, 49, 212
lack of autonomy, 227
lag, 12, 146, 237
law enforcement, 228
leader, 5, 15, 18, 42, 78, 154-155, 208, 242, 249, 266, 269, 272
leakage, 97, 238
leaking pipeline, 17, 98
lecturer, 59, 182, 187
legacy, 2, 10, 24, 53, 55, 77, 87, 102, 115, 175, 181
legal, 4, 9, 11, 16, 18, 41, 95, 107, 109-110, 114, 176, 196
legal guardian, 236
Leonard, Danusia, 237
lesbian, 24, 69, 227-228, 232, 273
levels of intimacy, 260
liaison, 122, 179
liberal, 9, 18, 40, 45, 95, 129, 150, 279
liberal multiculturalism, 228
liberate, 68, 88, 150-152, 154, 157, 172
liberty, 30, 110, 290
liminal, 153-154
literal Mothers, 14
literary critique, 3, 211-212
litigation, 96, 99, 109
livable wage, 63, 164, 166
lived experience, 219-220
loan, 62, 64, 69, 181-182
location, 3-4, 8-11, 14, 17-20, 23, 37-38, 41, 53, 72, 91-92, 94, 98, 102, 106, 114, 129-130, 175, 181, 269, 278
Lorde, Audre, 10, 24, 211-235, 273, 290

loving, 41, 148, 160-161
low-income, 228, 243, 270
lynching, 77

M
macho, 256, 291
mainstream, 41, 55, 81, 140, 173
male, 8, 19-20, 52, 75, 78-79, 82, 89, 102, 117-118, 130, 143-144, 166, 175-176, 179, 181, 193-194, 202, 237, 241-242, 257-259, 280, 290-291
Malina, Pauline, 237
manhood, 156
manifest, 95, 156, 176, 204, 206, 212, 221, 226, 269, 285
Manipulation, 2, 94, 229
manufacture, 7, 102, 114
manuscript, 134, 141
manymothering, 56
marginalization, 11, 15, 25-26, 66, 80-81, 100, 103-104, 109, 127, 140, 143, 145, 157, 176-177, 189, 193, 226, 251-252, 257-258, 262, 264-270, 273-275, 278, 283, 288
margins, 68, 115, 117, 119, 150, 255, 276
marital, 135, 179, 181
markers, 222 marketing, 2
marriage, 101, 128, 135, 157, 176, 178-180, 183, 189, 194-197, 236
Marshall, Paule, 211, 213, 235
masculine, 98, 103, 214, 229, 250
mask, 207, 248, 250-251, 254, 285
Mason, Mary Ann, 96-97, 110
master, 11, 20, 36, 38, 40-41, 45, 48, 77, 129, 142, 150, 164, 167, 178, 183, 212, 228, 263
Mater, 40, 112
material, 4, 7, 50, 53, 69, 104, 106, 146, 176, 215, 219-220, 231
maternal, 3-4, 8, 13-14, 16, 18, 22, 26, 49, 107, 111, 117, 121, 200, 212, 215, 220, 231, 264, 270
maternal guilt, 157, 170, 199
maternal labor, 2, 11, 15, 21, 217
maternal role, 2, 10
maternal subjectivities, 3, 220
maternal wall, 17, 20, 97-99, 108
maternalized, 2, 15-16, 266

maternity, 10, 214, 220-221
maternity leave, 21, 128, 131, 238
McCleod, Mary Bethune, 252
media, 70, 88, 180
media portrayals, 269
meditation, 173, 219
memoir, 3, 21-22, 128
mental health, 36, 46, 142, 153, 204-206, 240, 242
mentee, 269, 281-282
mentoring networks, 286-287
mentors, 13-14, 18, 24-26, 29, 42-44, 49-50, 52-53, 72, 78, 91, 101, 103, 115-116, 118, 122, 130, 152, 154, 157-158, 203, 242, 252, 257-271, 273-274, 278, 281-290
messy, 14, 30, 214, 231, 276, 281
metanarrative, 218
metaphor, 26, 99, 119, 223
methodology, 3, 20, 37, 50, 74, 77, 90, 100, 148, 179, 205, 225, 262, 272, 288
Mexicans, 66
Michaels, Meridith, 27-28
middle class, 1, 13, 19, 55, 68, 87, 95, 117, 128, 144, 212, 217, 219
middle class white women, 212
midwest, 62, 166, 171, 236, 245, 247
mind/body dualism, 1, 21
mindful, 119-120, 283
minority, 29-30, 42, 80, 84, 95, 113, 139, 173, 203, 206, 243, 253, 256, 258-259
miscarriages, 202
miseducation, 20, 78, 80, 82
misogynistic, 202
misperception, 242, 252
mobilization, 3, 87, 98, 231
model of mother involvement, 260
Modern Language Association, 227
monsters, 85, 153
Morgan, Joan, 247
mortgage, 135, 144
Moses, Yolanda, 7, 30
Moten, Fred, 220
mother-academics, 22, 95, 100, 106
mother-activism, 22
mother/daughter, 24-25, 28, 56, 107, 212, 214, 221-222, 234, 26

mothered, 9, 14, 18, 36-37, 39, 51, 147, 157
motherhood, 3-4, 8-11, 13-14, 20,22-25, 27-30, 35, 52, 56, 71, 75, 91-97, 99-101, 104, 106-108, 116, 120, 128, 131, 147-152, 154, 157-158, 160-161, 166, 169, 171, 176, 192, 199, 201-202, 205-207, 212, 234, 237-238, 245, 254, 257-258, 267, 271, 279, 289; motherhood penalty, 3, 12, 17; motherhood studies, 3, 17-18, 27
mothering, 1-4, 8-11, 13-14, 16-18, 23-29, 37-38, 45-46, 48-57, 84, 92-93, 95-96, 99-101, 103-104, 107-111, 116, 121, 137-138, 149-150, 156, 158, 160-161, 175-177, 179-181, 183, 185, 187, 189-192, 202, 211-217, 233-234, 237, 242-243, 255, 257, 260, 262, 267-269, 271, 273-274, 277-279
mothering and mentoring, 25, 257-261, 263, 265, 267, 269, 271, 273-275
mothering as resistance, 101
mothering as self-mothering, 274
mothering: single mother, 21-23, 31, 59, 69, 127, 129, 131, 133, 135, 137, 139-141, 143, 145, 164, 169, 172-173, 178, 183, 187, 189, 208, 249
mothering: sister mothering, 13, 152
mothering: student mother, 26
motherless, 150
motherwork, 10, 14, 21, 24, 95, 257, 278
movement, 5, 76-81, 84, 87, 110, 121, 128-129, 132-133, 140, 146, 153-154, 226
multicultural, 269, 271, 280
multigenerational, 48
multiplicities, 107, 122
Muslim, 176, 180-181, 183, 185, 189
Myers, Lena Wright, 15
Myers, Samuel, 5, 15, 30-31, 123

N
nanny, 119
narrative, 3, 10-12, 20-22, 51, 54, 77, 93, 105, 160, 172-173, 207, 222, 249, 262-263, 272, 274-276, 278-279, 287-288, 290
narrative of resistance, 25
nation-state, 274-276, 278
National Women's Law Center, 7
National Womens Studies Association (NWSA), 110, 271
nationalism, 77, 154, 289
native, 6, 66, 181
needy, 182, 185
nefarious stereotypes, 238
Negro, 29, 271
neoliberal, 6-7, 19
neophytes, 153
new media, 20, 76, 87
new momism, 10
newborn, 65, 167, 170
Nieman, Yolanda Flores, 109
Nigeria, 23, 175-190
nightmare, 215-219, 221, 223-224, 226-230, 233
nightmares of oppression, 232
no-involvement mentoring, 263
nontenure, 171
nonviolent, 83
normative behavior, 246
nurse, 64, 110, 119, 136, 148-149, 154-155, 160-161
nurturance, 2, 20, 27, 36, 45, 51, 69, 71, 73, 76, 78, 83, 120-121, 147-149, 153, 156, 158, 160-161, 177, 180, 182-183, 186, 190, 241, 243-244, 274, 285, 288

O
O'Brien, Lynn Hallstein, 15, 25, 28, 39, 42
O'Reilly, Andrea, 13, 27, 30
obesity, 247
objectified, 62, 98, 102, 105, 183, 216
obligations, 24, 69, 88, 193, 195, 205, 207, 247-248
obstacle, 42, 48, 113, 130, 167, 172, 187, 256
ontology, 274
oppression, 1, 4, 9, 11, 54, 66-69, 86, 89, 101, 107, 115, 160, 176, 212, 214, 221, 223-226, 228, 252, 255, 273, 277-278, 286
oppressive, 13, 84, 88, 100, 114, 168,

205, 214, 225-226, 231, 277-278, 286
oppressors, 225
opting out, 22, 97, 99, 110
orixas, 155, 158-159
ostracism, 179
other-mothering, 2, 9, 13-15, 18,27, 52, 55, 76, 82-83, 87, 95,113-114, 122, 235-236, 253
othered, 274, 278
outcast, 179
outsider, 6, 29, 93, 162, 176, 234, 290
overload, 259
overrepresentation, 5, 14
overtaxing, 166, 188
overwhelmed, 20, 36, 46, 78, 87, 90, 115, 144, 150, 167, 197, 242, 247, 249, 280

P
paid responsibilities, 112
paradigm, 127, 145, 268-269
paradox, 10, 23, 54, 78, 81, 88, 119, 243
parallel realities, 276
parental, 8, 35, 39, 79, 87, 117, 135, 166, 185, 192-193
parenthood, 26, 109, 165, 178, 260
parenting, 22-23, 38, 50, 54, 92-93, 108, 110, 128, 137, 141, 154, 172-173, 176, 182-184, 186, 189, 192, 196-197, 199, 203, 208, 230-232, 237, 257, 260-261, 270, 274
Parikh, Shanti, 245
part-time, 18, 22, 63, 113, 130-132, 259
participant observer, 158-159
partner, 20, 72, 82, 138, 169, 196-198, 229-230, 261, 263, 266-267, 274
patchwork of support, 285
path, 6, 12, 21, 40, 45, 53, 115, 120, 122, 189, 223, 226, 266, 268, 270
pathologies, 180, 252
patriarchy, 5, 8, 11, 16, 21, 23, 92, 94, 96, 127-128, 131, 145, 175, 180, 185, 212-213, 228
patrilineal, 178-179
pattern, 25, 96-97, 175-177, 194, 258, 270

Patton, Lori, 286
pedagogy, 6, 68, 74, 89, 117, 213, 217, 225
people of color, 6, 66, 68, 153, 272
Peoples, Witney, 45-47, 52-53, 89
personal relationships, 206-207
personal well-being, 8, 204
petition, 88, 90
phantoms, 24, 103, 107, 236-237, 239, 241, 243, 245, 247, 249, 251, 253, 255
police brutality, 225
policing, 94
policymakers, 139
political implications, 54, 150, 176, 275
polygamy, 154
positive racial identity, 281
post soul, 76
Post-civil Rights, 153
post-racialism, 273
postmodern, 65
poverty, 51, 136, 145, 164-165, 169, 182, 187
power dynamics, 59, 151, 229
powerless, 68, 121
practicing, 66, 204, 212
pragmatism, 29, 109, 255
praxis, 10-11, 15, 20, 24, 54, 212, 277, 286
prayer, 43-44, 51, 165, 197, 247
predecessors, 233
pregnancy, 12-13, 42, 91, 93, 96-97, 99, 103-105, 108-110, 155, 159, 165-166, 168-169, 171, 199, 202, 250, 279
Pregnancy Discrimination Act of 1978 (Title VII), 96
prejudices, 173, 238
reservationist, 120
primary breadwinner, 238, 247
primary caregiver, 261
prior generations, 6, 19, 24
priorities, 80, 151, 196-197, 204-207
privacy, 64, 142, 278
privatization, 7
privilege, 1, 3-4, 6, 9-13, 18-20, 37, 54-55, 66, 68, 76-77, 80, 93-94, 97, 99, 212, 259, 277, 285
professional, 4, 6, 11, 18-25, 27, 43-44,

62, 81, 87-88, 91-94, 96-98, 100-102, 104-106, 117, 119, 121-122, 128-129, 136-139, 142-145, 165, 168, 171, 176, 178-179, 183, 187, 189-190, 192, 195, 198, 200-201, 203, 205-207, 227, 243, 246, 257, 270-271, 278, 290
professional advancement, 237
professional development, 23, 132, 139, 175-176, 182, 259, 263-264, 267-269, 288
professional life, 170, 178
professionalism, 45
professionals, 109-110, 120, 139, 178, 289-290
professions, 18, 96
professor, 1, 5, 19, 21, 23, 25, 38-39, 63, 69, 80, 94, 100-101, 103, 105, 107, 111-112, 115-118, 120-121, 127, 130-131, 143, 145, 152, 157-158, 181, 192, 198, 201, 203, 205-206, 226, 237, 240, 243, 256, 279-280, 284, 290-291
professor-student dynamic, 21
professorship, 112, 164
profit, 1, 8, 15
progressive, 128, 226
prohibit, 168, 205
prolific, 6, 11, 156
promiscuous, 179
ronatalist, 95, 106
prophetic, 9, 43
proscribed, 150
prosperity, 76, 188
prostitute, 59
pseudo-mother, 120
psychoanalysis, 56, 108, 213, 217-218, 221-222
psychological availability, 282
psychological resistance, 25
psychological sterilization, 25
public and private realms, 278
public assistance, 105, 172
public education, 89, 114, 236
public transportation, 182
purposeful guidance, 262

Q

qualitative, 3, 23, 25, 31, 56, 89-90, 110, 260, 262, 271-272, 289
queer, 19, 26, 58, 68, 70, 95-96, 108; queer subjectivity, 217; queer theorists, 212

R

race, 1, 3, 13, 17, 21, 23, 28-31, 50, 54-57, 74, 85, 89-90, 93, 96, 98-100, 104, 107-110, 112, 114, 117, 119-123, 132, 144-145, 153, 162, 202, 214, 217, 228, 238, 246, 249, 253-258, 261-262, 267, 270-271, 274-277, 283, 286, 289-290
racial, 5, 13, 23, 31, 56, 69, 75, 214, 238, 240, 259, 269, 272, 276, 282, 286
racial uplift, 40, 56, 114, 151
racialized, 13-14, 17, 21, 24, 92-95, 99, 101, 103, 105, 116, 127, 139, 145, 273
racialized construction of gender, 248
racialized gender stereotypes, 241; Jezebel, 241; maids, 15, 29, 122, 255, 290; mammy, 24, 54, 69070, 107, 236-237, 240-244, 250-251, 256; matriarch, 24, 190, 236-237, 240, 244-245, 250-251; oversexed, 241; Sapphire, 244; superwoman, 127, 132, 199-201, 246- 248, 250-251, 256, 291; welfare queen, 241
racism, 5, 8-9, 12, 15, 47, 103, 115, 127-128, 130, 139, 143, 145, 151-152, 202, 224, 227-228, 267, 281, 283, 290
racist, 10, 16, 94, 202, 213
racist attitudes, 224
radical, 4, 10, 19, 24, 70, 74, 128, 130, 157, 162, 235, 277
rage, 224-225, 281
rank, 5, 91, 98, 131, 153, 181, 237, 259, 280, 285, 287
rape, 279
rapport, 117, 159
reciprocal relationship, 287
reciprocity, 286
recognition, 15, 35, 75, 111, 119, 148, 176, 179, 197, 200, 205, 239-240, 253, 264, 277-278, 286
recollection, 134, 239

reconstruction, 114, 194
reflexive, 21, 23, 54, 68, 159, 275
reform, 67, 81, 87
relational, 6, 97, 262, 265, 269, 271-272, 274
Relational Cultural Theory, 258
relational dynamics, 25, 257-260, 262, 265, 267, 269-270
relational theories, 258 101, 106
religious, 23, 37, 83, 154, 156-157, 184, 189
remarriage, 178-179
remembering, 134-135
reproduction, 8-9, 11, 20, 30, 92-95, 97, 105-106, 110, 194, 214, 221, 275, 290
reproduction of race, 214
reproductive freedom, 9-10, 94,
resignation, 131, 219
resilience, 64, 76, 183, 190, 199, 223, 282
resistance, 3-4, 6, 9-11, 13, 15-17, 19, 21, 25-27, 29, 58, 64, 66, 88, 91, 93, 95-97, 99, 101-103, 105-109, 127, 230, 256, 271, 273, 275, 277-281, 288
resisting marginality, 104, 288
resonance, 213, 232, 278
responsibility, 14, 23, 27, 84, 97, 115, 117-119, 121, 128, 131, 141, 143, 161, 172, 185-187, 192-193, 195-198, 203-204, 231, 236, 245, 247-248, 252-253, 270, 284
retention, 15, 253, 259, 288
retired, 53, 63, 142-143, 165, 247
retrograde, 10, 27
retrospective, 22, 234, 267
revolution, 30, 77, 87, 109, 220
rhetorical, 10, 50, 54-56, 72, 105, 276
Rich, Adrienne, 229 risk, 6, 8, 21, 91, 96-97, 99, 104, 113, 115, 119, 156, 189, 218, 282, 287
ritual, 153-154, 158-159, 163, 182, 184
roadblocks, 21
roadmaps, 24
Roberts, Dorothy, 9, 94, 102
role model, 48-49, 183, 186
roles of women, 175
rural, 51, 184-185, 263

S
sabbatical, 131, 141
sacred, 5, 25, 94, 152, 180
sacrifice, 6, 40, 48, 75, 86, 88, 119, 200, 206
salaries, 40, 127, 131, 135, 172, 180, 188
salary gap, 168
sanctions, 91
satisfaction, 62, 116, 118, 201, 266
scholar-mother, 15
scholars, 4, 9-11, 16-18, 22, 24-25, 27, 78, 86, 88, 92, 95, 97, 99, 101, 140, 150-151, 170, 190, 193, 211, 217, 233, 253-255, 257-259, 270
scholarship, 19, 22, 42, 56, 93-94, 110, 149-151, 190, 193, 205, 207, 227, 253, 289
secret, 41, 63, 108, 201, 255
secular, 153
segmentation, 7
segregated, 28, 41, 44, 53, 112, 114, 129-130, 276
Seitz, Victoria, 260, 270
self empowerment, 281
self-actualization, 149
self-care, 69, 204, 249, 274
self-definition, 151-152, 252, 278
self-determination, 149-150, 153
self-development, 222
self-esteem, 205
self-knowing, 215
self-narrative, 274
self-presentation, 276
self-sacrificing, 10, 26, 69, 75, 83, 96
selfhood, 120, 215
selfishness, 10 selfless, 26, 248
semi-structured interviews, 100, 192, 195, 261
semiotics, 215, 240
senior colleague, 25, 252, 260, 262-265, 267
senior positions, 260, 262
sexism, 5, 12, 47, 103, 115, 120, 128, 131, 145, 151-152, 194-195, 267, 290
sexist, 10, 127, 145, 213
sexual, 188, 243, 253, 279
sexual sexploitation, 241

INDEX

sexual harassment, 176, 179-180, 188
sexual violence, 242
sexuality, 69, 92, 94, 109, 150, 218, 274, 276, 283, 289
sexualized, 17, 93, 96, 103
sexually, 179-180
siblings, 148, 236
significant others, 206
signifier, 16, 81, 160, 217, 221
Silbergleid, Robin, 93
silence about motherhood, 238
sisterhood, 26, 63, 75
sites of resistance, 29, 69, 104, 109, 278, 290
slavery, 8-9, 76, 83-86, 94, 114-115, 212, 220-221, 251
sleep narratives, 220
Smith, Barbara, 150, 227
Smithsonian, 139, 141
social justice, 4, 6, 14-15, 21, 26, 54-55, 112, 269, 271, 286
social media, 50, 83, 87-88, 173, 285
social memory, 25, 239, 243
social organizing, 287
social taboo, 176, 178
socialization, 84, 114, 179-180, 184, 203, 261
socially constructed discourses, 257
societal, 114, 144, 189, 207
socio-cultural, 8, 100, 182, 184, 252, 258, 275, 278
socioeconomic, 18, 83, 114
sociopolitical, 4, 10, 16, 19, 22-23, 53, 55, 266
solidarity, 4, 75, 219, 229, 287
solution, 68, 71, 79-80, 88, 106, 110, 199, 222-223, 231, 237, 280
soul, 21, 68, 89, 247, 279
Spillers, Hortense, 8, 30, 57, 212, 217, 220, 235
spinster, 179, 235
spirit, 12, 29, 73, 148, 155, 159, 162, 218, 289
spiritual, 14, 22, 40, 46, 49, 148, 155, 158-159, 180, 214
standard bearer, 42-43
stereotype, 24, 80, 98-99, 102-103, 127, 157, 180, 182, 236, 238, 240-241, 244, 246, 250, 253, 256, 259, 272, 275-277
stereotypes, 246, 252
sterilization, 94-95
stewardship role, 213, 261
stigma, 63, 176, 179, 182-183, 189, 201-202, 218, 272
storyteller, 90, 148
strain, 7-8, 185, 206
strategic, 3, 30, 88, 190, 265-266
stress, 4, 25, 39, 42, 46, 127, 132, 138-139, 143, 145, 151, 160, 165, 167, 182, 185, 195, 202-204, 259
strive, 37, 161, 207, 274
strong Black woman, 21, 200, 207, 240, 246-249, 254s
structural barriers, 12, 17, 19, 22, 98, 106
struggle, 3-6, 9-10, 13, 15, 19, 21, 27, 36, 58-59, 65, 68-70, 72-74, 86, 93, 107, 112, 121-122, 127-128, 132, 134, 137, 141, 145-146, 151, 167, 170, 177, 180, 185, 189, 195, 219, 227, 237, 240, 249, 263, 284
stubbornness, 169-170
student achievement, 118
student loan, 129, 167
sub-standard housing, 183
subconscious, 212-215, 218-219, 224
subjectivities, 9, 23, 177, 183, 189, 212-213, 215, 218, 275
subordinate, 2, 12, 180, 257
subservience, 15, 117
success in academia, 259
suffer, 133, 142, 166, 168, 189, 204-205, 228, 241, 246, 248-250
sufficient, 86, 147, 249, 254
suffrage, 140
suicide, 117
supervise, 143, 185, 244, 262
superwoman, 21, 127, 132, 199-201, 206, 237, 240, 246-248, 250-251, 256, 291
supportive, 29, 40, 45-46, 49, 51, 54-55, 67, 79, 121, 136, 141, 152, 186, 202-203, 242, 253, 259, 265, 279, 284
suppress, 9, 19, 98, 225
surrogate, 9, 112, 115, 120, 142, 261, 264-266;

surrogate mentoring, 263
surrogate mistress and mother, 241
surrogate mother, 21, 111, 242-243
survival, 1-3, 12, 19, 21, 24-26, 29, 50, 54, 56, 58, 76, 86, 96-97, 115, 127, 136, 143, 148, 162, 171, 176-177, 180-181, 183, 185, 189, 213, 216, 219, 226, 230-231, 246, 258, 273, 275, 278, 280, 284-286, 288
survival dreams, 230
survival strategies, 14, 107, 162
Susan Bracken, 11, 30, 92, 109

T
technologies, 46, 95, 287
teen, 1, 42, 60, 147, 152, 189, 236, 261
temple, 158, 207, 254
tension, 13, 17, 45, 196, 260, 279, 285
tenure, 5-6, 18-19, 23, 81, 91, 101-102, 105, 107, 118, 121, 127, 130, 181, 192, 197-200, 202, 206-207, 237, 256, 259, 282, 286
tenure clock, 12, 23, 192, 206
tenure-track, 6, 22-23, 192-193, 195, 203, 205-206, 237, 245, 248
testimony, 2-3, 10, 12-13, 18-23, 91-92, 102-103, 125, 194-195, 278
Texeria, Mary, 105
Thailand, 40
theorization, 218, 220, 230
thesis, 9, 129, 244
third wave feminist, 14, 27
tokenism, 46, 228, 259
traditional, 8, 40, 43, 51-52, 72, 78, 85, 88, 128, 157, 176-178, 183, 185, 244, 271
traditions of exclusion, 105
transgressions, 17-18, 21, 30, 33, 74, 80, 89, 105
trauma, 22, 150, 195, 197, 224, 226
triangulation, 110
trope, 21, 26, 149, 161
truth, 4, 27, 62, 229-230, 232, 272, 278
Tubman, Harriet, 84
tuition, 131, 166, 187
Turner, Caroline, 5, 30, 153, 163, 207, 291
tutoring, 113, 118, 290
Twitter, 87, 90

twofers, 104

U
Ulrich, Laurel, 16
unborn, 160-161
unbound dimensions of work, 8-9, 13-14, 16, 18
uncompensated work, 15
under-achievers, 137
under-representation, 177
undercompensated, 119
underemployed, 7, 118, 167
undergraduate, 18, 41, 43-46, 48, 50-51, 67, 113, 128-130, 227
underpaid, 7, 17, 19, 127, 171
underrepresented, 3, 7, 92, 193
undervalued, 14, 118
undocumented, 3, 14
unemployment, 7, 136, 182
unfeminine, 10, 244
unfit parent, 240
uninsured, 17
unintelligent, 96, 101
uninvolved, 20, 77, 87
unionize, 171
university hierarchy, 181
unjust, 6, 84, 98, 276
unknown, 188-189, 282
unmarried, 128, 172, 176, 179, 205, 250
unmasked, 47
unpaid, 17, 144
unpaid duties, 164
unplanned, 170, 279
unwed mother, 250-251
upper middle-class, 219
U.S. Census Bureau of Labor Statistics Current Population Survey, 167
U.S.Department of Education (USDoE), 5, 7, 31, 50, 57, 106, 110

V
Valdez, Elsa, 105, 107
violence, 84, 149, 152, 214, 224, 226, 229 virtue, 116, 246 volunteer, 51, 54, 72, 219
vulnerability, 6-8, 12-14, 19, 21-22, 92, 104, 106, 128, 154, 158, 176, 282

INDEX

W
waking, 213, 222, 225-226, 229-233
Walker Alexander, Margaret, 38
Walker, Alice, 9, 160, 211
Wallace, Michelle, 246
Ward, Kelly, 205
warrior mother, 216-217
wealth, 7, 136, 144-145, 184, 192
welfare, 61-62, 69, 237, 241, 250-251
wellbeing, 10, 205, 247
western, 8, 13, 23, 95, 107, 178-179, 183-184
White men, 5, 139, 225
White privilege, 66
White supremacist, 228
White women, 2, 5-7, 35, 143-144, 146, 194-195, 212, 237, 242, 259, 270, 277
White women's Christian college, 242
whiteness, 90, 214
Whitney Peoples, 38, 44
William-White, Lisa, 16
Williams, Joan C., 97-98
Williams, Lorraine, 133
Wolf-Wendel, Lisa, 110, 205, 208
Wolfinger, Nicholas, 30, 96-97, 109-110
womanhood, 8, 13, 28, 150, 152-153, 157, 179, 275, 288
womanist, 3, 6, 8, 11, 19, 31, 36-37, 152
womanly, 244
womb, 112, 160
women of color, 3, 6-8, 12-16, 21, 25-26, 28, 38, 63, 74, 92-95, 98-100, 104, 106-107, 110, 136, 151, 193-194, 219, 228, 255, 258-259, 264, 284, 287-288
Women's Studies, 38-39, 44-45, 74, 146, 160, 227, 234, 271
work demands, 8, 199
work ethic, 76, 184, 186
work force, 205
work from home, 169
work-life, 1, 12-13, 97-98, 104, 106, 192-195, 201, 206
work-life balance, 12, 97, 201, 207
work-life policies, 104
work/life integration, 207
workaholic, 139, 196
workers, 2, 7, 10, 12, 17, 19, 22, 98-99, 102, 106-107, 109, 111, 118, 123, 127, 136, 206, 248
working class, 2, 88, 217, 228
workplace, 12, 16, 21, 96-100, 102, 104, 106, 122, 144-145, 184, 195, 201-202, 207, 253
workplace demands, 206
workplaces, 193, 205
Wright, Michelle, 214

X
xenophobia, 161

Y
Yahweh, 154
Yale, 29, 208, 256, 289
Yemaja, 211, 214-216
youth, 42, 54-55, 73, 78-80